Foundation

2

for **AQA, Edexcel** and **OCR two-tier GCSE mathematics**

CAMBRIDGE
UNIVERSITY PRESS

The School Mathematics Project

Writing and editing for this edition   John Ling, Paul Scruton, Susan Shilton, Heather West
SMP design and administration   Melanie Bull, Pam Keetch, Nicky Lake, Cathy Syred, Ann White

The following people contributed to the original edition of SMP Interact for GCSE.

Benjamin Alldred	David Cassell	Spencer Instone	Susan Shilton
Juliette Baldwin	Ian Edney	Pamela Leon	Caroline Starkey
Simon Baxter	Stephen Feller	John Ling	Liz Stewart
Gill Beeney	Rosemary Flower	Carole Martin	Biff Vernon
Roger Beeney	John Gardiner	Lorna Mulhern	Jo Waddingham
Roger Bentote	Colin Goldsmith	Mary Pardoe	Nigel Webb
Sue Briggs	Bob Hartman	Paul Scruton	Heather West

CAMBRIDGE UNIVERSITY PRESS
Cambridge, New York, Melbourne, Madrid, Cape Town, Singapore, São Paulo

Cambridge University Press
The Edinburgh Building, Cambridge CB2 8RU, UK

www.cambridge.org
Information on this title: www.cambridge.org/9780521694322

© The School Mathematics Project 2007

First published 2007

Printed in the United Kingdom at the University Press, Cambridge

A catalogue record for this publication is available from the British Library

ISBN 978-0-521-69432-2 paperback

Typesetting by The School Mathematics Project
Technical illustrations by The School Mathematics Project
Other illustrations by Robert Calow of Calow²Craddock Limited and Steve Lach
Cover design by Angela Ashton
Cover image by Jim Wehtje/Photodisc Green/Getty Images

The authors and publisher thank the following for supplying photographs:
page 52 © Dan Chung/Reuters/Popperphoto; page 59 David Parker/Science Photo Library (Barringer crater), English Heritage Photographic Library (Silbury Hill); pages 148, 151, 222–224 Graham Portlock

The authors and publisher are grateful to the following examination boards for permission to reproduce questions from past examination papers, identified in the text as follows.
AQA   Assessment and Qualifications Alliance
Edexcel   Edexcel Limited
OCR   Oxford, Cambridge and RSA Examinations
WJEC   Welsh Joint Education Committee

The map on page 171 consists of Ordnance Survey mapping with the permission of the Controller of Her Majesty's Stationery Office © Crown copyright. All rights reserved. Licence number 100001679.
Euro coins on page 148 reproduced by courtesy of the European Central Bank

Using this book

This book, *Foundation 2*, is the second of two main books for Foundation tier GCSE. It completes the course up to the level of grade C, and includes revision of topics from earlier in the course.

The contents list on the next few pages gives full details of the topics covered; after the contents list is a precedence diagram to help those who want to use chapters selectively or in a different order from that of the book.

Each chapter begins with a summary of what it covers and ends with a self-assessment section ('Test yourself').

Topics that can be used as the basis of teacher-led activity or discussion – with the whole class or smaller groups – are marked with this symbol.

There are clear worked examples – and past exam questions, labelled by board, to give the student an idea of the style and standard that may be expected, and to build confidence.

Questions to be done without a calculator are marked with this symbol.

Questions marked with a star are more challenging.

After every few chapters there is a review section, containing questions on work in that group of chapters; a special feature of the reviews in this book is that they also contain questions on work from *Foundation 1*, so that important skills and concepts can be 'kept alive' in the run up to the GCSE examination.

The resource sheets linked to this book can be downloaded in PDF format from www.smpmaths.org.uk and may be printed out for use within the institution purchasing this book.

Practice booklets

There is a practice booklet for each students' book. The practice booklet follows the structure of the students' book, making it easy to organise extra practice, homework and revision. The practice booklets do not contain answers; the answers can be downloaded in PDF format from www.smpmaths.org.uk

Contents

continues >

precedence diagram >

The precedence diagram below is designed to help with planning, especially where the teacher wishes to select from the material to meet the needs of particular students or to use chapters in a different order from that of the book.
A blue line connecting two chapters indicates that, to a significant extent, working on the later chapter requires competence with topics dealt with in the earlier one.

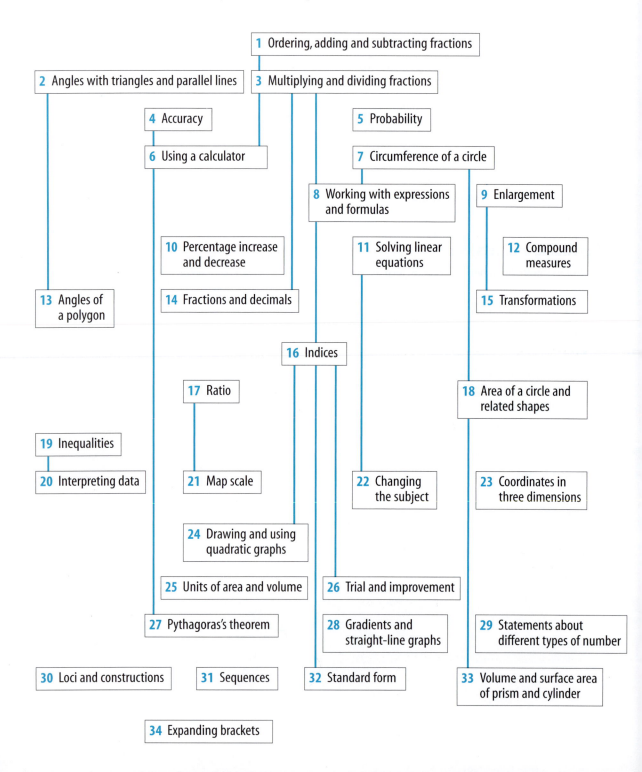

1 Ordering, adding and subtracting fractions

2 Angles with triangles and parallel lines

3 Multiplying and dividing fractions

4 Accuracy

5 Probability

6 Using a calculator

7 Circumference of a circle

8 Working with expressions and formulas

9 Enlargement

10 Percentage increase and decrease

11 Solving linear equations

12 Compound measures

13 Angles of a polygon

14 Fractions and decimals

15 Transformations

16 Indices

17 Ratio

18 Area of a circle and related shapes

19 Inequalities

20 Interpreting data

21 Map scale

22 Changing the subject

23 Coordinates in three dimensions

24 Drawing and using quadratic graphs

25 Units of area and volume

26 Trial and improvement

27 Pythagoras's theorem

28 Gradients and straight-line graphs

29 Statements about different types of number

30 Loci and constructions

31 Sequences

32 Standard form

33 Volume and surface area of prism and cylinder

34 Expanding brackets

1 Ordering, adding and subtracting fractions

You should know

- about equivalent fractions and mixed numbers
- how to simplify fractions

This work will help you

- put fractions in order of size
- add and subtract fractions using a common denominator

A Review: fractions

A1 Copy and complete each statement.

(a) $\frac{1}{2} = \frac{\blacksquare}{10}$ (b) $\frac{1}{4} = \frac{\blacksquare}{12}$ (c) $\frac{2}{5} = \frac{\blacksquare}{20}$ (d) $\frac{2}{3} = \frac{4}{\blacksquare}$

A2 What fraction of the circle is coloured blue?
Write this fraction in its simplest form.

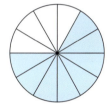

A3 Write these fractions in their simplest form.

(a) $\frac{4}{8}$ (b) $\frac{3}{15}$ (c) $\frac{2}{12}$ (d) $\frac{8}{10}$ (e) $\frac{9}{12}$

A4 Write down all the fractions in the bubble
that are equivalent to

(a) $\frac{1}{2}$ (b) $\frac{1}{4}$ (c) $\frac{3}{5}$

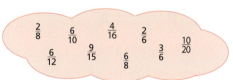

$\frac{2}{8}$ $\frac{6}{10}$ $\frac{4}{16}$ $\frac{2}{6}$ $\frac{10}{20}$ $\frac{6}{12}$ $\frac{9}{15}$ $\frac{6}{8}$ $\frac{3}{6}$

A5 Write each improper fraction as a mixed number in its simplest form.

(a) $\frac{4}{3}$ (b) $\frac{9}{6}$ (c) $\frac{14}{4}$ (d) $\frac{12}{5}$ (e) $\frac{24}{10}$

A6 Write each mixed number as an improper fraction.

(a) $2\frac{1}{2}$ (b) $1\frac{3}{4}$ (c) $4\frac{1}{3}$ (d) $2\frac{4}{5}$ (e) $3\frac{3}{8}$

A7 Write these fractions in order of size, smallest first.

$\frac{10}{3}$ $\frac{22}{5}$ $\frac{15}{6}$ $\frac{5}{4}$ $\frac{8}{2}$

A8 Work these out. Give each answer in its simplest form.

(a) $\frac{1}{5} + \frac{3}{5}$ (b) $\frac{9}{10} - \frac{3}{10}$ (c) $\frac{3}{4} + \frac{3}{4}$ (d) $\frac{7}{8} - \frac{3}{8}$

B Comparing (one denominator a multiple of the other)

It is easy to see from these diagrams that $\frac{1}{3}$ is larger than $\frac{1}{4}$.

- Which is larger, $\frac{1}{8}$ or $\frac{1}{5}$? Explain how you can tell.

B1 Write down the larger fraction in each pair.

(a) $\frac{1}{3}$ and $\frac{2}{3}$ (b) $\frac{1}{2}$ and $\frac{1}{4}$ (c) $\frac{1}{3}$ and $\frac{1}{5}$ (d) $\frac{2}{3}$ and $\frac{2}{6}$

B2 Write down two fractions that are larger than $\frac{1}{6}$ but smaller than $\frac{1}{2}$.

We can use equivalent fractions to compare fractions.

Example

Which is larger, $\frac{2}{3}$ or $\frac{11}{15}$?

$$\frac{2}{3} = \frac{10}{15}$$ with $\times 5$

15 is a multiple of 3, so change $\frac{2}{3}$ into fifteenths.

So $\frac{11}{15}$ is larger than $\frac{2}{3}$.

B3 For each pair of fractions, write down the smaller fraction and the letter that goes with it.
What word do you make?

$\frac{5}{6}$	$\frac{1}{2}$		$\frac{3}{12}$	$\frac{1}{3}$		$\frac{7}{20}$	$\frac{1}{4}$		$\frac{2}{15}$	$\frac{1}{5}$
M	**P**		**A**	**O**		**S**	**R**		**K**	**T**

B4 Twins Poppy and Daniel have identical birthday cakes.

Poppy and her friends eat $\frac{2}{3}$ of her cake.

Daniel and his friends eat $\frac{7}{12}$ of his cake.

Which group has eaten more cake?

B5 For each pair of fractions, write down the larger fraction and the letter that goes with it.
What word do you make?

$\frac{7}{9}$	$\frac{2}{3}$		$\frac{2}{5}$	$\frac{3}{10}$		$\frac{3}{4}$	$\frac{7}{8}$		$\frac{5}{16}$	$\frac{3}{8}$		$\frac{5}{7}$	$\frac{9}{14}$
C	**B**		**R**	**L**		**I**	**A**		**S**	**M**		**P**	**S**

B6 Write down a fraction that lies between $\frac{3}{4}$ and $\frac{14}{16}$.

B7 Write each set of fractions in order of size, starting with the smallest.

(a) $\frac{1}{2}, \frac{1}{5}, \frac{1}{4}$ (b) $\frac{2}{5}, \frac{1}{10}, \frac{1}{5}$ (c) $\frac{1}{3}, \frac{4}{9}, \frac{1}{6}$

C Adding and subtracting (one denominator a multiple of the other)

We can only add and subtract fractions that have the same denominator, so first write both fractions with the same denominator.

Examples

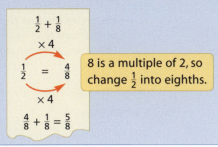

8 is a multiple of 2, so change $\frac{1}{2}$ into eighths.

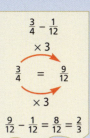

Give the answer in its simplest form.

C1 Work these out.

(a) $\frac{1}{2} + \frac{1}{4}$ (b) $\frac{1}{2} - \frac{1}{4}$ (c) $\frac{1}{4} + \frac{1}{8}$ (d) $\frac{1}{2} - \frac{1}{8}$ (e) $\frac{1}{5} + \frac{1}{10}$

C2 Work these out. Simplify your answers.

(a) $\frac{1}{2} + \frac{1}{10}$ (b) $\frac{1}{5} + \frac{3}{10}$ (c) $\frac{1}{2} + \frac{1}{6}$ (d) $\frac{1}{2} - \frac{1}{6}$ (e) $\frac{1}{2} - \frac{3}{10}$

C3 David and Sue share a bar of chocolate.

David eats $\frac{2}{5}$ of the bar.

Sue eats $\frac{3}{10}$ of the bar.

(a) What fraction of the bar have they eaten altogether?

(b) What fraction of the bar is left?

C4 Work these out.
Give your answers as mixed numbers and simplify them where possible.

(a) $\frac{1}{2} + \frac{3}{4}$ (b) $\frac{1}{2} + \frac{5}{8}$ (c) $1\frac{1}{2} + \frac{1}{4}$ (d) $2\frac{3}{4} - \frac{1}{2}$ (e) $1\frac{1}{4} - \frac{1}{8}$

(f) $\frac{11}{14} + \frac{2}{7}$ (g) $\frac{1}{2} + \frac{5}{6}$ (h) $\frac{2}{3} + \frac{5}{6}$ (i) $\frac{1}{3} + \frac{7}{9}$ (j) $1\frac{3}{4} - \frac{3}{8}$

*C5 The sketch shows three villages along a country road.

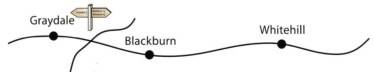

This signpost is at the crossroads between Graydale and Blackburn.
It shows some distances in miles.

What is the distance along the road

(a) from Graydale to Blackburn

(b) from Graydale to Whitehill

(c) from Blackburn to Whitehill

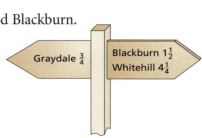

D Comparing (neither denominator a multiple of the other)

Dean wants to compare $\frac{2}{3}$ and $\frac{4}{7}$.

He writes out a set of equivalent fractions for both of them.

$\frac{2}{3} = \frac{4}{6} = \frac{6}{9} = \frac{8}{12} = \frac{10}{15} = \frac{12}{18} = \boxed{\frac{14}{21}} = \frac{16}{24} =$

$\frac{4}{7} = \frac{8}{14} = \boxed{\frac{12}{21}} = \frac{16}{28} = \frac{20}{35} =$

He circles the first pair of fractions that have the same denominator.

So $\frac{4}{7}$ is smaller than $\frac{2}{3}$.

$\frac{12}{21}$ is smaller than $\frac{14}{21}$ so $\frac{4}{7}$ is smaller than $\frac{2}{3}$.

D1 Dean has written down sets of equivalent fractions for $\frac{4}{5}$ and $\frac{3}{4}$.

Which fraction is smaller, $\frac{4}{5}$ or $\frac{3}{4}$? Explain how you decided.

$\frac{4}{5} = \frac{8}{10} = \frac{12}{15} = \frac{16}{20} = \frac{20}{25} =$

$\frac{3}{4} = \frac{6}{8} = \frac{9}{12} = \frac{12}{16} = \frac{15}{20} =$

D2 For each pair of fractions, write down the larger fraction and the letter that goes with it.
What word do you make?

$\frac{1}{3}$	$\frac{2}{5}$		$\frac{3}{4}$	$\frac{2}{3}$		$\frac{7}{10}$	$\frac{3}{4}$		$\frac{3}{7}$	$\frac{2}{5}$
T	**M**		**I**	**A**		**S**	**L**		**K**	**L**

D3 Work out which of the fractions $\frac{3}{5}$ or $\frac{2}{3}$ is larger.
Show all your working.

D4 Write these fractions in order of size, starting with the smallest.

$\frac{5}{8}$ $\frac{2}{3}$ $\frac{1}{2}$

D5 Write these fractions in ascending order.

$\frac{2}{3}$ $\frac{2}{5}$ $\frac{1}{3}$ $\frac{3}{5}$

D6 Which of these fractions is closest to $\frac{1}{2}$?
Explain how you know.

$\frac{4}{10}$ $\frac{11}{20}$ $\frac{3}{4}$

*D7 Find a fraction that lies between $\frac{5}{9}$ and $\frac{3}{5}$.

*D8 Find two different fractions that lie between $\frac{1}{5}$ and $\frac{1}{3}$.

E Adding and subtracting (neither denominator a multiple of the other)

Dean wants to work out $\frac{2}{5} + \frac{1}{4}$.

He writes out a set of equivalent fractions for both of them.

He circles the first pair of fractions with the same denominator.

$$\frac{2}{5} = \frac{4}{10} = \frac{6}{15} = \boxed{\frac{8}{20}} = \frac{10}{25} =$$

$$\frac{1}{4} = \frac{2}{8} = \frac{3}{12} = \frac{4}{16} = \boxed{\frac{5}{20}} = \frac{6}{24} =$$

So $\frac{2}{5} + \frac{1}{4} = \frac{8}{20} + \frac{5}{20}$

Now he can add them.

$$= \frac{13}{20}$$

E1 Dean has written down two sets of equivalent fractions for $\frac{2}{3}$ and $\frac{1}{5}$.

$$\frac{2}{3} = \frac{4}{6} = \frac{6}{9} = \frac{8}{12} = \frac{10}{15} = \frac{12}{18} = \frac{14}{21} = \frac{16}{24} =$$

$$\frac{1}{5} = \frac{2}{10} = \frac{3}{15} = \frac{4}{20} = \frac{5}{25} =$$

   (a) Write down two fractions, one from each set, that have the same denominator.

   (b) Work out $\frac{2}{3} + \frac{1}{5}$.

E2 (a) Copy and complete this to give a set of four equivalent fractions for $\frac{1}{2}$.
$$\frac{1}{2} = \frac{2}{4} = ? = ?$$

   (b) Copy and complete this to give a set of four equivalent fractions for $\frac{1}{3}$.
$$\frac{1}{3} = ? = ? = ?$$

   (c) Work out $\frac{1}{2} + \frac{1}{3}$.

E3 Work these out.

   (a) $\frac{1}{4} + \frac{1}{3}$ (b) $\frac{1}{3} + \frac{2}{5}$ (c) $\frac{1}{4} - \frac{1}{10}$ (d) $\frac{1}{2} - \frac{2}{7}$ (e) $\frac{3}{4} + \frac{2}{3}$

E4 Maya and George share a pizza.

Maya eats $\frac{1}{3}$ of the pizza.

George eats $\frac{3}{8}$ of the pizza.

   (a) What fraction of the pizza have they eaten altogether?

   (b) What fraction of the pizza is left?

E5 Tina buys a 2 pint carton of milk.

She uses $\frac{2}{3}$ pint of this to make a milkshake.

She uses another $\frac{1}{2}$ pint to make some pancakes.

How much milk does she have left?

Example

Work out $1\frac{2}{3} + 2\frac{3}{4}$.

> We need to change $\frac{2}{3}$ and $\frac{3}{4}$ into equivalent fractions with the same denominator.
> The denominator must be a multiple of 3 and also a multiple of 4. So 12 will do.

$$\overset{\times 4}{\frac{2}{3}} = \underset{\times 4}{\frac{8}{12}} \qquad \overset{\times 3}{\frac{3}{4}} = \underset{\times 3}{\frac{9}{12}}$$

$$1\frac{8}{12} = \frac{20}{12} \qquad 2\frac{9}{12} = \frac{33}{12}$$ Write the mixed numbers as improper fractions.

$$\frac{20}{12} + \frac{33}{12} = \frac{53}{12} = 4\frac{5}{12}$$ Give the answer as a mixed number.

E6 Work these out. Write the results as mixed numbers.

(a) $1\frac{1}{3} + \frac{1}{6}$ (b) $4 - 1\frac{1}{4}$ (c) $1\frac{3}{4} + \frac{2}{5}$ (d) $2\frac{2}{3} - \frac{3}{4}$ (e) $3\frac{1}{5} + 1\frac{1}{3}$

(f) $3\frac{3}{8} + 1\frac{1}{4}$ (g) $2\frac{3}{4} - 1\frac{1}{3}$ (h) $2\frac{5}{8} + 1\frac{2}{3}$ (i) $3\frac{1}{2} - 2\frac{1}{3}$ (j) $3\frac{3}{5} - 1\frac{5}{6}$

Test yourself

T1 Write the fractions $\frac{5}{8}, \frac{3}{4}, \frac{17}{24}, \frac{7}{12}$ in ascending order.   *Edexcel*

T2 (a) Here are three fractions.

$$\frac{3}{4} \qquad \frac{4}{5} \qquad \frac{5}{8}$$

Which of these fractions is the largest?
Show how you decide.

(b) Work out $\frac{1}{5} + \frac{2}{3}$.   *OCR*

T3 Work these out. Simplify your answers where possible.

(a) $\frac{1}{5} + \frac{3}{10}$ (b) $\frac{3}{4} - \frac{1}{8}$ (c) $\frac{5}{8} + \frac{2}{3}$ (d) $1\frac{5}{6} - \frac{1}{3}$ (e) $2\frac{1}{7} + 1\frac{2}{3}$

T4 Simon spent $\frac{1}{3}$ of his pocket money on a computer game.
He spent $\frac{1}{4}$ of his money on a ticket for a football match.
Work out the fraction of his pocket money that he had left.   *Edexcel*

T5 The sketch shows three villages and the distances between them.

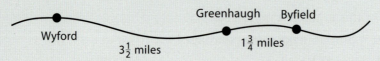

Work out the total distance along the road between Wyford and Byfield.

2 Angles with triangles and parallel lines

This work will help you find angles and explain your results using

- the sum of angles round a point, on a line and in a triangle (including an isosceles triangle)
- vertically opposite angles
- corresponding and alternate angles made with parallel lines

You will also meet a proof for the sum of the angles of a triangle.

A Giving reasons: angles on a line, round a point, in a triangle

 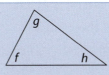 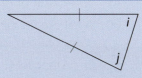

Angles around a point add up to 360°:
$a + b + c = 360°$

Angles on a straight line add up to 180°:
$d + e = 180°$

Angles in a triangle add up to 180°:
$f + g + h = 180°$

In an isosceles triangle, angles opposite equal sides are themselves equal: $i = j$

A1 Find the angles marked with letters, giving reasons chosen from the facts about angles above.
It is not enough to say, for example, 'Angles add up to 180°.'
You would also have to say the angles are 'on a straight line' or 'in a triangle'.

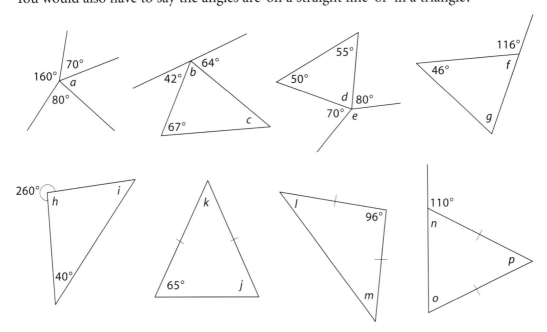

Labelling points with capital letters makes it easy to identify lines, shapes and angles.

We use 'line EF' to mean the straight line that goes from E to F.
(To be strictly correct we should say 'line segment EF'.)

'Triangle PQR' means the triangle with P, Q and R as its vertices.

'Angle DAB' means the angle with A at its vertex and
D and B along its arms.
You can also write ∠DAB or D̂AB.

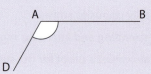

A2 (a) What kind of triangle is triangle ACD?

(b) Which triangle in this diagram is equilateral?

(c) What kind of quadrilateral is ACDE?

(d) What are the sizes of these angles?
(Give reasons in each case.)

(i) Angle BAC **(ii)** Angle BCD **(iii)** Angle BAD

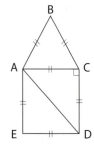

A3 (a) (i) What is the size of angle PSR? (Give reasons.)

(ii) Which other angle is the same size?

(b) What kind of quadrilateral is PQRS?

(c) Which line segment has the same length as SR?

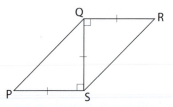

B Giving reasons: vertically opposite angles

Vertically opposite angles are equal angles like this 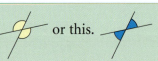 or this.

B1 (a) Which angle is vertically opposite to angle *g*?

(b) Which angle is vertically opposite to angle *b*?

(c) Give the letters for two more pairs of
vertically opposite angles.

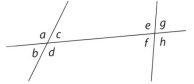

B2 The diagram shows three straight lines intersecting at point O.
Give the missing angles in these.

(a) Angles AOB and _____ are vertically opposite angles.

(b) Angles _____ and COD are vertically opposite angles.

(c) Angles FOE and _____ are vertically opposite angles.

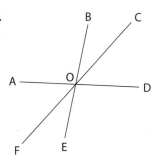

B3 Use vertically opposite angles to find the angles marked with letters here.

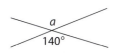
a
140°

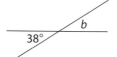
b
38°

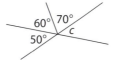
60° 70°
c
50°

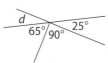
d
65° 90° 25°

B4 A furniture maker is designing a folding stool.

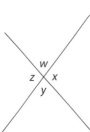
p
r
q

(a) When angle *p* is 100°, give the size of

    (i) angle *q*   **(ii)** angle *r*

(b) For safety reasons angle *p* must be greater than 110°.

    (i) Which one of these statements must be true for angle *r*?

r must be greater than 70°.	*r* must be less than 70°.	*r* must be greater than 110°.

    (ii) Write a statement that must be true for angle *q*.

B5 (a) In this diagram *w* is an **acute** angle.
What types of angle are *x*, *y* and *z*?

(b) If in this diagram *w* was an **obtuse** angle,
what types of angle would *x*, *y* and *z* be?

(c) If in this diagram *w* was a **right** angle,
what types of angle would *x*, *y* and *z* be?

w
z *x*
y

Points labelled with capital letters can be used to explain how you have found an angle.

Example

There are three straight lines in this diagram.
Work out the angle marked **?** here.

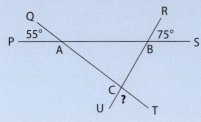
Q
55°
P
A
R
75°
B
S
C
?
U
T

Angle BAC = 55° (vertically opposite to angle QAP)
Angle ABC = 75° (vertically opposite to angle RBS)
So angle ACB = 180° – 55° – 75° = 50°
(angles of triangle ABC add up to 180°)
So angle UCT = 50° (vertically opposite to angle ACB)

B6 Work out the angles marked **?** here.
Give an explanation for each result, referring to each angle by three capital letters.

(a) (These are three
straight lines.)

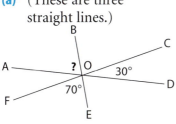
B
C
A ? O
30°
70° D
F
E

(b)
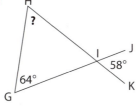
H
?
I
J
58°
64°
G
K

(c)
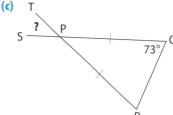
T
S ? P
Q
73°
R

C Angles from parallel lines crossing

If two lines go in the same direction and never meet,
we say they are **parallel** to one another.
We use arrows like these to show that lines are parallel.

If we have more than one set of parallel lines on a diagram
we can use double arrows for the second set of parallel lines.

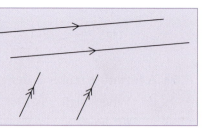

T Draw two sets of parallel lines like this.

Mark two **different-sized** angles on your diagram and
label them p and q.

- Mark with a p every angle that equals angle p.
- Mark with a q every angle that equals angle q.
- If you know the size of p, how do you work out q?

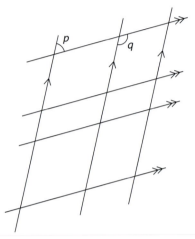

C1 Here are two more sets of parallel lines.
If this angle is 50°, what will each angle marked with a letter be?

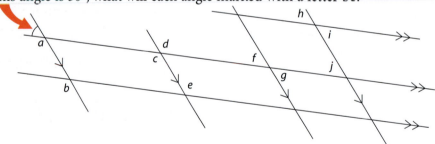

C2 Here are another two sets of parallel lines.
If this angle is 110°, what will each angle marked with a letter be?

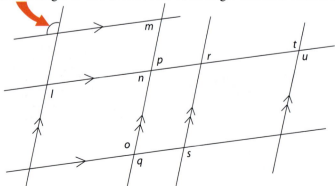

Corresponding angles are equal angles like these.

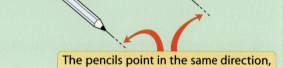

You can trace an F or a reverse F over them.

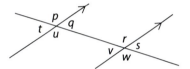

To see how corresponding angles work, think of two pencils in a straight line.

Now both pencils rotate 70° clockwise about their ends.

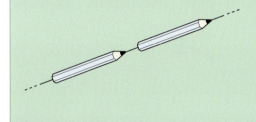

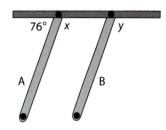

The pencils point in the same direction, so these lines are parallel.

C3 Give the missing letters for these.

(a) Angles p and ____ are corresponding angles.

(b) Angles ____ and t are corresponding angles.

C4 (a) Give the letters for five pairs of corresponding angles in the diagram for C1.

(b) Give the letters for four pairs of corresponding angles in the diagram for C2.

C5 In this mechanism the two bars A and B stay parallel. Find angles x and y.

C6 Use corresponding angles to find the angles marked with letters here.

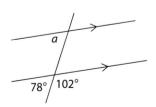

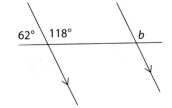

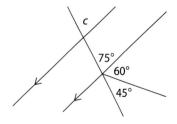

C7 Give the missing letters for these.

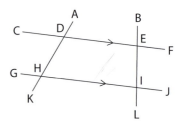

(a) Angles ADE and _____ are corresponding angles.

(b) Angles HIE and _____ are corresponding angles.

(c) Angles _____ and EIJ are corresponding angles.

(d) Angles _____ and KHI are corresponding angles.

Alternate angles are equal angles like these.

You can trace a Z or a reverse Z over them.

C8 Find four pairs of alternate angles in this diagram. Give their letters.

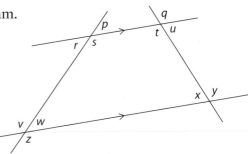

C9 Give the missing letters for these.

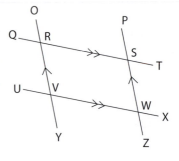

(a) Angles RSP and _____ are alternate angles.

(b) Angles SWV and _____ are alternate angles.

(c) Angles _____ and VWZ are alternate angles.

(d) Angles _____ and QRV are alternate angles.

C10 The diagram shows a lifting platform. The top always remains parallel to the base.

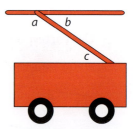

(a) When angle *c* is 20°, give the value of

  (i) angle *b*   (ii) angle *a*

(b) For safety reasons angle *c* must be smaller than 55°.

  (i) Which one of these statements must be true for angle *b*?

| *b* must be equal to 55°. | *b* must be greater than 55°. | *b* must be less than 55°. |

  (ii) Write a statement that must be true for angle *a*.

C11 Use alternate angles to find the angles marked with letters here.

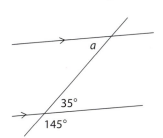 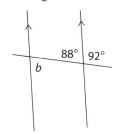 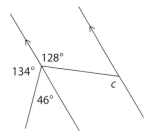

C12 Describe each of these pairs of angles. Choose from the boxes.

(a) Angles *b* and *d*

(b) Angles *b* and *f*

(c) Angles *c* and *g*

(d) Angles *a* and *b*

(e) Angles *c* and *e*

(f) Angles *e* and *g*

(g) Angles *a* and *e*

(h) Angles *d* and *g*

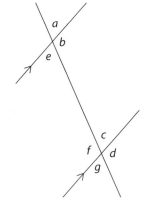

Vertically opposite angles

Corresponding angles (F)

Alternate angles (Z)

Angles on a straight line adding up to 180°

C13 Give the size of each lettered angle and the reason you know the angle.
(Choose each reason from one of the boxes in C12.)

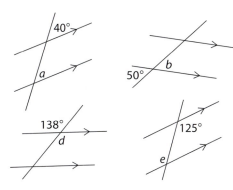 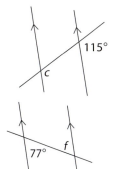

C14 Find the size of each lettered angle,
giving a reason.

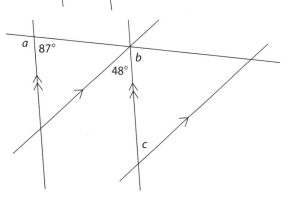

Sometimes two or more steps may be needed to find an angle.

Example

Work out angle x, giving reasons.

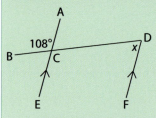

Angle ACD = 180° – 108° = 72° (angles on straight line BD add up to 180°)
Angle CDF = angle ACD = 72° (alternate angles), so x = 72°

OR

Angle BCE = 180° – 108° = 72° (angles on straight line AE add up to 180°)
Angle CDF = angle BCE = 72° (corresponding angles), so x = 72°

C15 Work out the angles marked in blue explaining your reasoning.
In your explanations, name the angles using capital letters.

(a)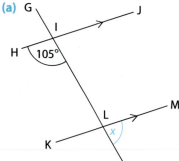

(b)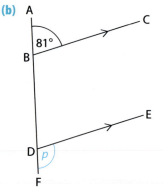

(c)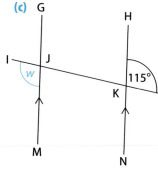

(d)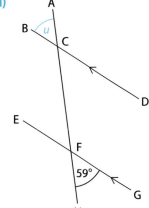

(e)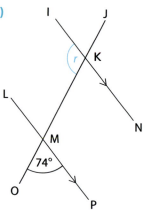

(f)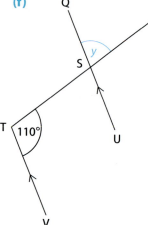

C16 This diagram shows a triangle ABC.
Side AC has been extended to D.
Line CE has been drawn parallel to line AB.

(a) Which other angle is equal to x, and why?

(b) Which other angle is equal to y, and why?

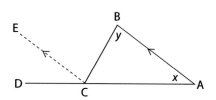

If one side of a triangle is extended, the angle formed is called an **exterior angle** of the triangle.

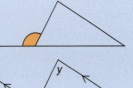

In question C16 you should have got these results (from corresponding and alternate angles).

So the exterior angle equals the sum of the **interior angles** x and y.
We have **proved** this whatever the values of x and y.

C17 Find the size of each lettered angle.

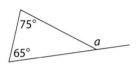
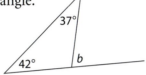
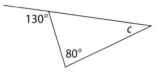

Let z stand for the third angle of the triangle in the panel above.

The angle marked blue is 180° (angles on a straight line).
So $x + y + z = 180°$.

But x, y and z are also the interior angles of the triangle.
So the interior angles of the triangle also add up to 180°.
We have **proved** this whatever the values of x, y and z.

D Mixed questions

D1 ABCE is a trapezium.
Work out angles x and y,
explaining your reasoning.

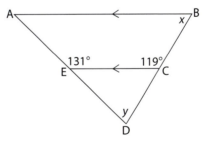

D2 Work out the angles marked in blue, explaining your reasoning.

(a)

(b)

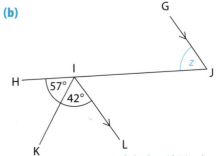

D3 In this diagram,
AB = BC,
AB is parallel to CE,
BCD is a straight line.

Find angle ECD, giving your reasons.

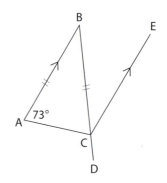

Test yourself

T1 The triangle in this diagram is isosceles.
Work out the angles marked with letters.

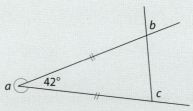

T2 Work out the angle marked x,
explaining your reasons.

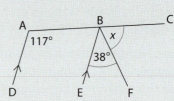

T3 Work out the values of a, b and c.

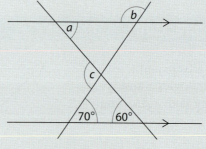

AQA

T4 PQRS is a parallelogram.

Angle QSP = 47°
Angle QSR = 24°
PST is a straight line.

(a) (i) Find the size of the angle marked x.

(ii) Give a reason for your answer.

(b) (i) Work out the size of angle PQS.

(ii) Give a reason for your answer.

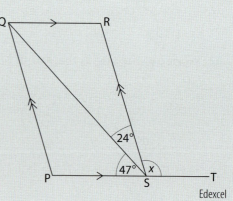

Edexcel

3 Multiplying and dividing fractions

You will revise how to

- find a fraction of a quantity
- multiply and divide a fraction by a whole number

This work will help you

- multiply and divide a fraction by any fraction
- understand what a reciprocal is

A Review: calculating with fractions

A1 Katy has £20. She spends a quarter of her money on a book.
What is the cost of the book?

A2 About two thirds of our body weight is water.
Estimate the weight of water in a person weighing 60 kg.

A3 Jan uses $\frac{1}{4}$ litre of milk to make a milkshake.
How much milk would she need to make 8 milkshakes?

A4 Work these out.

(a) $\frac{1}{4} \times 8$ (b) $12 \times \frac{1}{3}$ (c) $\frac{3}{4}$ of 4   (d) $\frac{2}{3} \times 6$ (e) $\frac{2}{5}$ of 15

A5 Ron does a $\frac{3}{4}$ hour walk each day as his exercise.
How many hours does he walk in

(a) 2 days   (b) 6 days   (c) a week

A6 Erica does a power walk of $3\frac{1}{2}$ km every day.
How far does she walk in one week?

A7 Work these out.
Give your answers as mixed numbers in their simplest form.

(a) $\frac{1}{8}$ of 6   (b) $\frac{2}{5} \times 4$ (c) $\frac{2}{3}$ of 5   (d) $\frac{3}{4} \times 6$ (e) $\frac{5}{6}$ of 3

A8 Jason picks $\frac{3}{4}$ kg of raspberries.
He shares them equally between his three children.
How much do they each get?

A9 Liam buys a pizza.
He eats $\frac{1}{2}$ of it and shares the rest between his 2 children.
What fraction of the pizza does each child get?

B Fraction of a fraction

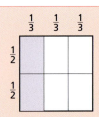 $\frac{1}{3}$ of this square is lightly shaded.

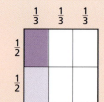 $\frac{1}{2}$ of $\frac{1}{3}$ of the square is heavily shaded.

• What fraction of the whole square is $\frac{1}{2}$ of $\frac{1}{3}$?

B1 What does each of these diagrams show?

(a)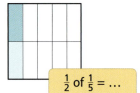

$\frac{1}{2}$ of $\frac{1}{5}$ = …

(b)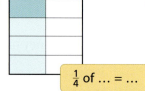

$\frac{1}{4}$ of … = …

(c)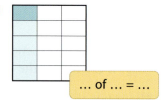

… of … = …

B2 Work these out without drawing diagrams.

(a) $\frac{1}{4}$ of $\frac{1}{3}$ (b) $\frac{1}{2}$ of $\frac{1}{6}$ (c) $\frac{1}{3}$ of $\frac{1}{2}$ (d) $\frac{1}{5}$ of $\frac{1}{4}$

B3 Work these out.

(a) $\frac{1}{4} \div 2$ (b) $\frac{1}{3} \div 4$ (c) $\frac{1}{10} \div 2$ (d) $\frac{1}{3} \div 3$ (e) $\frac{1}{6} \div 3$

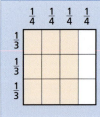 $\frac{3}{4}$ of this square is lightly shaded.

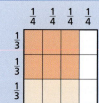 $\frac{2}{3}$ of $\frac{3}{4}$ of this square is heavily shaded.

• What fraction of the whole square is $\frac{2}{3}$ of $\frac{3}{4}$?

B4 What does each of these diagrams show?

(a)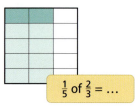

$\frac{1}{5}$ of $\frac{2}{3}$ = …

(b)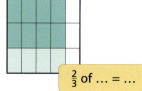

$\frac{2}{3}$ of … = …

(c)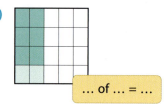

… of … = …

C Multiplying fractions together

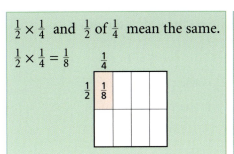

$\frac{1}{2} \times \frac{1}{4}$ and $\frac{1}{2}$ of $\frac{1}{4}$ mean the same.

$\frac{1}{2} \times \frac{1}{4} = \frac{1}{8}$

This diagram shows that $\frac{2}{3} \times \frac{4}{5} = \frac{8}{15}$

Notice that to multiply fractions, you can multiply the numerators and multiply the denominators.

$$\frac{2}{3} \times \frac{4}{5} = \frac{2 \times 4}{3 \times 5} = \frac{8}{15}$$

C1 Work these out.

(a) $\frac{1}{2} \times \frac{1}{3}$ (b) $\frac{1}{3} \times \frac{1}{5}$ (c) $\frac{1}{6} \times \frac{1}{4}$ (d) $\frac{1}{2} \times \frac{3}{5}$ (e) $\frac{1}{3} \times \frac{2}{5}$

(f) $\frac{3}{4} \times \frac{3}{5}$ (g) $\frac{2}{3} \times \frac{4}{7}$ (h) $\frac{4}{5} \times \frac{2}{3}$ (i) $\frac{3}{8} \times \frac{1}{5}$ (j) $\frac{2}{3} \times \frac{5}{7}$

C2 Choose fractions from the loop to make these multiplications correct.
You can use each fraction more than once.

(a) ■ × ■ $= \frac{1}{12}$ (b) ■ × ■ $= \frac{1}{20}$

(c) ■ × ■ $= \frac{1}{30}$ (d) ■ × ■ $= \frac{1}{18}$

(e) ■ × ■ $= \frac{1}{40}$ (f) ■ × ■ $= \frac{1}{24}$

$\frac{1}{4}$ $\frac{1}{8}$ $\frac{1}{3}$ $\frac{1}{6}$ $\frac{1}{5}$

When calculating with fractions, give your answer in its simplest form.

Examples

$\frac{2}{3} \times \frac{3}{8} = \frac{6}{24} = \frac{1}{4}$ (÷6)

$\frac{3}{5} \times \frac{4}{9} = \frac{12}{45} = \frac{4}{15}$ (÷3)

C3 Work these out, giving each result in its simplest form.

(a) $\frac{1}{2} \times \frac{2}{3}$ (b) $\frac{1}{4} \times \frac{2}{5}$ (c) $\frac{1}{3} \times \frac{6}{7}$ (d) $\frac{3}{4} \times \frac{2}{9}$ (e) $\frac{2}{5} \times \frac{3}{8}$

(f) $\frac{3}{7} \times \frac{2}{9}$ (g) $\frac{3}{4} \times \frac{2}{5}$ (h) $\frac{7}{8} \times \frac{2}{3}$ (i) $\frac{3}{10} \times \frac{2}{9}$ (j) $\frac{4}{5} \times \frac{7}{8}$

C4 Copy and complete these.

(a) $\frac{1}{2} \times$ ■ $= \frac{1}{12}$ (b) ■ $\times \frac{1}{5} = \frac{1}{15}$ (c) $\frac{2}{3} \times$ ■ $= \frac{2}{15}$ (d) ■ $\times \frac{5}{8} = \frac{15}{56}$

C5 Copy and complete this multiplication table.
Write each fraction in its simplest form.

×	$\frac{1}{2}$	$\frac{1}{3}$	$\frac{1}{4}$
$\frac{2}{5}$			$\frac{1}{10}$
$\frac{3}{10}$	$\frac{3}{20}$		

C6 Work these out.

(a) $2 \times \frac{1}{2}$ (b) $\frac{1}{3} \times 3$ (c) $5 \times \frac{1}{5}$ (d) $\frac{2}{3} \times \frac{3}{2}$ (e) $\frac{3}{4} \times \frac{4}{3}$

D Reciprocals

If two numbers multiply together to give 1, each is called the **reciprocal** of the other.

$$2 \times \tfrac{1}{2} = 1$$

$\tfrac{1}{2}$ is the reciprocal of 2.

2 is the reciprocal of $\tfrac{1}{2}$.

$$\tfrac{3}{4} \times \tfrac{4}{3} = 1$$

$\tfrac{4}{3}$ is the reciprocal of $\tfrac{3}{4}$.

$\tfrac{3}{4}$ is the reciprocal of $\tfrac{4}{3}$.

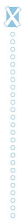

D1 Write down the reciprocal of each of these.

(a) 3 (b) $\tfrac{1}{3}$ (c) 5 (d) $\tfrac{2}{5}$ (e) $\tfrac{5}{6}$

(f) $\tfrac{1}{8}$ (g) $\tfrac{5}{7}$ (h) $\tfrac{5}{4}$ (i) 8 (j) 1

D2 (a) Write $1\tfrac{1}{2}$ as an improper fraction.

(b) Hence write down the reciprocal of $1\tfrac{1}{2}$.

D3 For each fraction below

(i) write it as an improper fraction

(ii) write down its reciprocal

(a) $3\tfrac{1}{2}$ (b) $1\tfrac{1}{3}$ (c) $2\tfrac{1}{4}$ (d) $1\tfrac{2}{5}$ (e) $2\tfrac{2}{3}$

E Dividing a whole number by a fraction

$3 \div \tfrac{1}{4}$ can mean

'how many $\tfrac{1}{4}$s make 3 whole ones?'

The answer is 12.

Notice that $3 \div \tfrac{1}{4} = 3 \times 4$

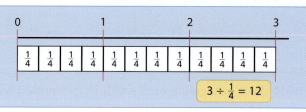

$3 \div \tfrac{1}{4} = 12$

E1 What is $3 \div \tfrac{1}{3}$?
This diagram may help.

E2 What is $4 \div \tfrac{1}{6}$?

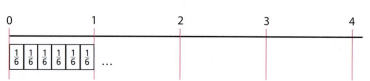

E3 Work these out. Imagine a diagram like those above if it helps.

(a) $4 \div \tfrac{1}{2}$ (b) $3 \div \tfrac{1}{5}$ (c) $2 \div \tfrac{1}{8}$ (d) $5 \div \tfrac{1}{4}$ (e) $6 \div \tfrac{1}{3}$

In every case so far, dividing by a fraction is the same as multiplying by its reciprocal.
We shall see whether it is true for dividing by, say, $\frac{2}{3}$.

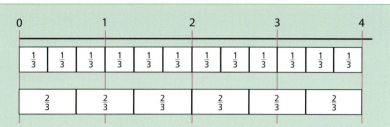

$4 \div \frac{1}{3} = 4 \times 3 = 12$

$4 \div \frac{2}{3} = 6$ (half of 12)

So $4 \div \frac{2}{3}$ is the same as $4 \times \frac{3}{2}$.

Dividing by a fraction is the same as multiplying by its reciprocal.

E4 (a) Work out $2 \div \frac{1}{5}$.
Check from the diagram.

(b) Work out $2 \div \frac{2}{5}$.
Check from the diagram.

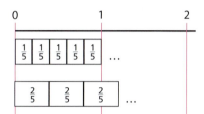

E5 Work these out.

(a) $6 \div \frac{1}{4}$ **(b)** $6 \div \frac{3}{4}$ **(c)** $6 \div \frac{1}{3}$ **(d)** $6 \div \frac{2}{3}$ **(e)** $4 \div \frac{2}{5}$

E6 Work these out. Give your answers as mixed numbers.

(a) $3 \div \frac{4}{5}$ **(b)** $2 \div \frac{3}{4}$ **(c)** $2 \div \frac{3}{5}$ **(d)** $1 \div \frac{3}{4}$ **(e)** $3 \div \frac{2}{5}$

E7 (a) Ashish's kitten eats $\frac{1}{3}$ of a tin of cat food each day.
Find out how many days 8 tins will last the kitten, by dividing 8 by $\frac{1}{3}$.

(b) The kitten's mother eats $\frac{2}{3}$ of a tin each day.
Find out how many days 8 tins will last the mother, by dividing 8 by $\frac{2}{3}$.

*E8 Max's ox pulls a heavy cart at $\frac{3}{4}$ m.p.h.
How long will it take the cart to travel 6 miles?

*E9 Only $\frac{4}{5}$ of the weight of apples is usable for making puddings,
because the peel and core are thrown away.
What weight do you need to start with in order to have 20 kg usable?

Here is another way to see why dividing is the same as multiplying by the reciprocal.

To multiply by $\frac{3}{4}$, multiply by 3 and divide by 4

Division is the **inverse** operation,

so to divide by $\frac{3}{4}$, multiply by 4 and divide by 3

F Dividing a fraction by a fraction

Example

Work out $\frac{3}{4} \div \frac{5}{8}$.

To divide by $\frac{5}{8}$, multiply by its reciprocal, $\frac{8}{5}$.

$$\frac{3}{4} \div \frac{5}{8} = \frac{3}{4} \times \frac{8}{5} = \frac{24}{20} = \frac{6}{5}$$

Give your answer in its simplest form.

F1 Work these out.

(a) $\frac{1}{2} \div \frac{1}{3}$ (b) $\frac{2}{3} \div \frac{3}{4}$ (c) $\frac{1}{5} \div \frac{4}{7}$ (d) $\frac{2}{5} \div \frac{3}{4}$ (e) $\frac{3}{8} \div \frac{2}{3}$

F2 Work these out, giving each result in its simplest form.

(a) $\frac{5}{6} \div \frac{1}{4}$ (b) $\frac{1}{4} \div \frac{5}{8}$ (c) $\frac{2}{5} \div \frac{9}{10}$ (d) $\frac{3}{4} \div \frac{5}{8}$ (e) $\frac{2}{3} \div \frac{4}{9}$

Test yourself

T1 (a) Ann eats three-quarters of a pound of fruit each day.
How much fruit does she eat in seven days?

(b) Tony eats $\frac{1}{4}$ kg of fruit each day.
He has 3 kg of fruit.
How many days will it take him to eat this fruit?   AQA

T2 Tom has £2200.
He gives $\frac{1}{4}$ to his son and $\frac{2}{5}$ to his daughter.

How much does Tom keep for himself?
You must show all your working.   AQA

T3 Write down the reciprocal of each of these.

(a) 4   (b) $\frac{1}{5}$ (c) $\frac{2}{3}$ (d) 10

T4 Work these out.

(a) $\frac{1}{5}$ of $\frac{2}{7}$ (b) $\frac{1}{4}$ of $\frac{3}{8}$ (c) $\frac{2}{5}$ of $\frac{1}{3}$ (d) $\frac{2}{3}$ of $\frac{5}{9}$ (e) $\frac{3}{4}$ of $\frac{5}{7}$

T5 Work these out, giving each answer in its simplest form.

(a) $\frac{1}{4} \times \frac{3}{8}$ (b) $\frac{2}{3} \times \frac{3}{8}$ (c) $\frac{1}{10} \times \frac{4}{7}$ (d) $\frac{2}{5} \times \frac{5}{6}$ (e) $\frac{5}{9} \times \frac{3}{4}$

T6 Work these out.

(a) $3 \div \frac{1}{6}$ (b) $3 \div \frac{5}{6}$ (c) $\frac{2}{3} \div \frac{1}{6}$ (d) $\frac{2}{3} \div \frac{5}{6}$ (e) $\frac{3}{8} \div \frac{2}{5}$

4 Accuracy

You will revise rounding.

This work will help you

- give quantities to a sensible degree of accuracy
- understand that measurements can be inaccurate by up to half a unit above or below

A Review: rounding

A1 Round each of these lengths to the nearest centimetre.

    (a) 6 centimetres and 2 millimetres   **(b)** 4 centimetres and 9 millimetres

    (c) 9 centimetres and 7 millimetres   **(d)** 12 centimetres and 1 millimetre

A2 Round each of these lengths to the nearest metre.

    (a) 5 metres and 13 centimetres   **(b)** 12 metres and 59 centimetres

    (c) 34 metres and 78 centimetres   **(d)** 2 metres and 8 centimetres

A3 Round each of these times to the nearest minute.

    (a) 2 minutes and 46 seconds   **(b)** 3 minutes and 29 seconds

    (c) 14 minutes and 36 seconds   **(d)** 21 minutes and 7 seconds

A4 Round each of these weights to the nearest kilogram.

    (a) 23 kilograms and 800 grams   **(b)** 167 kilograms and 235 grams

    (c) 29 kilograms and 532 grams   **(d)** 16 kilograms and 54 grams

A5 Round each of these to the nearest £1.

    (a) £5.63   **(b)** £7.80   **(c)** £9.07   **(d)** £24.52   **(e)** £20.42

A6 Round each of these to the nearest whole number.

    (a) 5.7   **(b)** 12.4   **(c)** 7.29   **(d)** 8.541   **(e)** 2.09

A7 Round each of these to one decimal place.

    (a) 1.24   **(b)** 4.08   **(c)** 72.152   **(d)** 2.308   **(e)** 1.397 291

A8 Round each of these to two decimal places.

    (a) 1.836   **(b)** 2.753   **(c)** 1.602   **(d)** 4.7209   **(e)** 4.3982

A9 Round each of these to one significant figure.

    (a) 0.6753   **(b)** 4.125   **(c)** 73.68   **(d)** 209.75   **(e)** 9.863

B Deciding on sensible accuracy

The measurements used in these statements are very accurate.

- How would you write each with more sensible accuracy?

A It takes Julie 8 minutes and 55 seconds to walk to the station.

B Hayleigh's height is 1 metre, 52 centimetres and 3 millimetres.

C Shawn has a sack of potatoes that weighs 56 kilograms and 231 grams.

D The distance from Amber's house to town is 38 kilometres and 824 metres.

E Ken took 2 weeks, 5 days, 7 hours and 4 minutes to build the wall.

F Tim is on a diet and lost 1.94 kg last week.

G The length of Kay's garden is 18.657 metres.

H The distance Hamish walked was 6.781 km.

I The church tower is 18.762 m high.

Big beast isn't he? And believe it or not this skeleton is **70 000 002** years old!

How do you know its age so accurately?

A scientist visited the museum and told me it was **70 000 000** years old …

… and that was **2 years ago**.

B1 The number of people at a football match is 47 231.
Which of these rounded values do you think would appear in a newspaper headline?

A 47 230 **B** 47 200 **C** 47 000 **D** 50 000

B2 The length of a road is measured as 26 kilometres, 817 metres and 64 centimetres.
Which of these values would be appropriate to give organisers of a sponsored walk?

A 26 km 818 m   **B** 26 km 800 m   **C** 27 km   **D** 30 km

B3 Dee drives from her home in Taunton to visit a friend in Glasgow.
The journey takes 7 hours, 37 minutes and 15 seconds.
If she was asked how long the drive took what do you think she would say?

A 7 hours 37 min   **B** 7 hours 40 min   **C** $7\frac{1}{2}$ hours   **D** 8 hours

B4 The weight of an elephant in a zoo is measured as 5826.9 kilograms.
Which of these values would you use in a leaflet about the animals in the zoo?

A 5827 kg   **B** 5830 kg   **C** 5800 kg   **D** 6000 kg

B5 Asif's height is measured as 1.674 metres.
Which of these values should he give as his height for his passport?

A 1.67 m   **B** 1.7 m   **C** 2 m

B6 The height of a room is measured as 2.357 metres.
Which of these values would be appropriate to give a painter and decorator?

A 2.36 m   **B** 2.4 m   **C** 2 m

B7 This has been written to be part of a leaflet about Bunchester.
Write each of the quantities in bold in what you think is the most appropriate way.
(You may not have to change them all.)

> The city of Bunchester is **243 kilometres and 673 metres** from the capital.
> The journey by train takes **2 hours, 28 minutes and 5 seconds**.
>
> The population of the city is **148 843**, and **32 422** of them are over the age of sixty.
>
> Bunchester covers an area of **11.8643 square kilometres**.
> The city is situated on the River Bunn, which is **186 metres and 23 centimetres** wide here.
> The distance from the coast is **35.270 km**.
>
> There are four bridges across the river. The newest of these is a suspension bridge with
> a span of **144.783 m** and towers that reach a height of **58.32 m** above the river bed.
> Each of the main cables of this bridge is **316.6 mm** in diameter.
>
> Bunchester Cathedral dates from **1284** and has a spire that is **87.63 m** high.
> Inside it is a bishop's throne that is made from solid granite and weighs **18 538.296 kg**.
>
> Bunchester is famous for its open air Rock Music Festival.
> Last year **184 529** people visited the festival and the final concert by The Maniacs
> could be heard up to a distance of **6.842 km** away.

C Giving answers to a sensible degree of accuracy

T
• Find the answer to each problem and write it using a sensible degree of accuracy.

Poppy is making fruit slices.

She cooks the mixture in a tin and cuts it into six slices as shown.

What is the width of each slice?

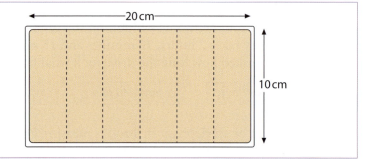

A piece of cheese weighs 6.517 kg.

It is cut into 11 equal pieces to sell in a supermarket.
What is the weight of each piece?

Solve each problem and give your answer to a sensible degree of accuracy.

C1 Emma has a piece of cheese that weighs 424 grams.
She cuts it into 12 equal pieces.
What is the weight of each piece?

C2 A sack of flour that weighs 10 kg is divided into 6 bags of equal weight.
What is the weight of each bag?

C3 A length of silk that is 22.53 m long is cut into 8 equal lengths.
What is the length of each piece?

C4 What is the area of this rug?

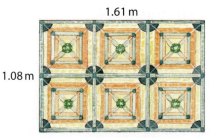

1.61 m

1.08 m

C5 These are the weights of seven people in a tug-of-war team.

84 kg   78 kg   87 kg   79 kg   91 kg   95 kg   93 kg

What is the mean of these weights?

D Lower and upper limits of rounded measurements

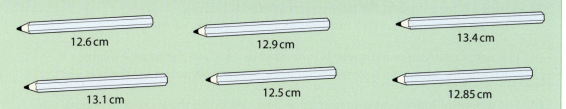

- What is the length of each pencil, to the nearest centimetre?

    12.6 cm   12.9 cm   13.4 cm

    13.1 cm   12.5 cm   12.85 cm

- What other lengths give the result 13 cm when rounded to the nearest centimetre?

- Measure the length of each line and write it correct to the nearest centimetre.

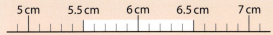

    A _____

    B _____

    C _____

    D _____

    E _____

    F _____

When you are measuring correct to the nearest centimetre,
any length **between** 5.5 cm and 6.5 cm will be measured as 6 cm.

    5 cm   5.5 cm   6 cm   6.5 cm   7 cm

So we say that a length rounded to 6 cm has a **minimum** value of 5.5 cm
and a **maximum** value of 6.5 cm.

D1 A piece of cheese is weighed as 42 g correct to the nearest gram.
What is the missing weight in the statement below?

   The weight of cheese must be between 41.5 g and ....

D2 The length of Polly's index finger is measured to the nearest centimetre as 8 cm.
What is the missing length in the statement below?

   The length of Polly's finger must be between .... and 8.5 cm.

D3 The weight of an apple is measured as 50 g, correct to the nearest gram.
What is the missing weight in the statement below?

   The weight of the apple must be between 49.5 g and ....

D4 The distance between two towns is measured as 20 km, correct to the nearest km. What is the missing distance in the statement below?

The distance between the towns must be between .... and 20.5 km

D5 A pencil is measured to the nearest centimetre as 7 cm. What are the minimum and maximum possible lengths of the pencil?

D6 The temperature of some water is measured as 13 °C, to the nearest degree. What are the minimum and maximum possible temperatures for the water?

D7 The weight of Mary's cat is measured as 2 kg, correct to the nearest kilogram. What is the maximum possible weight of the cat?

D8 The distance between two towns is given as 60 km, correct to the nearest kilometre. What is the minimum distance between the towns?

D9 A piece of cheese has been weighed correct to the nearest gram as 24 grams. Which of the weights below could be the weight of the cheese?

    A 24.4 g   **B** 24.7 g   **C** 23.8 g   **D** 23.1 g   **E** 25.1 g

D10 The length of a room has been measured correct to the nearest metre as 5 metres. Which of the lengths below could be the length of the room?

    A 5.24 m   **B** 5.56 m   **C** 4.75 m   **D** 5.49 m   **E** 4.39 m

D11 The length of an envelope is measured as 15 cm, correct to the nearest centimetre. The length of a birthday card is also measured as 15 cm, correct to the nearest centimetre.

Can you be sure that the card will fit in the envelope?
Explain your answer carefully.

Test yourself

T1 A piece of cheese that weighs 215 grams is cut into 6 equal pieces. What is the weight of each piece? Write your answer using a sensible degree of accuracy.

T2 In a chemistry experiment, a student produces a solution with a volume of 155 millilitres, correct to the nearest millilitre. Write down the greatest and least volume that the solution could have.

T3 The temperature in a room is measured as 20 °C, correct to the nearest degree. What is the minimum possible temperature?

5 Probability

You will revise how to find probabilities using equally likely outcomes.

You will learn how to

- **calculate a probability, using the fact that the probabilities of all the possible outcomes add up to 1**
- **estimate a probability from experimental data**

A Review: equally likely outcomes

Here are two unbiased dice.

A

B

Dice A

Dice B

+	1	2	3	4	5	6
1	2	3	4	5	6	7
2	3	4	5	6	7	8
3	4	5	6	7	8	9
4	5	6	7	8	9	10

Dice A has six faces numbered 1 to 6.

Dice B has four faces numbered 1 to 4. (The score is the number on the base.)

If both dice are rolled, there are 24 equally likely outcomes.

Each outcome is a cell on the grid, with its total score written in.

There are 4 outcomes where the total score is 7 (shown in red).

So the probability of getting a total score of 7 is $\frac{4}{24} = \frac{1}{6}$.

A1 Dice A and dice B are both rolled.
What is the probability that the total score is

(a) 5 **(b)** 3 **(c)** 9 **(d)** 2 **(e)** 1

A2 Dice C has eight faces numbered 1 to 8. It is also unbiased.

C

Dice B and dice C are rolled.

(a) Draw a grid showing the equally likely outcomes and total scores.

(b) How many equally likely outcomes are there?

(c) What is the probability that the total score is

(i) 9 **(ii)** 10 **(iii)** 11 **(iv)** 12 **(v)** 13

A3 These two spinners are spun.

A
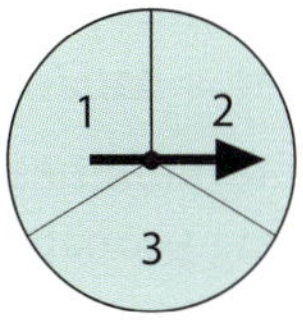

B

(a) Draw a grid showing the equally likely outcomes and total scores.

(b) What is the probability that the total score is

(i) 6 **(ii)** 7 **(iii)** an even number **(iv)** a multiple of 3

B Probabilities adding to 1

The four colours on this spinner are not equally likely.
Their probabilities are:

red	blue	yellow	green
$\frac{1}{10}$ or 0.1	$\frac{2}{10}$ or 0.2	$\frac{4}{10}$ or 0.4	$\frac{3}{10}$ or 0.3

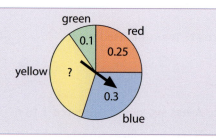

These probabilities add up to 1, because there are no other colours
on the spinner.

If we know the values of three of them, we can easily find the fourth.

Example

On this spinner the probabilities of red, blue and green
add up to $0.25 + 0.3 + 0.1 = 0.65$.

So the probability of yellow is $1 - 0.65 = 0.35$.

B1 A bag contains only red, yellow and green sweets.
A sweet is picked at random from the bag.

This table shows the probability of picking
each colour.
Find the probability of picking a green sweet.

Colour	Red	Yellow	Green
Probability	0.15	0.6	

B2 A spinner can show red, blue, green
or yellow.
Find the missing probability in this table.

Colour	Red	Blue	Green	Yellow
Probability	0.1	0.08		0.25

B3 The chocolates in a box have either hard or soft centres,
covered with milk, dark or white chocolate.

A chocolate is taken at random.
The table shows the probability of picking
each type of chocolate.

	Hard centre	Soft centre
Milk	0.16	0.2
Dark	0.08	
White	0.1	0.24

(a) What is the probability of picking a white chocolate with a hard centre?

(b) Find the missing probability in the table.

B4 A gambling machine has a dial that shows
an apple, a pear, a banana or a cherry.

Some of the probabilities are shown here.
Find the missing probability.

Fruit	Apple	Pear	Banana	Cherry
Probability	$\frac{1}{3}$	$\frac{1}{6}$	$\frac{1}{4}$	

C Using probability to estimate frequency

If an ordinary dice is thrown a large number of times, then you would expect each score 1 to 6 to come up the same number of times.

So you would expect $\frac{1}{6}$ of the throws to give a score of 1, $\frac{1}{6}$ to give a score of 2, and so on.

In practice, this does not happen exactly. Each score comes up in **roughly** $\frac{1}{6}$ of the throws.

For example, an ordinary dice was thrown 300 times.
The frequency of each score was as shown in this table.

Score	1	2	3	4	5	6
Frequency	48	44	55	51	53	49

The expected frequency of each score is $\frac{1}{6}$ of $300 = 50$.

Each actual frequency was fairly close to 50.
(If some scores were very different from 50, we might suspect that the dice is biased.)

C1 This spinner is spun 150 times.
Roughly how many spins would you expect to score 2?

C2 This spinner is spun.

(a) What is the probability that it shows red?

(b) The spinner is spun 500 times.
Roughly how many times would you expect it to show red?

C3 Two unbiased four-sided dice, each labelled 1 to 4, are rolled.

(a) Show all the possible outcomes, with the total scores, on a grid.

(b) Find the probability that the total score is 6.

(c) The two dice are rolled 400 times.
Roughly how many times would you expect the total score to be 6?

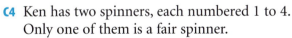

C4 Ken has two spinners, each numbered 1 to 4.
Only one of them is a fair spinner.

These tables show the results of spinning each spinner 80 times.

Which spinner do you think is fair, spinner A or spinner B?
Explain your decision.

A Score	Frequency
1	19
2	22
3	21
4	18

B Score	Frequency
1	15
2	18
3	15
4	32

D Relative frequency

In the last section we used a known probability to estimate the number of times something would happen.

Sometimes the probability is unknown, but we can estimate it by repeating an experiment a large number of times.

Suppose we drop a spoon on the floor. We can't tell by looking at the spoon whether the two outcomes are equally likely.

right way up

upside down

A particular spoon was dropped 200 times.
The table below shows the frequencies of the two possible outcomes.

	Right way up	Upside down	Total
Frequency	152	48	200

The results show that for this spoon 'right way up' is more likely than 'upside down'.

The fraction $\dfrac{\text{number of 'right way up'}}{\text{total number of drops}}$ is called the **relative frequency** of 'right way up'.

In this example, the relative frequency of 'right way up' is $\frac{152}{200} = 0.76$.
(Relative frequencies are usually given as decimals.)

The relative frequency is an estimate of the probability.
So the probability of 'right way up' is estimated as 0.76.

To get a better estimate, the spoon would need to be dropped more often.

D1 For the spoon above, estimate the probability of 'upside down' and check that the two probabilities add up to 1.

D2 In some games, sticks like the one shown here are thrown.  They are flat on one side and curved on the other.

Jade wanted to estimate the probability that a stick would land on its flat side. She threw it 80 times. It landed on its flat side 25 times.

(a) Estimate the probability that the stick lands on its flat side.

(b) Estimate the probability that it lands on its curved side.

(c) A stick is thrown 200 times.
Estimate the number of times you would expect it to land on its flat side.

D3 Darshat spins a spinner 140 times. It shows red 49 times.

(a) Estimate the probability that the spinner shows red.

(b) Estimate the probability that it does not show red.

(c) Estimate the number of times it will show red in 200 spins.

D4 Sean records the colour of each car that passes a point on a road.
After an hour, his record looks like this.

Colour	White	Red	Blue	Yellow	Green	Brown	Black	Other
Number of cars	37	31	18	8	6	6	4	10

(a) How many cars did Sean record?

(b) Calculate the relative frequency of blue cars.

(c) How many of the next 200 cars would you expect to be blue?

D5 Britalite is a company that make light bulbs.
They tested 250 of their bulbs to see how long they lasted.

24 bulbs lasted less than 1000 hours.
208 lasted between 1000 and 2000 hours.
The rest lasted over 2000 hours.

(a) Estimate the probability that a Britalite bulb lasts

    (i) less than 1000 hours   (ii) over 2000 hours

(b) A company orders 2000 light bulbs.
Estimate how many of them will last 1000 hours or over.

D6 Sue does an experiment to estimate the probability
that a spoon lands 'right way up'.

Her results are shown here, in groups of ten.
'R' means 'right way up' and 'U' means 'upside down'.

(a) Calculate the relative frequency of 'right way up'
after 10 drops.

(b) Check from the table that after 20 drops, the spoon
has landed 'right way up' 13 times.

Calculate the relative frequency of 'right way up'
after 20 drops.

(c) Continue for 30, 40, … drops and write the results
in a table.

Number of drops	10	20	30	40	50	…
Relative frequency of 'R'	0.8	0.65	…			

(d) Draw axes on squared paper using
the scales shown here.
Plot the points from your table.

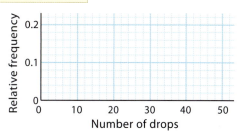

(e) What does the graph show about the relative
frequency as the number of drops increases?

Test yourself

T1 A dice is biased.
The table below shows the probability of obtaining each score when the dice is rolled.

Score	1	2	3	4	5	6
Probability	0.2	0.1	0.15	0.05	0.2	x

Find the value of x.   OCR

T2 A bag contains discs of different colours.
In an experiment Murinder took one disc out at random, noted its colour, then put it back into the bag.

He repeated this 50 times.
Here are Murinder's results.

Estimate the probability that the next time Murinder takes a disc it will be red.

Colour	Frequency
Blue	10
Green	12
Yellow	8
Red	20

                                                                                       OCR

T3 Bernadette's printer sometimes feeds in two sheets at a time (but never more than two).
When this happens, an extra blank sheet comes out with the copy.

Bernadette wants to estimate the probability that this happens.
After printing a run of 120 copies she finds 15 extra blank sheets among the copies.

(a) Estimate the probability that the printer feeds in two sheets at a time.

(b) After printing 800 copies, how many blank sheets should Bernadette expect to find?

T4 There are red, green, blue and yellow counters in a bag.
A counter is taken from the bag at random.
The colour is recorded and the counter is replaced.

This is repeated a number of times.
The table below shows the results.

Red	Blue	Green	Yellow
84	158	182	176

(a) What is the relative frequency of choosing a blue counter?

(b) Emma thinks that there are fewer red counters in the bag than any other colour.
Is she right? Justify your answer.   OCR

6 Using a calculator

You should know how to round to a given number of decimal places and to one significant figure.

This work will help you

- use a calculator for complex calculations
- use the unitary method to solve problems

A Order of operations

In calculations without brackets, do any multiplications before additions or subtractions.

Examples

$3 + 2 \times 4$	$11 - 3 \times 2$	$3 \times 5 + 2 \times 4$
$= 3 + 8$	$= 11 - 6$	$= 15 + 8$
$= 11$	$= 5$	$= 23$

Check that your calculator follows these rules.

A1 Do each of these in your head. Then check each one using a calculator.

(a) $2 + 6 \times 4$ (b) $10 - 3 \times 3$ (c) $8 + 5 \times 4 - 1$ (d) $7 \times 4 - 2 \times 6$

A2 Do each of these on a calculator.

(a) $34 + 16 \times 9$ (b) $84 - 26 \times 3$ (c) $17 \times 38 - 24$ (d) $762 - 23 \times 22 + 120$

A3 Do these on a calculator. Round each answer to the nearest integer.

(a) $29.4 + 13.6 \times 2.7$ (b) $83.4 - 16.5 \times 1.4$ (c) $25.3 + 76.4 \times 0.35$

A4 Do these on a calculator. Round each answer to one decimal place.

(a) $18.6 \times 2.6 + 41.7$ (b) $27.4 + 9.4 \times 13.2$ (c) $6.4 \times 3.9 - 7.4 \times 2.6$

B Division

In written calculations, a bar is often used for division.
Do any multiplications and divisions before additions or subtractions.

Examples

$6 + \dfrac{8}{2}$	$\dfrac{10}{2} - \dfrac{9}{3}$	$4 \times 2 - \dfrac{6}{3}$
$= 6 + 4$	$= 5 - 3$	$= 8 - 2$
$= 10$	$= 2$	$= 6$

Check that your calculator follows these rules.

B1 Do each of these in your head. Then check each one using a calculator.

(a) $4 + \dfrac{6}{2}$ (b) $\dfrac{12}{4} - 2$ (c) $\dfrac{24}{3} - \dfrac{28}{7}$ (d) $\dfrac{15}{3} + 4 \times 3$

B2 Do each of these on a calculator.

(a) $\dfrac{275}{25} + 38$ (b) $77 - \dfrac{286}{22}$ (c) $\dfrac{738}{18} - \dfrac{578}{34}$ (d) $345 + \dfrac{9018}{54}$

B3 Calculate these. Round each answer to the nearest integer.

(a) $45.2 + \dfrac{78.2}{6.8}$ (b) $112 - \dfrac{58.5}{15.6}$ (c) $\dfrac{34.6}{3.7} + 5.18$ (d) $23.6 - \dfrac{13.2}{0.72}$

B4 Do these on a calculator. Give each answer correct to two decimal places.

(a) $2.6 \times 5.4 + \dfrac{25.8}{6.4}$ (b) $\dfrac{11.34}{1.46} + \dfrac{23.54}{2.57}$ (c) $\dfrac{10.8}{3.56} + 0.65 \times 62.5$

C Negative numbers

Most calculators have a 'change sign' key $\boxed{+/-}$ or $\boxed{(-)}$ for entering negative numbers.
On some calculators you press this key after the number, on others before.
• Find out how to use your calculator to work out $1 + {}^-5$.

C1 Do each of these first without a calculator. Then use a calculator to check your answers.

(a) $7 + {}^-2$ (b) ${}^-1 + {}^-4$ (c) ${}^-7 + 3$ (d) ${}^-3 \times {}^-4$ (e) ${}^-2 \times {}^-5$

(f) ${}^-10 \div 2$ (g) ${}^-12 \div {}^-4$ (h) ${}^-1 + 2.5$ (i) $5 - {}^-2$ (j) ${}^-3 - {}^-5$

C2 Use a calculator to work these out.

(a) ${}^-17 + 54$ (b) $24 + {}^-67$ (c) ${}^-24 \times 15$ (d) ${}^-17 \times {}^-17$

(e) ${}^-45 \div 18$ (f) ${}^-56 - {}^-68$ (g) $2.5 + {}^-6.7$ (h) ${}^-3.5 \times {}^-6.7$

C3 The melting point of mercury is ${}^-38.9\,°C$.
The boiling point of mercury is $356.7\,°C$.
What is the difference between these two temperatures?

D Brackets

Written down	On the calculator	
$(4 + 5) \times 3$	$(4 + 5) \times 3 =$	
$7 \times (8 - 2)$	$7 \times (8 - 2) =$	
$\dfrac{7 + 8}{5}$	$(7 + 8) \div 5 =$	The division bar does a similar job to brackets.
$\dfrac{9 + 3}{6 - 4}$	$(9 + 3) \div (6 - 4) =$	Two sets of brackets are needed.

Check that you can work these out on your calculator.

D1 Do each of these in your head. Then check each one using a calculator.

(a) $7 \times (5 - 2)$ (b) $\dfrac{4 + 8}{3}$ (c) $\dfrac{15 - 3}{3 \times 2}$

D2 Do these on a calculator. Round the answers to one decimal place.

(a) $(5.67 + 2.95) \times 3.24$ (b) $2.64 \times (3.21 - 0.88)$ (c) $0.057 \times (34.2 + 12.8)$

(d) $\dfrac{12.55 - 3.68}{2.69}$ (e) $\dfrac{14.32 + 6.05}{0.15}$ (f) $\dfrac{9.86 \times 3.28}{1.43}$

D3 Do these on a calculator.

(a) $5 - (^-3 + 10)$ (b) $^-8 \times (^-5 + ^-7)$ (c) $^-2.7 \times (5.2 - 6.8)$

D4 Do these on a calculator. Round each answer to two decimal places.

(a) $\dfrac{4.86}{2.57 - 1.08}$ (b) $\dfrac{9.08 + 7.12}{6.48 - 3.25}$ (c) $\dfrac{4.72 \times 3.14}{6.82 - 4.01}$

D5 Each of these calculations should have a set of brackets.
Copy each calculation and add brackets to make the answer correct.

(a) $4.2 + 6.3 \times 4 = 42$ (b) $0.8 \times 1.4 + 3.6 \times 0.4 = 1.6$

E Squares and square roots

Squares

The squaring key is often labelled $\boxed{x^2}$. To do 4^2, press $\boxed{4}$ $\boxed{x^2}$.

Written down	On the calculator	
$9 + 5^2$	$9 + 5\,\boxed{x^2}\, =$	Only the 5 is squared.
$(9 + 5)^2$	$(9 + 5)\,\boxed{x^2}\, =$	The result of the bracket is squared.

E1 Calculate these, giving each answer correct to two decimal places.

(a) 4.74^2 (b) $(^-0.85)^2$ (c) $(1.56 - 0.28)^2$ (d) $1.85^2 - 0.72$

(e) $3.12 + 1.64^2$ (f) $(7.39 + 0.47)^2$ (g) $7.26 - 1.24^2$ (h) $3.44^2 - 1.63^2$

Square roots

The square root key is often labelled $\boxed{\sqrt{}}$.

On some calculators you press this key before the number, on others after.

So $\sqrt{9}$ may be $\boxed{\sqrt{}}$ $\boxed{9}$ or $\boxed{9}$ $\boxed{\sqrt{}}$.

E2 Use a calculator to find these.

(a) $\sqrt{784}$ (b) $\sqrt{18.49}$ (c) $\sqrt{0.2916}$ (d) $\sqrt{1049.76}$

E3 Use a calculator to evaluate these.

(a) $26.4 + \sqrt{57.76}$ (b) $5.5 \times \sqrt{77.44}$ (c) $\dfrac{\sqrt{12.96}}{1.6}$ (d) $4.5^2 + \sqrt{2.89}$

E4 (a) (i) Using the facts that $3^2 = 9$ and $4^2 = 16$,
estimate the nearest whole number to $\sqrt{10}$.

(ii) Use your calculator to find $\sqrt{10}$ correct to two decimal places.

(b) (i) Estimate the nearest whole number to $\sqrt{75}$.

(ii) Use your calculator to find $\sqrt{75}$ correct to two decimal places.

> The square root sign applies only to the number it is written by.
> $\sqrt{9} + 7$ means 'square root of 9, then add 7' which comes to $3 + 7 = 10$.
> $\sqrt{9+7}$ means 'do $9 + 7$ first, then find the square root'.

E5 Do these on a calculator. Give your answers correct to two decimal places.

(a) $\sqrt{\dfrac{19}{6}}$ (b) $\dfrac{\sqrt{2.6+3.7}}{1.5+2.8}$ (c) $\sqrt{4.4^2+1.9^2}$ (d) $\sqrt{\dfrac{9.8+7.2}{6.8-3.5}}$

E6 Many calculators have a cube root key. It is often labelled $\boxed{\sqrt[3]{}}$.
Use the cube root key to find the cube root of these numbers.

(a) 3375 (b) 6859 (c) 0.216 (d) 1.728

F Reciprocals

> You can work out $\tfrac{1}{4}$ on a calculator using $\boxed{1}$ $\boxed{\div}$ $\boxed{4}$ or $\boxed{4}$ $\boxed{\tfrac{1}{x}}$ or $\boxed{4}$ $\boxed{x^{-1}}$.
>
> Check that you get the answer 0.25.
>
> $\tfrac{1}{4}$ or 0.25 is the **reciprocal** of 4.
>
> • What is the reciprocal of 0.25?

F1 What are the reciprocals of these numbers?

(a) 2 (b) 8 (c) 20 (d) 100 (e) 0.125
(f) 0.05 (g) 0.4 (h) 0.025 (i) 1.6 (j) 64

F2 Use a calculator to work these out.

(a) $\dfrac{1}{16}$ (b) $\dfrac{1}{50}$ (c) $\dfrac{1}{3.2}$ (d) $\dfrac{1}{12.5}$ (e) $\dfrac{1}{0.64}$

F3 Use a calculator to work these out. Give your answers to two decimal places.

(a) $\dfrac{1}{3.2 + 4.7}$ (b) $7.4 + \dfrac{1}{16}$ (c) $\dfrac{1}{\sqrt{10.24}}$ (d) $5.6 + \dfrac{1}{2.5^2}$

G Checking by a rough estimate

G1 Amber had to calculate $\dfrac{8.3 + 3.8}{2.1}$. She got the answer 10.11, which is wrong.

She should have checked her answer by making a rough estimate:
8.3 is roughly 8, 3.8 is roughly 4 and 2.1 is roughly 2.

(a) Without using a calculator, use these approximations to get a rough estimate
for the answer to this calculation.

(b) Do the actual calculation on your calculator. Give your answer to two decimal places.

G2 Pat wants to get a rough estimate for $\dfrac{4.9 \times 22}{3.8}$.

(a) Write down a calculation Pat could do to get a rough estimate.

(b) Work out the rough estimate without using a calculator.

(c) Use a calculator to work out $\dfrac{4.9 \times 22}{3.8}$ and compare the result with your estimate.

G3 For each calculation below

      (i) work out a rough estimate   (ii) calculate the result, to two decimal places

(a) $\dfrac{58}{9.2 - 2.8}$ (b) $\dfrac{202 \times 0.48}{1.8}$ (c) $\dfrac{28 \times 4.2}{3.8 + 1.9}$

H Unitary method

Example

A pile of 15 identical books is 38 cm high.

How high is a pile of 35 of these books?
Give your answer to the nearest cm.

Keep all the figures on your calculator display.

15 books are 38 cm

÷ 15   ÷ 15

1 book is 38 ÷ 15 = 2.53333... cm

× 35   × 35

35 books are 2.53333... × 35 cm

So the height of 35 books is 88.66666...
= 89 cm (to the nearest cm)

Only round when you get to the final answer.

H1 Lucy was paid £88.50 for 15 hours' work.

(a) How much was she paid for each hour?

(b) How much would she be paid for 26 hours' work, at the same hourly rate?

H2 Martin bought 4.5 m of curtain fabric for £30.60.

(a) How much would 1 m of this fabric cost?

(b) How much would 2.5 m of the same fabric cost?

H3 50 ml of milk contains 60 mg of fat.
How much fat is in 568 ml of milk?
Give your answer correct to the nearest mg.

H4 A Caesar salad recipe for 6 people uses 250 g of diced potatoes.
How much diced potato would you need for a Caesar salad for 11 people?
Give your answer correct to the nearest 10 g.

H5 Hayley bought 250 g of olives for £1.89.
What would 160 g of these olives cost?

H6 This is a recipe to make 12 pieces of shortbread.
Write out a recipe to make 25 pieces of shortbread.
Give each quantity to the nearest 10 g.

> **Shortbread**
> (makes 12 pieces)
>
> 175 g butter
> 75 g soft light brown sugar
> 250 g plain flour

H7 On average a certain diesel car travels 100 km on fuel costing £4.40.

(a) Calculate the cost of fuel for a journey of 720 km.

(b) The fuel for another journey cost £14.30. Calculate the length of this journey.

Test yourself

T1 Work out
(a) $\dfrac{14.6 - 8.72}{0.014}$
(b) $(5.1)^2 \times \sqrt{6.2 - 3.6}$
Edexcel

T2 Use your calculator to work out $\dfrac{1}{0.2^2}$.
AQA

T3 (a) Estimate the value of $\dfrac{7.74 + 3.8}{5.8 \times 9.8}$.
Show all your approximations and working.

(b) Use a calculator to work out the result, correct to two decimal places.

T4 (a) Put a pair of brackets into this calculation so that the answer of 6 is correct.
$$4.1^2 + 1.79 \div \sqrt{9.61} = 6$$

(b) Calculate $\dfrac{12.74 - 4.35}{1.58 + 7.16}$.

Give your answer correct to two decimal places.
OCR

T5 Beth bought 250 g of tuna steak for £4.95.
What would 350 g of this tuna cost?

Review 1

1 Luke drinks $\frac{1}{3}$ of a pint of milk each day he is at school.
How much milk does he drink at school in a week, from Monday to Friday?
Give your answer as a mixed number.

2 In the diagram, the two angles marked w are equal.

Are they • vertically opposite angles

• alternate angles

or   • corresponding angles?

3 (a) Find $\frac{2}{3}$ of 12.

(b) For this pattern write down

(i)   the fraction of the shape that is shaded

(ii) the order of rotation symmetry

4 Write down a number that is a multiple of both 5 **and** 3.

5 This bus is 2.5 metres high.

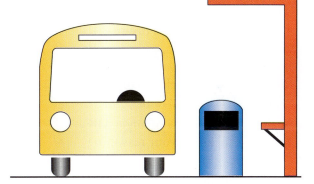

(a) Estimate the height in metres of

(i)   the top of the bus shelter

(ii) the waste bin

(b) Roughly, what is the height
of the bus in **feet**?

6 Write these fractions in order of size, starting with the smallest.

$\frac{1}{2}$ $\frac{3}{10}$ $\frac{2}{5}$ $\frac{7}{20}$

7 50 rows of chairs are set out in a school hall.
There are 30 chairs in each row.
How many chairs are there altogether in the hall?

8 (a) Which is larger, $\frac{4}{5}$ or $\frac{5}{8}$?

(b) Calculate $\frac{3}{8} - \frac{1}{5}$.

9 The midnight temperature in Glasgow is $^{-}5\,°C$.
The midnight temperature in London is $4\,°C$.

(a) In which city is the temperature lower?

(b) What is the difference between these two temperatures?

10 Calculate the angles marked with letters in these diagrams. Give an explanation for each result.

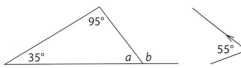 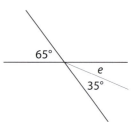

11 A ribbon that is 2.6 metres long is cut into 5 equal pieces. How long is each piece?

12 A cat eats $\frac{1}{2}$ of a can of cat food each day. How long will 14 cans of cat food last?

13 What is the value of each expression when $k = 5$?

(a) $3k + 1$ (b) $k - 7$ (c) $\dfrac{1 + 3k}{2}$ (d) $\dfrac{k + 3}{5}$

14 Write down the reciprocal of 10, giving your answer as a fraction.

15 How many sides has a pentagon?

16 A class raised £184 for charity, correct to the nearest pound. What was the minimum possible amount raised?

17 (a) Write 45% as a decimal.   (b) Write 20% as a decimal.

    (c) Write 0.3 as a fraction.   (d) Write 0.03 as a fraction.

18 ABC is an isosceles triangle. ACDE is a trapezium.

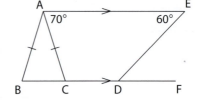

(a) Find the size of angle ABC, explaining your reasoning.

(b) Find the size of angle CDE, explaining your reasoning.

19 Work these out.

(a) $\frac{1}{5} \times \frac{1}{3}$ (b) $\frac{3}{4} \times \frac{3}{5}$ (c) $\frac{1}{2} \div 2$ (d) $3 \div \frac{1}{3}$

20 Estimate the answer to each of these calculations. Show clearly the values you use.

(a) $\dfrac{\sqrt{102.3}}{0.49}$ (b) $\dfrac{28.72 \times 3.15}{(2.95)^2}$ (c) $\dfrac{7.82}{2.08} - 1.81$ (d) $7.82 - \dfrac{1.81}{2.08}$

21 Calculate these.

(a) 23×45 (b) 781×32 (c) $273 \div 13$ (d) $756 \div 21$

22 Work these out, giving each answer in its simplest form.

(a) $\frac{3}{4} \times \frac{2}{3}$ (b) $10 \div \frac{2}{5}$ (c) $3\frac{1}{2} - 1\frac{2}{3}$ (d) $\frac{3}{5} \div \frac{7}{10}$ (e) $20 \times \frac{3}{5}$

23 What is an eight-sided shape called?

24 **(a)** Is angle x an obtuse angle or an acute angle?

   (b) What type of angle is

   (i) y **(ii)** z

25 Find the volume of this cuboid.
Remember to include the units in your answer.

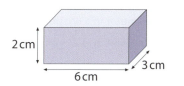

26 This diagram shows the net of a cube.
It is folded up to make a fair dice.

   (a) What colour is the face on
   the opposite side to the grey face?

   (b) The dice is rolled once.
   What is the probability that it lands with blue on the top face?

   (c) The dice is rolled 90 times.
   How many times would you expect it to land with yellow on the top face?

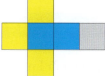

27 Calculate these, giving your answers to two decimal places.

   (a) $\dfrac{2.42 + 1.68}{0.28}$ **(b)** $\dfrac{29}{3.25 - 1.42}$ **(c)** $5.22 + 1.64^2$ **(d)** $\dfrac{\sqrt{10.4} - 3.1}{6.92 + 1.3}$

28 Find the area of this triangle.
Give your answer to an appropriate degree of accuracy.

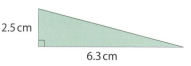

29 In a school, there are 167 students in year 11.
73 of them are boys.
Find the percentage of year 11 that are boys, correct to 1 d.p.

30 A row of 11 one-pound coins is 24.6 cm long.
How long is a row of 7 one-pound coins (to the nearest 0.1 cm)?

31 At a road junction cars can turn left, turn right or go straight on.
The probability of a car turning left is 0.15.
The probability of a car going straight on is 0.58.

   (a) Calculate the probability of a car turning right at this junction.

   (b) One day 1534 cars go through this junction.
   Estimate how many of them turn right.

32 Marie's suitcase weighs 22 kg to the nearest kg.
What is the maximum possible weight of this suitcase?

7 Circumference of a circle

This work will help you find

- the circumference of a circle from its radius or diameter
- the radius or diameter of a circle from its circumference
- the perimeter of a shape involving part of a circle

You need scissors and a cylindrical object such as a food can.

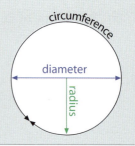

A Finding the circumference of a circle

A1 The clock face of Big Ben in London is being cleaned.

Use the height of a cleaner to estimate

(a) the radius of the clock face

(b) the diameter of the clock face

(c) the distance the **tip** of the minute hand moves in five minutes

(d) the distance the tip of the minute hand moves in one hour

T Make a 'circumference strip' for a cylindrical object.

Mark the diameter on it.

Fold to see how many times the diameter goes into the circumference.

What do you find?
Is it true for cylindrical objects of any size?

A rough rule is

circumference = 3 × diameter

Use this rule to answer the following questions.

A2 What is the circumference of each of these, roughly?

(a)

diameter = 7 cm

(b)

diameter = 10 cm

(c)

diameter = 6 cm

A3 Roughly how much sticky tape is needed to go once round the curved part of each of these parcels?

(a)

15 cm

(b)

8 cm

(c)

23 cm

A4 What is the circumference of each of these circles, roughly?

(a)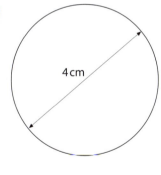

4 cm

(b)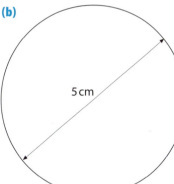

5 cm

(c)

2.5 cm

A5 The circles below are not drawn true size, and their **radius** is given, not their diameter.

For each circle,

(i) give the diameter

(ii) use the rule above to get the rough circumference

(a)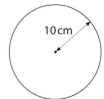

10 cm

(b)

6 cm

(c)

9 cm

(d)

8.5 cm

B Using π

When you did the experiment with the 'circumference strip' you may have found
that the circumference was a little bit more than three times the diameter.

For thousands of years, people have tried to work out this '3-and-a-bit' number,
always searching for a more accurate value. We now use the Greek letter π
(pronounced pie) to stand for this number and we know that it is 3.141 59...

A scientific calculator gives π to more decimal places than shown above.
Find out how to get π on your calculator (it may involve the SHIFT or second function key).

The value on the calculator seems very accurate; 3.14 or 3.142 is accurate enough
for most practical purposes. But in fact you can never write π exactly:
however many decimal places you write, you will never have the exact value.

Do a web search for the word pi. There is a lot about the history of π and
how mathematicians have calculated it to more and more decimal places.

You'll also see that it plays an important part in advanced mathematics.

But there are also some simple things you can do for fun, like searching
for your phone number – or your birth date in figures – in the first
two hundred million decimal places of π.

Because of the way π fascinates people, you'll find some eccentric websites.

This arrow diagram shows how you work out a circumference from a diameter.

diameter → ⟨ × π ⟩ → circumference

A formula connecting C (the circumference) with d (the diameter) is $C = \pi d$.
We could write $C = d\pi$ but we usually write numbers (including the number π)
before letters when things are multiplied together in algebra.

Use the π key on your calculator or 3.142 for the calculations in this section.

B1 For each of these circles

    (i)   calculate the circumference and write down the answer your calculator shows

    (ii) round the answer to one decimal place and show the correct units

(a)
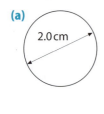
2.0 cm

(b)
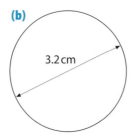
3.2 cm

(c)
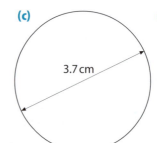
3.7 cm

(d)
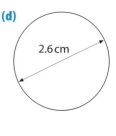
2.6 cm

B2 Calculate the circumference of these circles.
Write each answer to one decimal place (1 d.p.).

(a) 2.2 cm

(b) 3.4 cm

(c) 1.8 cm

(d) 4.4 cm

B3 On your calculator, work out the distance round these,
rounding your answers to one decimal place.

(a) A pipe with diameter 8.0 cm

(b) A pipe with diameter 4.2 cm

(c) A pipe with diameter 11.2 cm

B4 A circular pond has a diameter of 23 metres.
Calculate its circumference to the nearest metre.

B5 Petra wants to make a bracelet by forming a piece of silver wire into a circle.
What length of wire will she need for a bracelet with diameter 8.5 cm?

Since the diameter of a circle is twice the radius, this is the arrow diagram for
working out the circumference C from the radius r.

radius — $\boxed{\times 2}$ — $\boxed{\times \pi}$ → circumference

A formula connecting C with r is $C = 2\pi r$.
We could write $C = r2\pi$ but we usually write numbers (including the number π)
before letters when things are multiplied together in algebra.

B6 Calculate the circumference of each circle to 1 d.p.

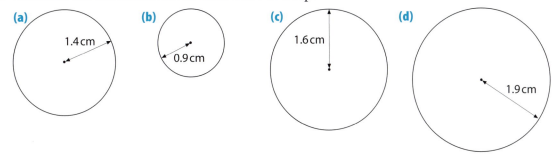

(a) 1.4 cm

(b) 0.9 cm

(c) 1.6 cm

(d) 1.9 cm

B7 A circular plate has radius 14.0 cm.
Calculate its circumference to the nearest 0.1 cm.

B8 The distance from the centre of a large wind turbine to the tip of a blade is 46 metres. How far does the tip of the blade travel in one rotation?

B9 The Earth goes round the Sun once every year, roughly in a circle.
The Earth is about 150 million kilometres from the Sun.
How far does the Earth travel round the Sun in a year?

C Finding a diameter from a circumference

If you need to find **a diameter from a circumference**, the easiest way is to start with the arrow diagram you used earlier.

diameter — $\boxed{\times \pi}$ → circumference

Then reverse it.

diameter ← $\boxed{\div \pi}$ — circumference | Dividing is the **inverse** of multiplying. |

Then use π (or 3.142) and division on your calculator to get the diameter.

C1 A circle has circumference of 48.0 cm. Calculate its diameter to 1 d.p.

C2 Here are the circumferences of some circles.
Calculate the diameter of each circle to 1 d.p.
   (a) Circumference = 25.2 cm   **(b)** Circumference = 1.5 cm

C3 One lap of a circular racing track is 500 m.
What is its diameter roughly?

C4 Here again is the arrow diagram for finding a circumference from a **radius**.

radius — $\boxed{\times 2}$ — $\boxed{\times \pi}$ → circumference

   (a) Draw a reverse arrow diagram for finding a **radius from a circumference**.
   (b) Calculate the radius (to 1 d.p.) of a circle with circumference 14.2 cm.

C5 Here are the circumferences of some circles.
Calculate the radius of each circle to 1 d.p.
   (a) Circumference = 34.2 cm   **(b)** Circumference = 2.2 cm

C6 A conker is swung in a circle. It travels 240 cm each full turn.
How long is the straight part of the string?

*C7 The planet Neptune goes round the Sun in roughly a circle.
It travels 28 billion kilometres every time it goes round.
How far is it from the Sun?

D Checking that a circumference answer makes sense

It helps to be able to check whether answers to circle calculations are sensible.

A circle has radius 5 cm.
(It is not drawn true size in this diagram.)

The sides of the square touch the circle.

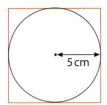

5 cm

- What is the perimeter of the square?
- Which is greater, the perimeter of the square or the circumference of the circle?

This regular hexagon is drawn inside the same circle.

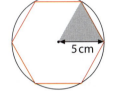

5 cm

- What kind of triangle is the shaded triangle?
- What is the perimeter of the hexagon?
- Which is greater, the perimeter of the hexagon or the circumference of the circle?
- Calculate the circumference of the circle to 1 d.p.
- Does your answer seem sensible compared with the perimeter of the square and the perimeter of the hexagon?

D1 A circle has a **diameter** of 8 cm.
(It is not drawn full size here.)

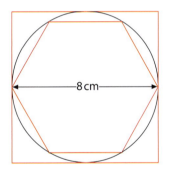

8 cm

   (a) Use the appropriate rule to calculate the circumference of the circle, to 1 d.p.

   (b) What is the perimeter of the square?

   (c) What is the perimeter of the hexagon?

   (d) Use your answers to (b) and (c) to say whether your answer to (a) is sensible.

D2 Find the circumference of each of these circles (they are not drawn accurately).
Each time, use the square and hexagon method to check that your answer is sensible.

(a)

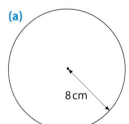

8 cm

(b)

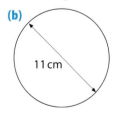

11 cm

(c)

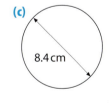

8.4 cm

(d)

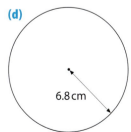

6.8 cm

D3 In 1985 a beefburger was made with diameter 2.7 m.
What was the circumference of the beefburger?
Give your answer to an appropriate degree of accuracy and check that it is sensible.

E Finding the perimeter of a shape that involves part of a circle

When you find the perimeter of part of a circle, or of a shape made from part of a circle and another shape, it is important to do these things.

- On a diagram, label key points with letters if they are not already there.
- Show all your working, referring to the lettered parts of the shape.

In this way you can keep track of your calculations and they can be checked later.

Example

Find the perimeter of this quarter circle, to 1 d.p.

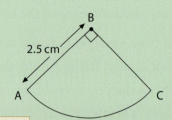

> The perimeter of this shape has three pieces.
> So you add three lengths together.

The circumference of a whole circle with radius 2.5 cm would be
$2\pi r = 2 \times \pi \times 2.5 = 15.7079\ldots$ cm

So length of arc AC = $15.7079\ldots \div 4 = 3.9269\ldots$ cm
Length of line segment AB = 2.5 cm
Length of line segment BC = 2.5 cm

So total perimeter = $\underline{8.9269\ldots}$ cm = 8.9 cm (to 1 d.p.)

> An **arc** is part of the circumference of a circle.

E1 Find the perimeter of this semicircle to 1 d.p.

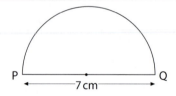

E2 This shape is three-quarters of a circle.
Find the total perimeter to 1 d.p.

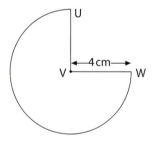

E3 This shape consists of a square with a semicircle attached.
Find the perimeter of the whole shape to 1 d.p.

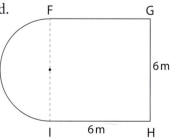

E4 This shape consists of a quarter circle with a square attached. Find the perimeter of the whole shape to 1 d.p.

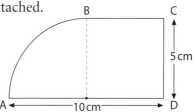

Test yourself

T1 Calculate the circumference of this circle.
Give your answer correct to one decimal place.

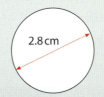

2.8 cm

T2 The Barringer crater in Arizona is circular.
It has a diameter of 1.6 km.

Calculate the circumference of
the Barringer crater.

OCR

T3 A bicycle has a wheel with radius 30 cm.

(a) What is the diameter of the wheel?

(b) What is the circumference of the wheel?

T4 A fence 240 m long is to make a circular pen for sheep.
Roughly what will the diameter of the pen be?

T5 This shape is made from a semicircle and an equilateral triangle.
Find its perimeter, giving your answer to one decimal place.

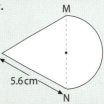

5.6 cm

T6 Silbury Hill in Wiltshire is a prehistoric mound
with a circular base.
The distance round the base of the mound
is 530 m.

In 1968 archaeologists dug a tunnel at the base
to the centre of the mound.
Roughly how long was their tunnel?

8 Working with expressions and formulas

You will revise

- calculating with and without brackets
- simplifying expressions

This work will help you

- substitute numbers, including decimals and fractions, into expressions and formulas
- form and solve equations from given formulas
- form and use formulas

You need sheet F2–1.

A Review: calculating

A1 Work out each of these.

(a) $10 - 4$ (b) $4 - 10$ (c) $^-2 + 9$ (d) $^-1 + ^-5$

(e) $^-1 - 3$ (f) $1 - ^-3$ (g) $^-2 \times 5$ (h) $3 \times ^-4$

(i) $^-4 \times ^-5$ (j) $^-10 \div 2$ (k) $12 \div ^-3$ (l) $^-8 \div ^-4$

A2 Work out each of these.

(a) $\frac{1}{2} + \frac{1}{4}$ (b) $4 \times \frac{1}{2}$ (c) $\frac{1}{4} \times 6$ (d) $\frac{1}{2} \div 2$

A3 Work out each of these.

(a) $(6 - 1) \times 2$ (b) $2 \times (3 + 4)$ (c) $3 \times (10 - 8)$ (d) $20 \div (2 \times 5)$

(e) $\frac{20}{4}$ (f) $\frac{12}{2} + 4$ (g) $\frac{12 + 4}{2}$ (h) $\frac{14}{9 - 2}$

A4 Copy and complete: $8 + 5 \times 2 = 8 + \blacksquare$

$= \blacksquare$

A5 Work out each of these.

(a) $4 + 2 \times 3$ (b) $10 + 4 \times 5$ (c) $12 - 3 \times 2$ (d) $15 - 2 \times 4$

(e) $5 \times 2 + 3 \times 4$ (f) $6 \times 3 + 2 \times 9$ (g) $4 \times 6 - 3 \times 7$ (h) $4 \times 2 - 3 \times 3$

Sometimes you can simplify a calculation.

Example

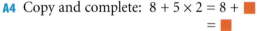

$6 \times 23 + 4 \times 23$

$= 10 \times 23$

$= 230$

It can help to think of this as '6 lots of 23' + '4 lots of 23' which is equivalent to '10 lots of 23'.

A6 Work these out.

(a) $3 \times 14 + 7 \times 14$ (b) $43 \times 15 + 57 \times 15$ (c) $13 \times 27 - 3 \times 27$

B Review: simplifying

B1 Find five pairs of matching expressions.

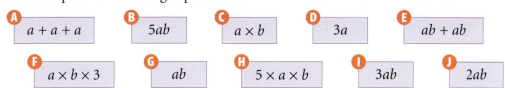

| **A** $a + a + a$ | **B** $5ab$ | **C** $a \times b$ | **D** $3a$ | **E** $ab + ab$ |
| **F** $a \times b \times 3$ | **G** ab | **H** $5 \times a \times b$ | **I** $3ab$ | **J** $2ab$ |

B2 Which two of these expressions cannot be simplified?

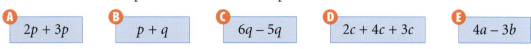

| **A** $2p + 3p$ | **B** $p + q$ | **C** $6q - 5q$ | **D** $2c + 4c + 3c$ | **E** $4a - 3b$ |

B3 Simplify each of these.

(a) $h + h + h + h$ (b) $3x + 4x$ (c) $8k - 3k$ (d) $2p + 7p + p$

(e) $6a - a$ (f) $5n + 2n - 3n$ (g) $7x - 2x + 3x$ (h) $10b - 3b + b$

B4 Find four pairs of matching expressions.

| **A** $2a + 3b + 4a + 5b$ | **B** $3a + b + 5b + 2a$ | **C** $6a + 5b + a - 3b$ | **D** $3a + 2b - a - 3b$ |
| **E** $5a + 6b$ | **F** $2a - b$ | **G** $6a + 8b$ | **H** $7a + 2b$ |

B5 Simplify each of these.

(a) $2h + 3k + h + 4k$ (b) $2a + 3b - a + 7b$ (c) $6x + 3y - 2y + 3x$

(d) $3m + 2n - m + n$ (e) $8x + 4y - 3x + 2y$ (f) $5p + 8q - 2p - 10q$

B6 Find and simplify an expression for the perimeter of this shape.

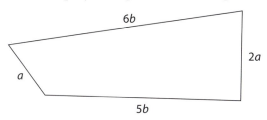

B7 Find four pairs of matching expressions.

| **A** $3 \times 2a$ | **B** $4a \times 5$ | **C** $\dfrac{18a}{2}$ | **D** $\dfrac{12a}{6}$ | **E** $2a$ | **F** $6a$ | **G** $9a$ | **H** $20a$ |

B8 Simplify each of these.

(a) $5 \times 3p$ (b) $2a \times 7$ (c) $\dfrac{16k}{8}$ (d) $\dfrac{27c}{9}$

c Substituting into expressions

When $a = 2$ and $b = 7$,

$5a + 3b$
$= 5 \times a + 3 \times b$
$= 5 \times 2 + 3 \times 7$
$= 10 + 21$
$= 31$

$6(b - a)$
$= 6 \times (b - a)$
$= 6 \times (7 - 2)$
$= 6 \times 5$
$= 30$

$\dfrac{5ab}{2}$
$= \dfrac{5 \times a \times b}{2}$
$= \dfrac{5 \times 2 \times 7}{2}$
$= \dfrac{70}{2}$
$= 35$

$\frac{1}{3}(a + b)$
$= \frac{1}{3} \times (a + b)$
$= \frac{1}{3} \times (2 + 7)$
$= \frac{1}{3} \times 9$
$= 3$

Check that you can use your calculator to work out each of these.

C1 Work out the value of each expression when $a = 3$ and $b = 5$.

(a) ab (b) $2a + 3b$ (c) $3(a + b)$ (d) $2a - b$ (e) $2b - 3a$

(f) $\dfrac{a + b}{4}$ (g) $2ab$ (h) $\dfrac{a + 7}{b}$ (i) $a - b$ (j) $\frac{1}{2}(a + b)$

C2

A	W	H	C	K	L	B	R	O	I
1	2	3	4	18	20	30	36	⁻4	⁻24

Work out the value of each expression below when $p = 2$, $q = 3$ and $r = ⁻6$.
Find the letter in the box above.
Unjumble the letters in each part to make the name of a tree.

(a) $3p + 4q$ $p + r$ $\dfrac{pq}{6}$

(b) $10q + 3p$ $3q + r$ $5pq$ $4r$ $5p + r$

(c) $4(p + q)$ $\dfrac{pr}{3}$ $r + 26$ $2pr$ $\dfrac{r}{p} + 5$ $7p + 2r$

C3 Work out the value of each expression when $x = \frac{1}{2}$ and $y = 4$.

(a) $2(x + y)$ (b) $y - x$ (c) xy (d) $8x - y$ (e) $\dfrac{x}{y}$

C4 Work out the value of each expression when $d = ⁻2$, $e = 3$ and $f = ⁻8$.

(a) df (b) $e - d$ (c) $\dfrac{ef}{2}$ (d) $\dfrac{d + f}{5}$ (e) $3e - 2d$

C5 Work out the value of each expression when $n = 4.6$.

(a) $9n - 5$ (b) $\frac{1}{2}n - 1$ (c) $\dfrac{n + 3}{5}$ (d) $3(n - 2)$ (e) $11 - 2n$

C6 Work out the value of each expression when $a = 1.5$ and $b = 3.6$.

(a) ab (b) $0.5b$ (c) $\dfrac{a + b}{10}$ (d) $5a - 2b$ (e) $\dfrac{2b}{a}$

C7 You are given that $a = \frac{1}{4}$, $b = \frac{1}{2}$ and $c = 6$.

Find the value of

(a) $a + b$ (b) $5bc$ (c) $ac - b$ (d) $ab + c$ (e) $\dfrac{a + b}{3}$

C8 Work out the value of $2x + xy$ when $x = 4$ and $y = {}^-3$.

D Substituting into formulas

Examples

$c = 2(a + b)$

Find the value of c
when $a = 5$ and $b = {}^-2$.

$$c = 2(a + b)$$
$$= 2 \times (a + b)$$
$$= 2 \times (5 + {}^-2)$$
$$= 2 \times 3$$
$$= 6$$

$F = \dfrac{40 - 3V}{2}$

Find the value of F
when $V = 1.5$.

$$F = \frac{40 - 3V}{2}$$
$$= \frac{40 - 3 \times V}{2}$$
$$= \frac{40 - 3 \times 1.5}{2}$$
$$= \frac{40 - 4.5}{2}$$
$$= \frac{35.5}{2}$$
$$= 17.75$$

$A = \pi xy$

Find the value of A
when $x = 3$ and $y = 2.5$.

$$A = \pi \times x \times y$$
$$= \pi \times 3 \times 2.5$$
$$= 23.6 \text{ (to 1 d.p.)}$$

Here, the π key on a calculator
was used and the result
rounded to one decimal place.

Check that you can use your calculator
to work out each of these.

D1 $V = 7 + 5W$
Work out V when $W = 1$.

D2 $R = 3x + 4y$
Work out R when $x = 4$ and $y = {}^-2$.

D3 Work out the value of P in each of the following formulas
when $a = 1.6$ and $b = 2.5$.

(a) $P = 2a + 4b$ (b) $P = 5(a + b)$ (c) $P = \dfrac{a}{2} + 5b$ (d) $P = \pi ab$

D4 $A = \dfrac{\pi uv}{5}$

Work out A when $u = 2.1$ and $v = 3.9$.

D5 A formula to convert British shirt size (B) into Continental shirt size (C) is

$$C = 2B + 8$$

Use this formula to find the value of C when $B = 15\frac{1}{2}$.

D6 A formula to estimate the number of rolls of wallpaper, R, for a room is

$$R = \frac{ph}{5}$$ where p is the perimeter of the room in metres and h is the height of the room in metres.

The perimeter of Carol's bedroom is 15.5 m and it is 2.25 m high.
How many rolls of wallpaper will she have to buy?

AQA

D7 This question is on sheet F2–1.

D8  This candle was lit at 12 o'clock.
Its height h in cm after t hours is given by the formula $h = 20 - 4t$.

(a) Find the value of h when $t = 0$.

(b) How high will the candle be after 1 hour?

(c) How high will it be at 4 o'clock?

(d) How high was it after $\frac{1}{2}$ hour?

(e) What was its height at a quarter past 12?

(f) At what time will the candle burn out?

D9 An exact formula to convert between °C and °F is $C = \dfrac{5(F - 32)}{9}$

where C is the temperature in °C and F the temperature in °F.

Use the formula to convert these temperatures to Celsius, correct to the nearest degree.

(a) 80°F   (b) 150°F   (c) ⁻35°F   (d) 19.5°F

D10 It can be dangerous to give a child an adult's dose of medicine.
There are several formulas which help doctors to give a safe children's dose.

Here is one. It is called Cowling's rule.

$$C = \frac{(A + 1)D}{24}$$

C is the safe dose for a child aged A years. D is the adult dose.

(a) The adult dose for a certain medicine is 30 mg.
Use Cowling's rule to find the safe dose for an eleven-year-old.

(b) For the same medicine, what dose would Cowling's rule
give for a one-year-old baby?

(c) Why would it be dangerous to use Cowling's rule for someone over 23?
Support your answer with some figures.

OCR

D11 The area A of a trapezium is given by the formula

$$A = \tfrac{1}{2}h(a + b)$$

Calculate the area of a trapezium for which
$a = 1.5$ metres, $b = 2$ metres and $h = 1.2$ metres.

Include the units in your answer.

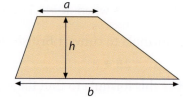

E Forming and solving an equation from a formula

The formula $y = 4x + 3$ gives you a rule for working out y when you know the value of x. You can work out x when you know the value of y by forming and solving an equation.

For example, if $y = 12$ then	$y = 4x + 3$
gives	$12 = 4x + 3$
Subtracting 3 from each side gives	$9 = 4x$
and dividing both sides by 4 gives	$2.25 = x$

E1 Given that $y = 3x + 1$, work out the value of x when $y = 10$.

E2 Given that $y = 2x + 5$, work out the value of x when

  (a) $y = 13$ **(b)** $y = 35$ **(c)** $y = 16$

E3 For the formula $l = 5r - 8$, find r when $l = 27$.

E4 $A = 4p - 3$
$A = 29$

Find the value of p.

E5 Sue is an author. The formula for her weekly wage £W is $W = 2.5P + 50$, where P is the number of pages she writes.

  (a) One week she writes 50 pages. What is her wage?

  (b) She gets paid £170 one week. How many pages did she write?

E6 $C = 180R + 2000$

The formula gives the capacity, C litres, of a tank needed to supply water to R hotel rooms.

  (a) $R = 5$. Work out the value of C.

  (b) $C = 3440$. Work out the value of R.

  (c) A water tank has a capacity of 3200 litres.
  Work out the greatest number of hotel rooms it could supply.   Edexcel

E7 Given that $y = 2x + 9$, work out the value of x when $y = 5$.

E8 $h = 3k - 10$
Work out the value of k when $h = {}^-1$.

E9 Use $a = 2b + c$ to work out the value of c when $a = 12$ and $b = 5$.

E10 $v = u + 10t$
Find the value of u when $v = {}^-5$ and $t = 3$.

F Forming and using formulas

A company uses this rule to work out
the cost in pounds to hire a car.

Add 2 to the number of days.
Multiply your answer by 30.

You could write the formula in shorthand
using C for the cost in pounds and
d for the number of days hired.

$C = 30(d + 2)$

Brackets are needed
to show that we add 2
before multiplying by 30.

This is sometimes called writing C **in terms of** d.

F1 This rule gives the sum of the interior angles of any polygon.

Subtract 2 from the number of sides.
Multiply your answer by 180.

(a) What is the sum of the interior angles of a hexagon?

(b) Find a formula for S (the sum of the angles)
in terms of n (the number of sides).

(c) What is the value of S when $n = 20$?

The blue angles are the interior angles.
The sum is the result of adding the angles.

F2 A cookbook gives this rule to work out the number of minutes to roast a chicken.

Multiply the weight in kilograms by 50 and then add 15.

(a) Write down a formula for T (the time in minutes) in terms of w (the weight in kg).

(b) Using this rule, how long will it take to roast a chicken that weighs 2.5 kg?
Give your answer in hours and minutes.

(c) Using this rule, Tom roasts a chicken for 90 minutes.
Write down an equation and solve it to find the weight of the chicken.

(d) Find the value of w when $T = 110$.

F3 Potted Palms sell palm trees on their website.
Each palm tree costs £6, and for each order you have to pay
a £7 postage charge.

(a) What is the total cost of buying 10 palm trees
(including postage)?

(b) Write down a formula for the total cost £C of buying n palm trees.

(c) Chelsea buys some palm trees.
The total bill is £85.
Use your formula from part (b) to write down an equation in n showing this.
Solve your equation to find how many palm trees Chelsea bought.

(d) Find the value of n when $C = 151$.

Test yourself

T1 Work out

    (a) $2 \times 3 + 4$ **(b)** $10 - 2 \times 5$ **(c)** $16 \div (2 \times 4)$ Edexcel

T2 Work out $4 \times 6 - 3 \times 5$.

T3 Use the formula $G = 7t - 6$ to find G when $t = 4.3$.

T4 $v = u + 10t$

    Work out the value of v when

    (a) $u = 10$ and $t = 7$ **(b)** $u = {}^{-}2.5$ and $t = 3.2$ Edexcel

T5 An approximate rule for converting degrees Fahrenheit into degrees Centigrade is

$$C = \frac{F - 30}{2}$$

    Use this rule to convert $22\,°F$ into $°C$.   AQA

T6 Given that $r = 2$, $s = 4$ and $t = \frac{1}{4}$, work out the value of

    (a) $r - 2s$ **(b)** $s + r + 6t$

T7 Using the formula $A = \dfrac{\pi x y}{2}$, calculate the value of A when $x = 5.4$ and $y = 3.2$.

    Give your answer correct to two decimal places.

T8 An approximate conversion between temperatures in Fahrenheit (F) and Celsius (C) is given by the formula

    $F = 2C + 30$

    Use this formula to find the value of C when $F = 68$.   OCR

T9 Use the formula $y = 5x - 7$ to find the value of x when $y = 9$.

T10 **(a)** Find the value of $2x - 5y$ when $x = 3$ and $y = {}^{-}2$.

    (b) Find the value of $\dfrac{a}{b}$ when $a = {}^{-}40$ and $b = 8$.

T11 $S = 2p + 3q$

    $p = {}^{-}4$, $q = 5$

    (a) Work out the value of S.

    $T = 2m + 30$

    $T = 40$

    (b) Work out the value of m.   Edexcel

T12 Find the value of $x - y$ when $x = 5$ and $y = {}^{-}2$.

9 Enlargement

You will revise the enlargement of a shape by a positive integer scale factor.

This work will help you

- enlarge a shape by a fractional scale factor
- see how the angles, perimeter, area and volume are affected by enlargement
- decide when two shapes are similar

A Enlargement, angle and perimeter

In any enlargement, the length of each side of a shape is multiplied by the scale factor.

Shape B is an enlargement of shape A using a scale factor of 2.

The length of each side has doubled so the perimeter has doubled too.

In any enlargement, the angles in a shape do not change so, for example, the two angles marked here are equal.

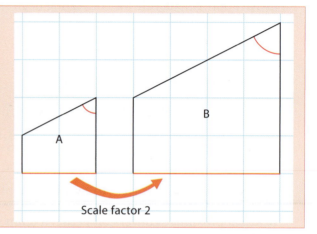

Scale factor 2

A1 On centimetre squared paper, enlarge each of these shapes using a scale factor of 3.

(a)   (b)   (c)

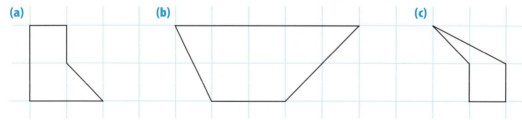

A2 This rectangle is 6.1 cm long and 1.5 cm wide.

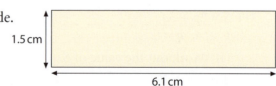

1.5 cm

6.1 cm

(a) Find the perimeter of this rectangle.

(b) The rectangle is enlarged by scale factor 5.

    (i) Work out the length and width of the enlarged rectangle.

    (ii) What is the perimeter of the enlarged rectangle?

A3 Leo draws shapes P and Q as shown.

He says, 'The length of each side in shape Q is double the length of each side in shape P. So Q is an enlargement of P.'

(a) What is wrong with what Leo says?

(b) Draw a correct enlargement of P using a scale factor of 2.

Shape Y is a copy of shape X where the length of each side has been halved.

We say that shape Y is an enlargement of shape X using a scale factor of $\frac{1}{2}$.

Even though shape Y is smaller than shape X we still call this an enlargement.

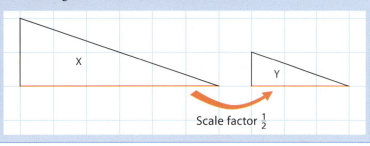

Scale factor $\frac{1}{2}$

A4 On centimetre squared paper, enlarge each of these shapes by a scale factor of $\frac{1}{2}$.

(a)   **(b)**   **(c)**

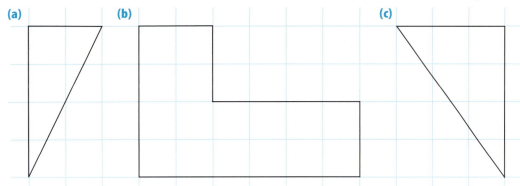

A5 **(a)** Which four shapes below are enlargements of A?

(b) Give the scale factor for each shape that is an enlargement of A.

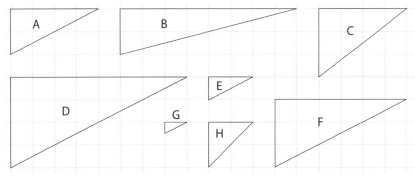

B Similar shapes

If one shape is an enlargement of another, then the two shapes are **similar**.

B1 Find a pair of similar shapes.

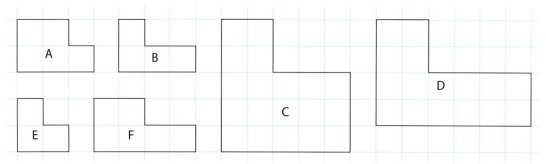

B2 Squares B, C and D are all enlargements of square A.

    (a) Find the scale factor of each enlargement from A.

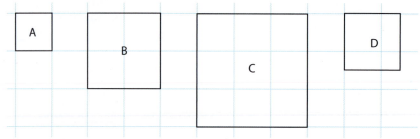

    (b) Is it possible to draw a square that is not an enlargement of A?

B3 Circle Q is an enlargement of circle P.

    (a) What is the scale factor of
this enlargement?

    (b) Is it possible to draw a circle that
is not an enlargement of P?

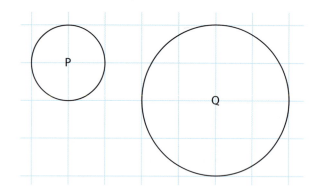

B4 Draw a rectangle that measures 4 cm by 3 cm.
Draw another rectangle that is not an enlargement of this one.

B5 Decide whether each statement is true or false.

    (a) Any two squares are similar.   **(b)** Any two circles are similar.

    (c) Any two rectangles are similar.   **(d)** Any two triangles are similar.

C Enlargement and area

C1 This diagram shows a rectangle.

(a) Draw an accurate copy of the rectangle on centimetre squared paper.

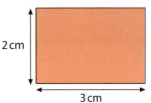

(b) This rectangle is enlarged by scale factor 2. Draw an accurate copy of the enlarged rectangle.

(c) (i) Calculate the area of each rectangle, using the correct units for this area.

(ii) How many times will the smaller rectangle fit into the larger one?

C2 This right-angled triangle has a base that measures 4 cm and a height of 1 cm.

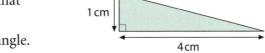

(a) Draw an accurate copy of the triangle.

(b) This triangle is enlarged by a scale factor of 2. Draw an accurate copy of the enlarged triangle.

(c) (i) Calculate the area of each triangle.

(ii) What is the area of the small triangle multiplied by to give the area of the enlarged triangle?

C3 This rectangle is 4 cm long and 1.5 cm wide. It is enlarged by scale factor 2.

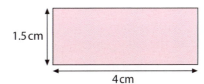

(a) Work out the length and width of the enlarged rectangle.

(b) What is the area of the small rectangle multiplied by to give the area of the enlarged rectangle?

C4 This right-angled triangle has a base that measures 2 cm and a height of 2 cm.

(a) Draw an accurate copy of the triangle.

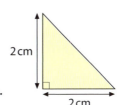

(b) The triangle is enlarged by scale factor 3. Draw an accurate copy of the enlarged triangle.

(c) (i) Calculate the area of each triangle.

(ii) What is the area of the small triangle multiplied by to give the area of the enlarged triangle?

C5 A rectangle is 5 cm long and 2.4 cm wide. It is enlarged by scale factor 3.

What is the area of the small rectangle multiplied by to give the area of the enlarged rectangle?

C6 A rectangle has an area of 8 cm².
It is enlarged by scale factor 3.
What is the area of the enlarged rectangle?

*C7 A triangle with an area of 3 cm² is enlarged by scale factor 4.
What is the area of the enlarged triangle?

D Enlargement and volume

These diagrams show two boxes.
Each box is in the shape of a cuboid.

Box B is an enlargement of box A.

- What is the scale factor
  of the enlargement?

- How many of the smaller boxes could
  fit inside the larger box?

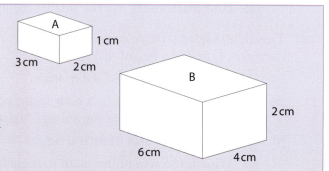

D1 Cuboid Q is an enlargement of cuboid P.

   (a) What is the scale factor
      of the enlargement?

   (b) **(i)** Calculate the volume of each box,
          using the correct units for each volume.

      (ii) What is the volume of the small box
           multiplied by to give the volume of
           the enlarged box?

   (c) How many of the smaller boxes could
      fit inside the larger box?

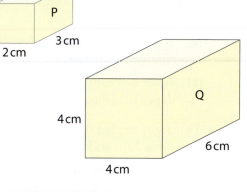

D2 Cube Z is an enlargement of cube Y.

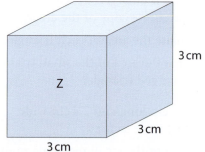

   (a) What is the scale factor of the enlargement?

   (b) How many of the smaller cubes could fit inside the larger cube?

D3 Both these boxes are in the shape of cuboids.
The larger box is full of boxes identical to the smaller box.

1 cm   4 cm   3 cm

5 cm   20 cm   15 cm

Work out how many smaller boxes are inside the larger box.

Test yourself

T1 A shape has been drawn on a grid of centimetre squares.

(a) Work out the area of the shape.
State the units with your answer.

(b) Copy the shape on to centimetre squared paper and
enlarge the shape with a scale factor of 2.

Edexcel

T2 This rectangle is 4 cm long by 2.5 cm wide.

It is enlarged by a scale factor of 3.
Work out the length and width of the
enlarged rectangle.

4 cm

2.5 cm

T3 The diagram shows two squares P and Q.

Q

P

6 cm   12 cm

Decide whether each statement is true or false.

(a) Squares P and Q are similar.

(b) The perimeter of square Q is twice the perimeter of square P.

(c) The area of square Q is twice the area of square P.

10 Percentage increase and decrease

You will revise how to work out a percentage of a quantity.

This work will help you

- calculate an amount after a percentage increase or decrease
- calculate an amount after an increase or decrease by a fraction
- calculate an increase or decrease as a percentage
- use percentages in real-life situations

A Review: percentage of a quantity

10% of £45 is £4.50.

- Explain how you would find these.

| 20% of £45 | 5% of £45 |

| 1% of £45 | 65% of £45 |

A1 Work these out.

(a) 5% of £24   (b) 15% of £24   (c) 35% of £24   (d) 1% of £24

A2 Work these out.

(a) 5% of 60 kg   (b) 25% of £14   (c) 70% of 120 m   (d) 45% of £600

1% is the same as $\frac{1}{100}$.
To work out 1% of something, divide by 100.

$$1\% \text{ of } 350 = 350 \div 100 = 3.5$$

Once you know what 1% is you can easily work out 2%, 3%, …

$$2\% \text{ of } 350 = 2 \times 3.5 = 7$$
$$3\% \text{ of } 350 = 3 \times 3.5 = 10.5$$

A3 Work these out.

(a) 1% of 200   (b) 1% of £8   (c) 1% of £650   (d) 1% of £1260

A4 Work these out.

(a) 2% of £500   (b) 3% of £1400   (c) 4% of £25   (d) 6% of £2400

To find a percentage of a quantity with a calculator, you can change the percentage to a decimal and then multiply.

Find 23% of £140.

$$23\% = \frac{23}{100} = 0.23 \longrightarrow$$

$$0.23 \times 140 = 32.2$$
So 23% of £140 = £32.20

A5 Calculate these.

    (a) 42% of £54   (b) 35% of 48 kg   (c) 49% of £2500   (d) 8% of 3750

A6 Calculate these, rounding your answers to the nearest penny.

    (a) 9% of £7.50   (b) 12% of £8.60   (c) 15% of £24.99   (d) 26% of £15.49

A7 There are 1250 pupils in a school.

    (a) 14% of the pupils wear glasses. How many pupils wear glasses?

    (b) 52% of the pupils walk to school. How many pupils walk to school?

    (c) 46% of the pupils have school dinners. How many pupils is this?

B Percentage increase

Example

The price of a camera is to be increased by 10%.
If the original cost was £140, what will its new price be?

BUY NOW!
Prices go up 10%
next week

Increase is 10% of £140 = £14
New price = old price + increase
        = £140 + £14
        = £154

B1 A television costs £250. Its price is to be increased by 10%.

    (a) How much is 10% of £250?   (b) What is the new price of the television?

B2 A bottle of cola contains 500 ml. A special-offer bottle will have 10% extra free.

    (a) How much is 10% of 500 ml?   (b) How much cola is in the special-offer bottle?

B3 How much will each of these amounts be when they have been increased by 10%?

    (a) £240   (b) £600   (c) £18   (d) £5400   (e) £1.90

B4 Anna's pocket money is £3.50 per week. It goes up by 20%.

    (a) How much is 20% of £3.50?

    (b) How much pocket money will Anna now receive?

B5 Pete earns £6 per hour. He gets a pay rise of 5%. What is Pete's new rate of pay?

B6 A test is due to last 90 minutes.
The teacher allows Kevin 20% extra time because of a broken arm.
How much time can Kevin take in total to complete the test?

B7 A roll of kitchen foil normally contains 50 m.
How much foil is there on this special-offer roll?

Kitchen foil

Normally 50 metres.
20% extra free!

Investing money

When you save money in a bank or building society, they pay you interest on the money in your account. The interest rate is given as a percentage.

A rate of 5% per annum (p.a.) means you get an extra 5% of your savings added to your account at the end of the year.

B8 Sanjay has £1200 invested. The interest rate is 5% per annum.

   (a) Find how much interest Sanjay will receive after one year.

   (b) Find how much his investment will be worth after one year.

B9 Karen invests £200 in a savings account with an interest rate of 4% per annum. How much is her investment worth after one year?

B10 For each pair, find which gives the greater amount after the increase.

   (a) £40 increased by 15% or £42 increased by 10%

   (b) £2000 increased by 25% or £2200 increased by 10%

C Percentage decrease

Example

The price of a television is to be reduced by 10%.
If the original cost was £240, what will its new price be?

Decrease is 10% of £240 = £24
New price = old price – decrease
        = £240 – £24
        = £216

Special offer
10% off all prices

C1 A jacket originally cost £40. The price is reduced by 10% in a sale.

   (a) Find 10% of £40.   **(b)** Find the sale price of the jacket.

C2 The population of a village is 5600.
It is expected that the population will decrease by 10% over the next five years.
What is the population expected to be in five years?

C3 Jan used to work for 40 hours each week. She now works 5% fewer hours.
How many hours does she now work each week?

C4 Match these up.

A Decrease £10 by 30%.

B Increase £4 by 25%.

P £3   **Q** £4   **R** £5

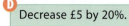

C Increase £2 by 50%.   **D** Decrease £5 by 20%.

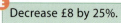

E Decrease £8 by 25%.

S £6   **T** £7

C5 Find the sale price of each item.

Blue Cross Sale

All prices reduced by 20%

Shirt £24

Vest £15

Jeans £36

Shorts £19

Jacket £56

D Increase and decrease with fractions

Example

The price of a jumper is to be reduced by $\frac{1}{4}$ in a sale.
The original price of the jumper is £24.
What will the sale price be?

Decrease is $\frac{1}{4}$ of £24 = £24 ÷ 4 = £6
New price = old price – decrease
= £24 – £6
= £18

D1 Prices are to be **reduced** by $\frac{1}{4}$ in a sale. Find the sale price of each of these.

(a) A skirt costing £32

(b) A pair of trousers costing £40

(c) A jacket costing £60

(d) A T-shirt costing £14

D2 A packet of pasta normally contains 500 g.

(a) How much **extra** pasta is in the special-offer packet?

(b) How much pasta is there altogether in the special-offer packet?

Special offer Pasta
$\frac{1}{2}$ EXTRA FREE

D3 Find the total amount in each of these special offers.

(a)

Cereal
Normally 1.5 kg
$\frac{1}{3}$ EXTRA FREE

(b)

Orange juice
Normally 500 ml
$\frac{1}{4}$ EXTRA FREE

(c)

Tea
Normally 125 g
$\frac{1}{5}$ EXTRA FREE

D4 The price of a computer is £840.
In a sale the price is **reduced** by one third.
What is the sale price of the computer?

E Increasing using a multiplier

If prices go up by 15%, this means that 15% of the old price is added on to make the new price.

Gas prices to rise by 15%

Pensioners will be hit hard this winter as gas companies are expected to increase prices by 15%. The elderly spend a higher proportion of their income on

15% of old price

15%

100%   →   100%

old price   new price

15% or $\frac{15}{100}$ of the old price is added on.

So the new price is $1\frac{15}{100}$ or 1.15 times the old price.

old price → × 1.15 → new price

To increase by 15%, you can multiply by 1.15.

E1 Calculate the new price after a 15% increase on each of these old prices.

(a) £42   (b) £25.60   (c) £36.80   (d) £15   (e) £17.80

E2 (a) If bus fares go up by 12%, what number should you multiply by to get the new fare?

(b) Calculate the new fare after a 12% increase on these old fares.

(i) £2.50   (ii) £36.75   (iii) £60   (iv) £15.75   (v) £7.50

E3 A company increases the prices of all of its holidays by 18%.
Calculate the new price after an 18% increase on each of these old prices.

(a) £200   (b) £260   (c) £185   (d) £325   (e) £380

E4 A shop buys coffee for £2.50 per kilogram.
It adds 55% on when it sells the coffee.
To the nearest penny, what is the selling price of one kilogram of coffee in this shop?

E5 At the start of 2007, Mary had 140 budgies.
During the year the number of budgies went up by 35%.
How many budgies did Mary have at the end of the year?

E6 A population in a town is expected to rise by 8%.

(a) Tina says you should multiply the present population by 1.8.
Tim says you should multiply by 1.08.
Who is right?

(b) If the present population is 56 000, what will the population be after a rise of 8%?

E7 The puffin population on a small island is estimated to be 1500 birds.
This year the population is expected to rise by 6%.
What would the new puffin population be after a rise of 6%?

F Decreasing using a multiplier

If prices are reduced by 25%, this means that 25% of the old price is taken off to make the new price.

TODAY ONLY

Fantastic value

Take 25% off all ticket prices

That leaves 75% or $\frac{75}{100}$ of the old price.

So the new price is $\frac{75}{100}$ or 0.75 times the old price.

F1 Reduce each of these prices by 25%.

    (a) £16.80　　**(b)** £5.60　　**(c)** £90　　　**(d)** £3.40　　**(e)** £0.20

F2 **(a)** What number should you multiply by to reduce prices by 16%?

    (b) Reduce each of these prices by 16%.

        (i) £4.50　　**(ii)** £6.25　　**(iii)** £35.50　　**(iv)** £280　　**(v)** £86

F3 **(a)** In a sale, prices are reduced by 35%.
        What number should you multiply by to reduce prices by 35%?

    (b) Calculate the sale prices, to the nearest penny, of items with these original prices.

        (i) £25　　**(ii)** £29.60　　**(iii)** £50　　　**(iv)** £16.99　　**(v)** £39.99

F4 What should you multiply by to reduce prices by these percentages?

    (a) 72%　　**(b)** 23%　　**(c)** 30%　　**(d)** 5%　　**(e)** 2%

F5 Reduce

    (a) £240 by 13%　　**(b)** £620 by 82%　　**(c)** £2.50 by 22%　　**(d)** £430 by 8%

F6 Sally is interested in buying a car that is priced at £6200.
She is offered a 7% reduction in the price if she pays cash.
How much would the car cost her if she pays cash?

F7 The value of a car decreased by 18% over the last year.
The car was worth £4500 a year ago.
How much is the car worth now?

F8 Between 2000 and 2005, the number of school-age children in a town
went down by 23%.
The number of children in this town in 2000 was 9560.
How many children were living in this town in 2005, correct to the nearest 10?

G Finding an increase as a percentage

On an island the number of great skuas goes up from 39 to 54 birds one year.
What is the percentage increase in the number of birds?

You need to find the multiplier from 39 to 54.   39 ⟶ ×? ⟶ 54

To find the multiplier, **divide** 54 by 39. ⟶ 54 ÷ 39 = 1.38 (to 2 d.p.)
So the percentage increase is 38%.

The multiplier 1.38 corresponds to an increase of 38%.

G1 The price of a camera goes up from £250 to £270.
  (a) Find the multiplier from £250 to £270.
  (b) What is the percentage increase in the price of the camera?

G2 Jake buys a painting for £400 and sells it for £540.
  (a) Find the multiplier from £400 to £540.
  (b) What is the percentage increase in the value of the painting?

G3 Match each increase to the correct percentage.

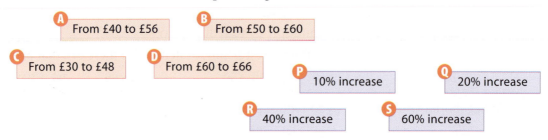

A From £40 to £56   **B** From £50 to £60

C From £30 to £48   **D** From £60 to £66

P 10% increase   **Q** 20% increase

R 40% increase   **S** 60% increase

G4 Calculate the percentage increase in each case below.
  (a) From £25 to £28.50   **(b)** From £150 to £247.50
  (c) From 69 kg to 117.3 kg   **(d)** From 2 metres to 2.14 metres

G5 Meena sells a book for £22.20 that she bought for only £12.
By what percentage has its price increased?

G6 From 1975 to 2006, the number of UK public libraries increased from 3714 to 4515.
What was the percentage increase in the number of libraries, correct to the nearest 1%?

G7 In 1980 there were 2556 km of motorway in the UK.
In 2005 there were 3519 km of motorway.
Find the percentage increase, correct to one decimal place.

H Finding a decrease as a percentage

On an island the number of arctic skuas goes down from 78 to 64 birds one year.
What is the percentage decrease in the number of birds?

You need to find the multiplier from 78 to 64.   78 ⟶ ×? ⟶ 64

To find the multiplier, **divide** 64 by 78.   64 ÷ 78 = 0.82 (to 2 d.p.)
So the percentage decrease is 18%.

The multiplier of 0.82 means that the new number is 82% of the old number. This corresponds to a decrease of 18%.

H1 In a sale, the price of a jumper is cut from £42 to £27.30.
  (a) Find the multiplier from £42 to £27.30.
  (b) What is the percentage decrease in the price of the jumper?

H2 In a sale, the price of a sofa is reduced from £875 to £630.
  (a) Find the multiplier from £875 to £630.
  (b) What is the percentage reduction in the price of the sofa?

H3 Match each decrease to the correct percentage.

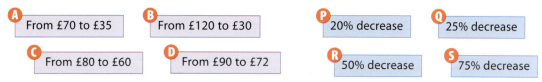

A From £70 to £35   **B** From £120 to £30   **P** 20% decrease   **Q** 25% decrease

C From £80 to £60   **D** From £90 to £72   **R** 50% decrease   **S** 75% decrease

H4 Calculate the percentage decrease in each case below.
  (a) From £75 to £57   **(b)** From £8.50 to £3.23
  (c) From 84 kg to 58.8 kg   **(d)** From 6.5 metres to 6.24 metres

H5 Between 1981 and 2001, the population of Sheffield fell from 538 000 to 513 000.
What was the percentage decrease in the population, correct to the nearest 1%?

H6 Sanjay is buying a car that is priced at £6450.
The saleswoman reduces the price to £5700 as Sanjay is paying cash.
What percentage discount is this?

H7 Calculate the percentage change in each case below, correct to the nearest 1%.
Say whether it is an increase or a decrease.
  (a) From £560 to £476   **(b)** From 20 kg to 28.6 kg
  (c) From 58 kg to 75.2 kg   **(d)** From 82 m to 60 m

Percentages in the real world

VAT

VAT is short for Value Added Tax.
You usually pay it when you buy something or pay for a service.
VAT is a percentage of the cost of something. The government sets the percentage.
VAT is currently set at $17\frac{1}{2}\%$ for most things.

Example

The cost of a printer is £140 + VAT. Find the total cost of the printer.

Method 1

VAT = 17.5% of £140 = 0.175×140
= £24.50
Total price = £140 + £24.50 = £164.50

Method 2

Price including VAT is 117.5% of £140
Total price = £140 × 1.175 = £164.50

I1 Work out the price of each of these items if the rate of VAT is $17\frac{1}{2}\%$.
Round each answer to the nearest penny.

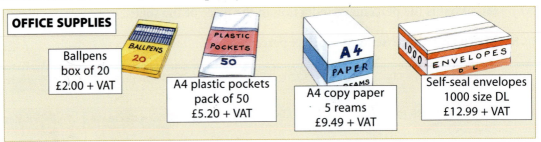

OFFICE SUPPLIES

Ballpens box of 20 £2.00 + VAT

A4 plastic pockets pack of 50 £5.20 + VAT

A4 copy paper 5 reams £9.49 + VAT

Self-seal envelopes 1000 size DL £12.99 + VAT

I2 At which shop is this television cheaper?

VISIONPLUS
£249.99 inc VAT

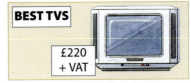

BEST TVS
£220 + VAT

I3 Which of these sofas is cheaper?

A Normally £650 Now 40% off!

B SALE Was £500 Save 25%!

I4 A shop has this special offer on packets of biscuits.
Randeep buys two packets of biscuits.
How much does he pay altogether?

SPECIAL OFFER
Normally 68p
BUY ONE GET THE SECOND
HALF PRICE!

Example

Anita invested £260 for one year at an interest rate of 3.5% per annum.
What was the value of her investment at the end of the year?

Method 1

Interest = 3.5% of £260 = 0.035 × 260 = £9.10
Total investment = £260 + £9.10 = £269.10

Method 2

Total investment is 103.5% of £260
Total investment = £260 × 1.035 = £269.10

I5 Hilda invested £3800 in an account with an interest rate of 3.2% per annum.

   (a) How much interest will her investment have earned after one year?

   (b) How much in total will her investment now be worth?

I6 Rajesh puts £500 into a building society account that pays 5% interest per annum.

The interest is paid on the amount in the account at the start of that year.

Copy and complete this table showing the amount in the account at the end of each year for 4 years. (Round to the nearest penny.)

Number of years	Amount
0	£500.00
1	£525.00
2	
3	
4	

I7 Sonia works in a shop where she gets 12% staff discount. How much would she pay if she bought one duvet cover, one sheet and two pillowcases?

Price list	
Duvet cover	£29.50
Sheet	£14.50
Pillow	£8.99
Pillowcase	£3.25

I8 Patrick gets paid £8.60 an hour.
He gets paid 'time and a quarter' for any overtime he works.
How much would he get paid for 6 hours of overtime?

I9 An electricity company supplies electricity to a family with the following charges.

   Standing charge: 9.13 pence per day

   Electricity used: 6.19 pence per unit

VAT of 5% is added to the total.

The Green family receives a bill for 91 days.
In that time they have used a total of 1272 units of electricity.
Calculate the amount the Greens have to pay. Show your working clearly.   OCR

I10 A shopkeeper reduced prices by 12% in a sale.
After a week the sale prices were themselves reduced by 20%.
Before the sale, a suit cost £150.

   (a) What was the final price of the suit?

   (b) Calculate the overall reduction in the price of the suit.

Test yourself

T1 A running club has 240 members.

   (a) 40% of the members are female. How many female members are there?

   (b) 15% of the members are over 50. How many members are over 50?

T2 Ben invests £60 in a bank account.
Interest of 5% is added at the end of each year.
Work out the money in Ben's account after one year.　　　　　　　　　　*Edexcel*

T3 Abby sees the same model of digital camera for sale in two different shops.

DIGICAM	**Pictures4u**
Our price	Our price
15% off normal price	$\frac{1}{6}$ off normal price
of £288	of £288

Calculate the final cost of the camera from

   (a) Digicam　　　　　　　　　　**(b)** Pictures4u　　　　　　*AQA*

T4 The cash price of a saxophone is £740.
Tom buys the saxophone using a credit plan.
He pays a deposit of 5% of the cash price and
12 monthly payments of £65.

Saxophone
£740 for cash
Credit plan available

Work out the difference between the cost when
he used the credit plan and the cash price.　　　　　　　　　　*Edexcel*

T5 A shop increases the price of a television from £480 to £648.
What is the percentage increase in price?

T6 Miss Evans earns £240 per week.
She is awarded a pay rise of 3.5%.
How much does she earn each week after the pay rise?　　　　　　　*AQA*

T7 Calculate the percentage change in each case below.
Say whether it is an increase or a decrease.

   (a) From 60 kg to 66 kg　　**(b)** From £1200 to £1176　　**(c)** From 150 m to 90 m

T8 Sam wants to buy a Hooper washing machine.
Hooper washing machines are sold in three different shops.

Washing Power	**Whytes**	**Clean Up**
$\frac{1}{4}$ OFF	15% OFF	£240
usual price of £370	usual price of £370	plus VAT at $17\frac{1}{2}$%

Find the difference between the maximum and minimum prices
Sam could pay for a washing machine.　　　　　　　　　　*Edexcel*

11 Solving linear equations

You will revise how to solve simple linear equations, including those formed from problems.

This work will help you

- solve equations that involve fractions, such as $\frac{n}{5} + 3 = 9$

- solve equations that use brackets, such as $3(x + 1) = 15$

- solve equations where unknowns are subtracted, such as $10 - 3x = 4$ and $8 - x = x + 4$

A Review: simple linear equations

A1 Solve each of these equations.

(a) $5 + x = 8$ (b) $x - 2 = 5$ (c) $3x = 15$

(d) $x + 3 = 1$ (e) $2x = 9$ (f) $x + 1.5 = 4$

A2 Solve each of these equations.

(a) $2x + 5 = 17$ (b) $4x - 2 = 10$ (c) $3x + 1 = 10$

(d) $6 + 4x = 18$ (e) $6x - 5 = 25$ (f) $27 = 5x + 2$

A3 Solve each of these equations.

(a) $2x + 3 = 10$ (b) $4x + 7 = 13$ (c) $10x - 3 = 22$

(d) $4x - 1 = 1$ (e) $2x + 7 = 5$ (f) $3x + 8 = 2$

A4 Write an equation for each puzzle.
Solve it to find the weight of each animal.

(a)   (b)

A5 Use balancing to solve these equations.

(a) $5n + 2 = 2n + 14$ (b) $3w + 1 = 11 + w$ (c) $4m + 14 = 7m + 2$

(d) $3x - 4 = x + 2$ (e) $n + 8 = 4n - 10$ (f) $6h - 12 = 8 + 4h$

(g) $6x + 2 = 4x + 7$ (h) $2b + 8 = b + 5$ (i) $5a + 9 = 3a + 1$

A6 Solve these equations.

(a) $5n = 32$ (b) $2x - 7 = 51$ (c) $8y - 3 = 93$

(d) $7x - 9 = 3x$ (e) $7n + 3 = 2n + 11$ (f) $5m + 5 = m - 1$

B1 (a) What do the angles of a triangle add up to?

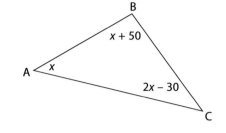

(b) The angles shown in this triangle are in degrees. Write down and simplify an expression for the sum of the angles of the triangle.

(c) Use your answers to parts (a) and (b) to form an equation in x.

(d) Solve your equation to find x.

(e) Hence write down the size of angles A, B and C, in degrees.

B2 Write an equation involving x for each triangle. Solve each equation.

(a)   **(b)**   **(c)**

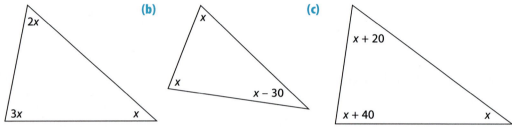

B3 In the diagram all measurements are in centimetres. The lengths of the sides of a triangle are $2x$, $x + 6$ and $x - 1$, as shown.

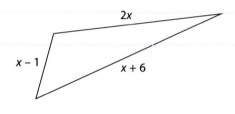

(a) Write an expression, in terms of x, for the perimeter of the triangle. Give your answer in its simplest form.

(b) The perimeter of the triangle is 21 cm. Write down an equation in x and use it to find the value of x.

B4 The length of a rectangle is x centimetres. The width of the rectangle is $(x - 5)$ centimetres.

(a) Find an expression, in terms of x, for the perimeter of the rectangle. Give your expression in its simplest form.

(b) The perimeter of the rectangle is 50 centimetres. Work out the width of the rectangle.

B5 A biscuit costs x pence. A bun costs 30 pence more than a biscuit.

(a) Write down, in terms of x, the cost of a bun.

(b) Two biscuits and a bun cost 90p. Form an equation in x and solve it to find the cost of a biscuit.

C Equations that involve a fraction

Examples

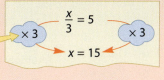

Multiplying by 3 'undoes' dividing by 3.

$$\frac{x}{3} = 5$$

×3   ×3

$$x = 15$$

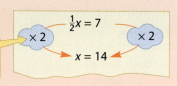

Multiplying by 2 'undoes' multiplying by $\frac{1}{2}$.

$$\frac{1}{2}x = 7$$

×2   ×2

$$x = 14$$

C1 Solve these equations.

(a) $\dfrac{y}{3} = 6$ (b) $\frac{1}{2}m = 4$ (c) $\dfrac{n}{5} = 4$

Examples

Each operation in brackets shows what is done to **both** sides to get the next line.

$$\frac{x}{3} + 5 = 9$$
$$\frac{x}{3} = 4 \quad [-5]$$
$$x = 12 \quad [\times 3]$$

$$\frac{1}{2}x - 9 = 3 \quad [+9]$$
$$\frac{1}{2}x = 12 \quad [\times 2]$$
$$x = 24$$

$$\frac{3x + 5}{4} = 2$$
$$3x + 5 = 8 \quad [\times 4]$$
$$3x = 3 \quad [-5]$$
$$x = 1 \quad [\div 3]$$

Multiply by 4 first here as the whole expression $3x + 5$ has been divided by 4.

C2 Solve these equations.

(a) $\dfrac{y}{3} + 2 = 6$ (b) $\dfrac{k}{4} + 8 = 10$ (c) $\dfrac{n}{5} + 3 = 9$

(d) $\frac{1}{2}x - 1 = 3$ (e) $\dfrac{p}{8} - 2 = 1$ (f) $\frac{1}{3}m - 1 = 4$

C3 Solve these equations.

(a) $\dfrac{x + 1}{3} = 4$ (b) $\dfrac{x - 3}{2} = 5$ (c) $\dfrac{1 + x}{2} = 1.5$

(d) $\dfrac{x - 5}{7} = 1$ (e) $\dfrac{3x + 1}{5} = 2$ (f) $\dfrac{2x - 7}{3} = 3$

C4 (a) Which equation below fits this number puzzle?

$$\frac{n}{3} + 5 = 6 \qquad \frac{n + 5}{3} = 6$$

I think of a number.
I add 5.
I divide by 3.
My answer is 6.
What was my number?

(b) Use the correct equation to solve the puzzle.

C5 Solve these equations.

(a) $\dfrac{n}{9} - 7 = 11$ (b) $\dfrac{n + 5}{6} = 12$ (c) $\dfrac{4n + 1}{3} = 9$

D Brackets in equations

An equation that involves brackets can be solved by first multiplying out the brackets.

Examples

$$3(x + 5) = 36 \quad \text{[multiply out brackets]}$$
$$3x + 15 = 36 \quad \text{[− 15]}$$
$$3x = 21 \quad \text{[÷ 3]}$$
$$x = 7$$

$$2(3x − 1) = x + 8 \quad \text{[multiply out brackets]}$$
$$6x − 2 = x + 8 \quad \text{[− x]}$$
$$5x − 2 = 8 \quad \text{[+ 2]}$$
$$5x = 10 \quad \text{[÷ 5]}$$
$$x = 2$$

D1 Solve each of these equations by first multiplying out the brackets.

(a) $3(x + 1) = 15$ (b) $4(x − 2) = 12$ (c) $2(x − 6) = 20$

(d) $5(4 + n) = 25$ (e) $14 = 2(1 + n)$ (f) $3(n + 5) = 36$

(g) $2(p − 1) = 3$ (h) $3(p + 4) = 6$ (i) $2(3p + 1) = 14$

(j) $4(2y − 5) = 12$ (k) $5(2y − 4) = 10$ (l) $3(4y + 1) = 9$

D2 The solution to each equation below stands for a letter.
Use the table on the right to find the letters.
Rearrange them into the name of an animal.

A $2(x + 1) = 10$ **B** $3(x − 2) = 9$

C $4(x − 1) = 12$ **D** $5(2x − 3) = 15$

E $2(3x + 2) = 10$ **F** $3(2x − 9) = 21$

1	T
2	D
3	A
4	B
5	R
6	G
7	E
8	I

D3 (a) Which equation below fits this number puzzle?

$3(n + 6) = 21$ $3n + 6 = 21$

> I think of a number.
> I add 6.
> I multiply by 3.
> My answer is 21.
> What was my number?

(b) Use the correct equation to solve the puzzle.

D4 Solve each of these equations by first multiplying out the brackets.

(a) $2(p + 5) = 3p$ (b) $3(n − 1) = 2n$ (c) $2(r + 5) = r + 13$

(d) $6(x + 1) = 2x + 16$ (e) $4(z − 1) = 2(z + 1)$ (f) $3(2k + 7) = k − 4$

(g) $3(n + 2) = 4(n − 1)$ (h) $4(3x − 1) = 2x + 1$ (i) $3(y + 7) = 5(2y + 7)$

*D5 Solve these.

(a) $\dfrac{x + 8}{5} = x$ (b) $\dfrac{x − 7}{3} = x − 7$ (c) $\dfrac{x + 5}{3} = x + 3$

E Equations with x subtracted

Some equations may involve terms like $-2x$.

Examples

$14 - 3x = 5$	[+ 3x]
$14 = 5 + 3x$	[− 5]
$9 = 3x$	[÷ 3]
$x = 3$	

$5x + 1 = 15 - 2x$	[+ 2x]
$7x + 1 = 15$	[− 1]
$7x = 14$	[÷ 7]
$x = 2$	

$7 = 9 - 5x$	[+ 5x]
$5x + 7 = 9$	[− 7]
$5x = 2$	[÷ 5]
$x = \frac{2}{5}$	

If you are not using a calculator, it can be easier to leave your answer as a fraction.

E1 (a) Solve $2 = 8 - 3a$ by first adding $3a$ to both sides.

(b) Solve $20 - 2b = 12$ by first adding $2b$ to both sides.

E2 Solve these.

(a) $10 - x = 7$ (b) $1 = 15 - x$ (c) $2 = 12 - 2x$

(d) $13 - 3n = 7$ (e) $19 - 4n = 7$ (f) $7 - 5n = 5$

E3 Copy and complete this working to solve $2x + 7 = 19 - 4x$.

$2x + 7 = 19 - 4x$	[+ 4x]
$\blacksquare + 7 = 19$	[− 7]
$\blacksquare = 12$	[÷ 6]
$x = \blacksquare$	

E4 Solve each of these equations.

(a) $3x = 15 - 2x$ (b) $7x = 18 - 2x$ (c) $8 - 3x = x$

(d) $20 - 3n = 2n$ (e) $3n + 2 = 27 - 2n$ (f) $2n + 4 = 19 - 3n$

(g) $7k + 1 = 28 - 2k$ (h) $16 - k = 1 + 2k$ (i) $4 - 3k = 1 + k$

E5 Solve each of these equations by first multiplying out the brackets.

(a) $2(x + 1) = 8 - x$ (b) $5(10 - f) = 15$ (c) $8 = 2(10 - v)$

(d) $4(6 - d) = 2d$ (e) $3(n - 5) = 13 - n$ (f) $11 - 2a = 3(a + 1)$

E6 Solve these equations.

(a) $\dfrac{10 - x}{3} = 2$ (b) $\dfrac{21 - 2x}{5} = 3$ (c) $\dfrac{5 - x}{2} = 4$

*E7 Solve these equations.

(a) $\dfrac{15 - x}{2} = x$ (b) $\dfrac{22 - 3x}{4} = 2x$ (c) $\dfrac{16 - x}{3} = x - 4$

Test yourself

T1 Solve

    (a) $5 + x = 9$ **(b)** $8x = 80$ **(c)** $4x - 5 = 17$ OCR

T2 Solve the equations.   **(a)** $8z - 5 = 11$ **(b)** $3(w - 2) = 9$ AQA

T3 In the diagram, all measurements are in centimetres.

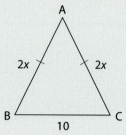

ABC is an isosceles triangle.
AB = 2x
AC = 2x
BC = 10

    (a) Find an expression, in terms of x, for the perimeter of the triangle. Simplify your expression.

The perimeter of the triangle is 34 cm.

    (b) Find the value of x.   Edexcel

T4 Solve these.   **(a)** $3x - 5 = 16$ **(b)** $5(y + 3) = 40$ Edexcel

T5 **(a)** Write down an equation involving x.

    (b) Solve your equation to find the value of x.   Not to scale

    $4x°$ $x°$ $x°$ OCR

T6 Solve these equations.   **(a)** $3x + 2 = 14$ **(b)** $4 = 10 - x$ OCR

T7 Solve

    (a) $5w = 90$ **(b)** $3y + 8 = 2$ **(c)** $7 = 4p - 3$ OCR

T8 Solve   **(a)** $5x + 2 = x + 8$ **(b)** $2(x + 3) = 4$ OCR

T9 Solve   **(a)** $\dfrac{x}{4} + 3 = 11$ **(b)** $5x - 7 = 3x$ OCR

T10 **(a)** Solve $\dfrac{x}{2} = 10$.

    (b) A cream cake costs x pence.
    A chocolate cake costs 50 pence more than a cream cake.

      (i) Write down, in terms of x, the cost of one chocolate cake.

      (ii) Three cream cakes and one chocolate cake cost £4.30 in total.
        Form an equation in x and solve it to find the cost of one cream cake.   OCR

T11 **(a)** Solve $7x + 18 = 74$.   **(b)** Solve $4(2y - 5) = 32$.

    (c) Solve $5p + 7 = 3(4 - p)$.   Edexcel

12 Compound measures

You will revise working with speed, distance and time.

This work will help you to work with a range of compound measures, including density.

A Review: speed, distance and time

A car travels at a speed of 46 m.p.h. for 4 hours.
How far does it travel in this time?

> $46 \times 4 = 184$
> So the car travels 184 miles.

> Speed is in miles per hour and time in hours, so distance is in miles.

To calculate distance, use the formula distance = speed × time .

A train travels a distance of 468 km in 3 hours.
What is its average speed?

> $468 \div 3 = 156$
> So the average speed of the train is 156 km/h.

> Distance is in kilometres and time in hours, so speed is in kilometres per hour.

To calculate speed, use the formula speed = distance ÷ time .

A bird flies 270 metres at a speed of 12 m/s.
How long does this journey take?

> $270 \div 12 = 22.5$
> So the journey takes 22.5 seconds.

> Speed is in metres per second and distance in metres, so time is in seconds.

To calculate time, use the formula time = distance ÷ speed .

A1 A dolphin swims a distance of 80 kilometres in two hours.
What is the dolphin's average speed in kilometres per hour?

A2 A penguin swims at a speed of 8 metres per second for 20 seconds.
How far does it swim in this time?

A3 A slug crawls across a path at a speed of 0.5 cm per second.
How long does it take to crawl 10 cm?

A4 A jumbo jet flies for 5 hours at a speed of 975 km/h.
How far does it travel during this time?

A5 A cyclist travels a distance of 54 miles at an average speed of 18 m.p.h.
How long has this journey taken the cyclist?

A6 How long does it take Paul to cycle 330 metres at a speed of 6 m/s?

A7 A car travels 400 miles in 7 hours.
Work out the car's average speed in m.p.h., correct to one decimal place.

A8 A zebra takes 6 seconds to cover 98 metres.
Calculate its average speed in m/s, correct to one decimal place.

B Hours and minutes on a calculator

When using a calculator, you need to be able to change between hours and minutes and decimals of an hour.

There are 60 minutes in an hour,

so 30 minutes = $\frac{1}{2}$ hour = 0.5 hour

15 minutes = $\frac{1}{4}$ hour = 0.25 hour

> Remember $\frac{1}{2}$ is equivalent to 0.5 and $\frac{1}{4}$ is equivalent to 0.25.

• What fraction of an hour is 45 minutes?
How would you write 45 minutes as a decimal of an hour?

B1 Which **two** of these are equivalent to 3 hours 15 minutes?

A $3\frac{1}{4}$ hours   **B** 3.4 hours   **C** $3\frac{1}{15}$ hours   **D** 3.25 hours

B2 Write each of these times in hours, using decimals of an hour.

(a) 1 hour 30 minutes   (b) 2 hours 15 minutes   (c) 1 hour 45 minutes

Example

A train travels a distance of 120 miles in $1\frac{1}{2}$ hours.
What is its average speed in m.p.h.?

$1\frac{1}{2}$ hours = 1.5 hours   First write the time as a decimal.
Distance ÷ time = 120 ÷ 1.5 = 80
So the average speed of the train is 80 m.p.h.

B3 A train travels at 75 m.p.h for 30 minutes.
How far does it travel during this time?

B4 Work out the average speeds in km/h of these.

    (a) A coach that takes $2\frac{1}{2}$ hours to travel 200 km

    (b) A cyclist who travels 42 km in 1 hour 45 minutes

B5 Simon sets out from home at 8:00 a.m. to drive 65 miles to a meeting.
He arrives at the meeting at 9:15 a.m.
What is his average speed?

B6 A coach leaves London at 4:00 p.m. and travels at 55 m.p.h.
How far has it travelled at 6:30 p.m.?

Example

A ferry travels a distance of 54 km at a speed of 24 km/h.
How long does the journey take, in hours and minutes?

Distance ÷ speed = 54 ÷ 24 = 2.25
0.25 hours = $\frac{1}{4}$ hour = 15 minutes
So the journey takes 2 hours 15 minutes.

Change the decimal part into minutes.
Remember 0.25 hours is **not** the same as 25 minutes.

B7 Write each of these times in hours and minutes.

    (a) 2.75 hours   **(b)** 3.5 hours   **(c)** 1.25 hours

B8 Work out the time taken for each of these journeys.
Give your answers in hours and minutes.

    (a) A cyclist who travels at a steady speed of 40 km/h for 30 km

    (b) A ferry that travels at 12 m.p.h. for 21 miles

    (c) A lorry that travels for 130 miles at an average speed of 52 m.p.h.

B9 A train travels 84 miles at a speed of 56 m.p.h.
What time does it arrive at its destination if it left at 08:45?

*B10 Brooke drove for 15 minutes at an average speed of 40 m.p.h. and
then for $1\frac{3}{4}$ hours at an average speed of 60 m.p.h.

    (a) Calculate the total distance of her journey.

    (b) Calculate her average speed for the whole journey.

To convert a decimal part of an hour to minutes, you can multiply by 60.

For example, 0.2 hours = 0.2 × 60 minutes = 12 minutes

        1.2 hours = 1 hour + 0.2 × 60 minutes = 1 hour 12 minutes

---

*B11 Write each of these times in hours and minutes.

    (a) 0.15 hours   **(b)** 0.4 hours   **(c)** 2.6 hours   **(d)** 4.65 hours

C Rates

Speed is measured in miles per hour, metres per second, and so on.
It is an example of a **rate**.

Other examples are:

- the rate at which water flows from a pipe, measured in litres per second
- the rate at which a photocopier makes copies, measured in copies per minute
- the rate at which a household uses water, measured in litres per day

When calculating with rates, it is sometimes difficult to decide on the correct calculation.

You have to decide whether to multiply or divide, or which way round to divide.
Sometimes a mental picture can help you think more clearly.

Which is the correct calculation in each of these?

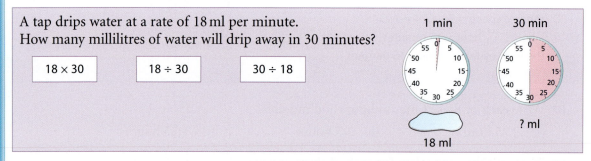

A tap drips water at a rate of 18 ml per minute.
How many millilitres of water will drip away in 30 minutes?

| 18 × 30 | 18 ÷ 30 | 30 ÷ 18 |

1 min   30 min

18 ml   ? ml

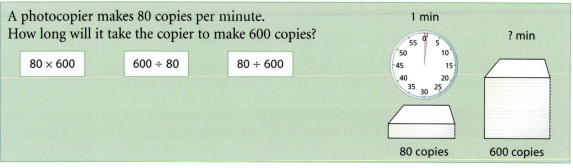

A photocopier makes 80 copies per minute.
How long will it take the copier to make 600 copies?

| 80 × 600 | 600 ÷ 80 | 80 ÷ 600 |

1 min   ? min

80 copies   600 copies

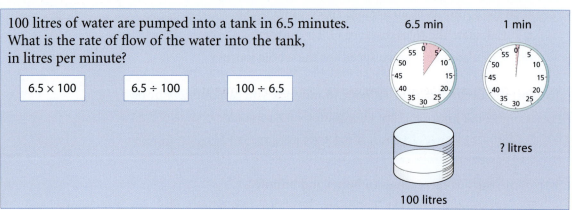

100 litres of water are pumped into a tank in 6.5 minutes.
What is the rate of flow of the water into the tank,
in litres per minute?

| 6.5 × 100 | 6.5 ÷ 100 | 100 ÷ 6.5 |

6.5 min   1 min

100 litres   ? litres

Give the answers to the following questions to an appropriate degree of accuracy.
Remember to state the units (e.g. hours, litres, millilitres per minute) in each case.

C1 Connor is paid at a rate of £6.50 per hour.
How much does he earn for 14.5 hours' work?

C2 Moles can dig at a rate of 10 metres per hour.
At this rate, how long would it take a mole to dig
a tunnel that is 25 metres long?

C3 A dripping tap fills a bowl with 300 ml of water in 12 minutes.
At what rate is the tap dripping in millilitres per minute?

C4 Lucy's heart beats at a rate of 77 beats per minute.
How long does it take her heart to beat 1000 times?

C5 Water comes out of a tap at a rate of 0.4 litres per second.
How much water would come out of the tap in 20 seconds?

C6 Jack is paid by the hour.
He works for 5.5 hours and earns a total of £40.15.
What is his hourly rate of pay?

C7 A person in the UK uses water in their home at the rate of about 150 litres per day.
About how much water would a household of five people use in a week?

C8 A furnace burns fuel at a rate of 5.5 kg per hour.
How long will 40 kg of fuel last?

C9 A printer takes 35 minutes to print 800 copies of a leaflet.
What is its rate of printing in copies per minute?

C10 A water pump operates at a rate of 13.6 litres per minute.
How long will it take to pump 150 litres of water out of a tank?

C11 A machine wraps 4000 bars of chocolate in an hour.
At what rate does it wrap, measured in chocolate bars per minute?

C12 Water comes out of a tap at the rate of 0.7 litre/second.
How long will it take to fill an 8 litre bottle?

D Compound measures

A rate is an example of a **compound measure**.

Other examples are:

- population density measured in people per square kilometre
- fuel consumption measured in miles per gallon
- density measured in grams per cubic centimetre

Example

Iceland has an area of $103\,000\,\text{km}^2$.
In 2005 its population was about $297\,000$.
What was its population density?

> Population ÷ area = $297\,000 ÷ 103\,000 = 2.883\,495\,\ldots$
> So the population density is 3 people per km^2 (to the nearest person).

Give the answers to the following questions to an appropriate degree of accuracy. Remember to state the units (e.g. people per km^2) in each case.

D1 The UK has an area of $244\,820\,\text{km}^2$.
In 2005 its population was $60\,441\,457$.
What was its population density?

D2 Australia has an area of $7\,686\,850\,\text{km}^2$.
In 2005 its population was $20\,090\,437$.
What was its population density?

D3 The Orkneys are a group of islands that lie to the north of mainland Scotland.
The table below has some information about six of the smaller inhabited islands.

Island	Area in km^2	Population in 1891	Population in 1991
Eday	27.45	647	166
Rousay	48.60	774	217
Sanday	50.43	1929	533
Shapinsay	29.48	903	322
Stronsay	32.75	1275	382
Wyre	3.11	67	28

Draw up a table to show the population density of each of these islands in 1891 and 1991.

D4 Jane drives a distance of 400 miles and uses 11 gallons of petrol.
What was her petrol consumption in miles per gallon?

D5 In town the fuel consumption of Prakash's car is about 25 miles per gallon.
How many miles will he be able to drive in town on 4.2 gallons of petrol?

D6 On a long journey the fuel consumption of Mark's car is about 45 miles per gallon.
How many gallons of fuel will he use on a journey of 250 miles?

D7 On a long journey, Sam's car uses 7.5 gallons of petrol to travel 315 miles.
   (a) What is her petrol consumption in miles per gallon?
   (b) Estimate the distance Sam could travel on 12 gallons of petrol.

The **density** of an object is usually given as the mass in grams of $1\,cm^3$.

So density in grams per cm^3 (g/cm^3) is found by using the rule

   density = mass in grams ÷ volume in cm^3

For example, the mass of this piece of wood is 380 grams.

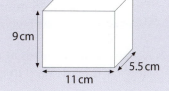

It is in the shape of a cuboid so its volume is $\quad 11 \times 9 \times 5.5$

$\qquad\qquad\qquad = 544.5\,cm^3$

So the density of this wood is $\quad 380 \div 544.5$

$\qquad\qquad\qquad = 0.697\,887\ldots$

$\qquad\qquad\qquad = 0.7\,g/cm^3$ (to one decimal place)

Density can also be found in kilograms per m^3 (kg/m^3) by using the rule

   density = mass in kilograms ÷ volume in m^3

D8 (a) Work out the volume of the block of tin.

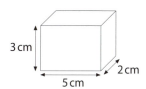

(b) The block weighs 220 grams.
What is the density of the block of tin in g/cm^3, correct to one decimal place?

D9 Find the density of each of these cuboids.

(a)

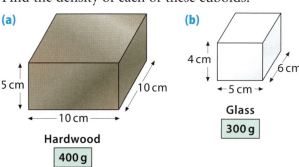

(b)
(c)

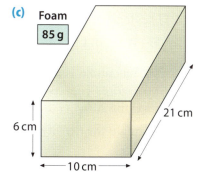

D10 A certain stone has a density of 3 g/cm^3.
The volume of the stone is 92 cm^3.
Find the mass of the stone.

D11 Gold has a density of 19.3 g/cm^3.
The mass of this ingot of gold is 40 g.
What is the volume of this ingot of gold?

Test yourself

T1 Alan drove 12 miles.
The journey took 15 minutes.
What was Alan's average speed?   AQA

T2 A giant tortoise crawls at a speed of 0.17 m/s for 34 seconds.
How far does it travel in metres, correct to one decimal place?

T3 (a) An athlete runs 15 miles at an average speed of 6 miles per hour.
How long does he take to run the 15 miles?
Give your answer in hours and minutes.

(b) Another athlete runs 18 miles in $2\frac{1}{4}$ hours.
What is her average speed?   AQA

T4 Cheryl works for 35 hours one week and is paid £253.75.

(a) What is her hourly rate of pay?

(b) At the same hourly rate, how much would she get paid for working 28 hours?

T5 The area of Trinidad and Tobago is 1980 square miles.
The population density is 460 people per square mile.
Work out the population of Trinidad and Tobago.   OCR

T6 The mass of 5 m^3 of copper is 44 800 kg.

(a) Work out the density of copper.

The density of zinc is 7130 kg/m^3.

(b) Work out the mass of 5 m^3 of zinc.   Edexcel

T7 A solid cuboid is made from brass.
It measures 4 cm by 2 cm by 3 cm.
It weighs 204 g.
Calculate the density of the brass.   OCR

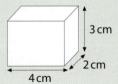
3 cm
2 cm
4 cm

13 Angles of a polygon

You should know about the sum of angles around a point, on a line and in a triangle.

This work will help you use the interior and exterior angles of a regular or irregular polygon.

You need a pair of compasses and an angle measurer.

A Angles of a regular polygon

A **regular polygon** is one that has all its angles and all its sides equal.
Follow these instructions to draw a regular hexagon inside a circle.

Draw a circle of radius 6 cm.

Mark a point on the circle and two spaced 6 cm each side.

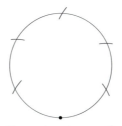

Repeat, using each mark as the centre for another mark.

Join the marks up to make a hexagon.

Join the vertices of the hexagon to the centre.

- How many of these angles are there at the centre?
- What must the sum of these angles be?
- So how big is each of the angles? Check by measuring.

A1 For a regular pentagon you need five points spaced equally around a circle.

   (a) When lines are drawn from the points to the centre of the circle, how many angles are there at the centre?

   (b) What must these angles add up to?

   (c) Work out the size of one angle at the centre.

> Each of these lines is a **radius** of the circle (plural **radii**).

A2 Copy and complete this table.

Regular polygon	Pentagon	Hexagon	Octagon	Decagon	Dodecagon
Number of sides	5	6	8	10	12
Angle at the centre					

A3 Use your table from A2 to draw each of the regular polygons in a 6 cm radius circle. Use an angle measurer to draw the angles at the centre.

You should have found that in a regular polygon each angle at the centre is 360° ÷ n, where n is the number of sides of the polygon.

You can use this fact to find the **interior angles** in a regular polygon.

This is part of a regular pentagon with centre O.

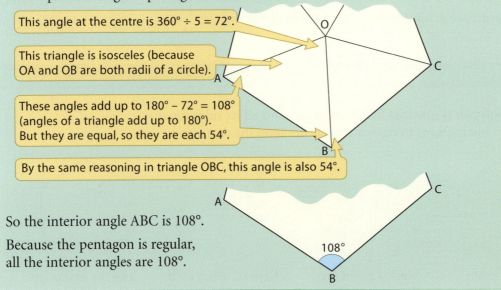

This angle at the centre is 360° ÷ 5 = 72°.

This triangle is isosceles (because OA and OB are both radii of a circle).

These angles add up to 180° − 72° = 108° (angles of a triangle add up to 180°). But they are equal, so they are each 54°.

By the same reasoning in triangle OBC, this angle is also 54°.

So the interior angle ABC is 108°.

Because the pentagon is regular, all the interior angles are 108°.

A4 Copy this table and use the approach above to complete it.

Regular polygon	Pentagon	Hexagon	Octagon	Decagon	Dodecagon
Size of interior angle	108°				

Measure the interior angles of the polygons you drew in A3 and see how well they correspond to these answers.

A5 In this question you will use the table you completed for A4. So first make sure that it is correct.

(a) Three regular hexagons will fit exactly round a point. Explain why.

(b) Now decide whether each of these combinations of shapes will fit exactly round a point, giving a reason in each case.

(i) Three regular octagons

(ii) Six equilateral triangles

(iii) Two regular octagons and a square

(iv) A regular octagon, a regular hexagon and a regular pentagon

(v) Two regular hexagons and two equilateral triangles

(vi) Two regular dodecagons and an equilateral triangle

(vii) Two regular decagons and a regular pentagon

(viii) Two regular pentagons and a regular decagon

B Interior angles of a quadrilateral

A **quadrilateral** is a shape with four straight sides.

A quadrilateral can be divided into two triangles. The sum of the angles in each triangle is 180°.

The angles of the two triangles make up the interior angles of the quadrilateral. So the interior angles of a quadrilateral add up to 360°.

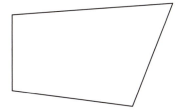 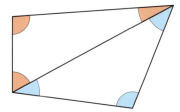 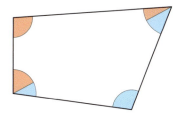

B1 (a) What do these three angles add up to?

(b) What must the fourth angle of the quadrilateral be to make all four angles add up to 360°?

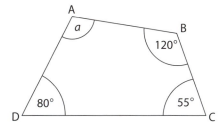

B2 ABCD is a quadrilateral. Work out the value of *a*.

Not drawn accurately

AQA

B3 Find the angles labelled by letters in these quadrilaterals.

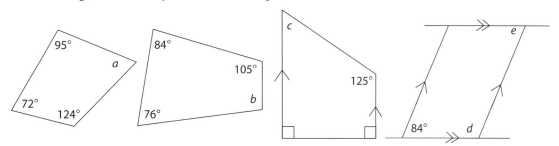

B4 This diagram shows a kite.

(a) What is angle *f*? Explain how you know.

(b) Calculate angle *g*.

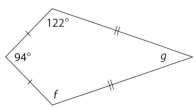

B5 Find the angles marked x, y and z.
Explain how you worked out each angle.

(a)

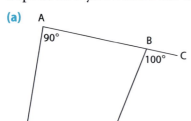

(b)

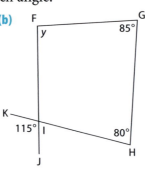

(c)

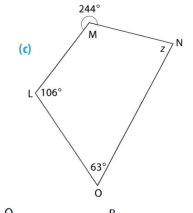

B6 In this diagram lines PS and TW are parallel.

(a) What kind of quadrilateral is QRVU?

(b) What is the size of angle PQU?

(c) What is the size of angle RQU?

(d) What is the size of angle QRV?

(e) Check that the sum of the angles of quadrilateral QRVU is what you expect.

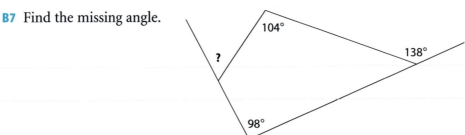

B7 Find the missing angle.

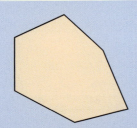

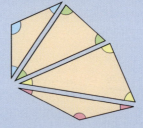

C Interior angles of any polygon

This is an irregular hexagon.

Here it has been split into triangles by cutting from one vertex to the other vertices.

- How many triangles has the hexagon been split into?
- What is the sum of all the interior angles of these triangles?
- What is the sum of the interior angles of the hexagon?

C1 Find the missing angle in each of these hexagons.

(a)

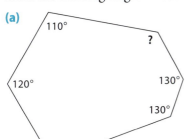

(b)

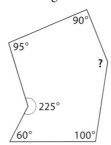

(c)

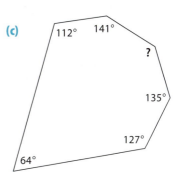

C2 In question A4 you should have found that each interior angle of
a **regular** hexagon is 120°.
Use this to find the sum of the interior angles of a regular hexagon.

Check that this answer agrees with sum of the angles of a hexagon
that you used in question C1.

C3 **(a)** Draw a pentagon with a ruler: it does not have to be regular.
Draw lines from a single vertex to all the other vertices.

(b) How many triangles are there inside your pentagon?

(c) What is the sum of all the interior angles of a pentagon?

C4 Find the missing angle in each of these pentagons.

(a)

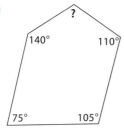

(b)

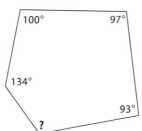

(c)

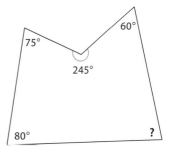

C5 On page 100 you saw that each interior angle of a **regular** pentagon is 108°.
Use this to find the sum of the interior angles of a regular pentagon.

Check that this answer agrees with sum of the angles of a pentagon
that you found in question C3.

*C6 **(a)** If a polygon is split into triangles by lines drawn from a single vertex to
all the other vertices, what rule connects the number of sides of the polygon
with the number of triangles produced? (Draw sketches and experiment.)

(b) What rule connects the number of sides of a polygon with the sum of
its interior angles?

D Exterior angles of any polygon

If you extend a side of a polygon, the angle made is called an **exterior angle**.

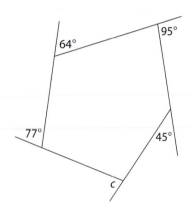

If a pencil is moved around the sides of a polygon, at each vertex it turns through the exterior angle.

- When the pencil gets back to where it has started from, it will point in the same direction as before. What angle has it turned through?
- What is the sum of the exterior angles of a polygon?

Start and finish

D1 Find the angles labelled by letters.

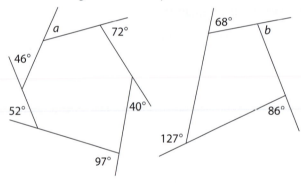

D2 This diagram shows a regular octagon.

(a) How many exterior angles are shown here?

(b) What must be the size of one exterior angle?

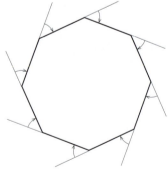

D3 In section A you should have found that each **interior** angle of a regular octagon is 135°.
With the help of a diagram, explain how this value relates to the size of an exterior angle that you have just found.

D4 This is a regular 12-sided polygon (a dodecagon).

(a) How many exterior angles are shown here?

(b) What must be the size of one exterior angle?

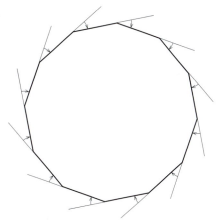

D5 Copy this table. Calculate the missing exterior angles and complete the table.

Regular polygon	Pentagon	Hexagon	Octagon	Decagon	Dodecagon
Size of exterior angle			45°		30°

D6 Each exterior angle of a certain regular polygon is 40°.
How many sides must this polygon have?

D7 How many sides does a regular polygon have if each exterior angle is

(a) 9°   (b) 24°   (c) 10°   (d) 18°

E Mixed questions

E1 PQRST is a regular pentagon.

(a) Calculate angle STP, giving your reasons.

(b) What kind of triangle is triangle STP?

(c) Calculate angle TSP, giving your reasons.

(d) Calculate angle PSR, giving reasons.

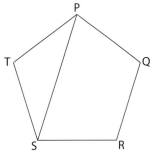

E2 Two sides of this regular octagon have been extended
to make a triangle on one of the sides.

Find angles a, b and c.

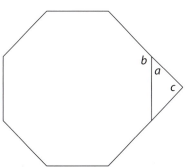

E3 Calculate the size of angle GIK, giving full reasons for your answer.

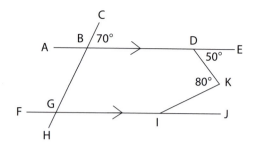

A **tangent** is a line that touches a circle at one point only.

Think of a wheel touching horizontal ground.
The centre of the wheel is above the point of contact, so the radius is at right angles to the horizontal tangent.

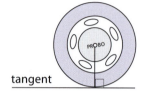

tangent

If the entire diagram is rotated it will make no difference to the fact that **the angle between the radius and tangent is a right angle**.

You will need this fact in the following question.

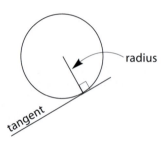

radius

tangent

E4 The sides of the triangle ABC are tangents that touch a circle at points P, Q and R as shown.
O is the centre of the circle.

(a) Give the sizes of angles ARO and APO, explaining your reasons.

(b) By considering the angles of the quadrilateral APOR, calculate angle RAP.

(c) Find angle RCQ.

(d) Find angle POQ and hence find angle PBQ.

(e) Do the three angles of the triangle have the total you expect?

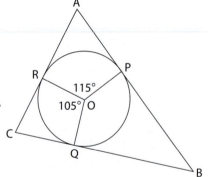

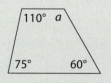
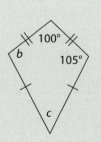

T2 Find the angles labelled by letters.

T3 Calculate the lettered angles.

T4 (a) What is the sum of the interior angles of any pentagon?

(b) Calculate the missing interior angle in this pentagon.

T5 (a) What is the sum of the interior angles of any hexagon?

(b) Calculate the missing interior angle in this hexagon.

T6 Katya has started to draw a regular polygon by marking points round a circle.

(a) How many sides will her polygon have?

(b) What size will each exterior angle of her polygon be?

(c) What size will each interior angle be?

T7 Each exterior angle of certain regular polygon is 8°.

(a) How many sides does this regular polygon have?

(b) What is the size of an interior angle of this polygon?

14 Fractions and decimals

You should know how to

- add and subtract decimals
- multiply and divide by a two-digit number

This work will help you

- convert between decimals and fractions
- multiply and divide by a decimal
- solve problems involving decimals

A Changing between decimals and fractions

> **Example**
>
> Change each of these decimals to a fraction in its lowest terms. **(a)** 0.32 **(b)** 0.275
>
> (a) 0.32 means the same as $\frac{32}{100}$. (b) 0.275 means the same as $\frac{275}{1000}$.
>
> $$\frac{32}{100} = \frac{8}{25} \qquad (\div 4)$$
>
> $$\frac{275}{1000} = \frac{55}{200} = \frac{11}{40} \qquad (\div 5)(\div 5)$$

A1 Change each of these decimals to a fraction in its lowest terms.

(a) 0.6 (b) 0.64 (c) 0.35 (d) 0.08 (e) 0.96

A2 Match each decimal with an equivalent fraction.

| 0.04 | 0.025 | $\frac{1}{25}$ | $\frac{1}{40}$ |

0.45 $\frac{9}{20}$

A3 Change each of these decimals to a fraction in its lowest terms.

(a) 0.125 (b) 0.035 (c) 0.004 (d) 0.152 (e) 0.625

> **Example**
>
> Change $\frac{3}{8}$ to a decimal.
>
> You need to divide 3 by 8.
> To allow for decimal places, write 3 as 3.00…
>
>
>
> $\frac{3}{8} = 0.375$

A4 Change each of these fractions to a decimal.

(a) $\frac{5}{8}$ (b) $\frac{7}{8}$ (c) $\frac{6}{5}$ (d) $\frac{11}{8}$

B Recurring decimals

When you change $\frac{1}{3}$ to a decimal, you do not get an exact answer.

The decimal carries on forever.

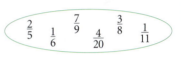

$\frac{1}{3} = 0.33333\ldots\ldots$

This is called a **recurring decimal**.

A decimal such as 0.1, which is equivalent to $\frac{1}{10}$, is called a **terminating decimal**.

- Use division to change $\frac{1}{6}$ to a decimal.
  Is this a terminating decimal or a recurring decimal?

Any decimal that is either recurring or terminating is equivalent to an exact fraction.

B1 Change these fractions to recurring decimals.

 (a) $\frac{2}{3}$ (b) $\frac{5}{6}$ (c) $\frac{1}{9}$ (d) $\frac{4}{9}$

B2 Write down all the fractions in the loop that are equivalent to recurring decimals.

$\frac{2}{5}$ $\frac{1}{6}$ $\frac{7}{9}$ $\frac{4}{20}$ $\frac{3}{8}$ $\frac{1}{11}$

B3 Jo uses her calculator to change $\frac{2}{3}$ to a decimal.
For $2 \div 3$ her calculator gives 0.6666667.
What is wrong with this answer?
Why has this happened?

*B4 Change each of these fractions to recurring decimals.
What do you notice about the results?

 (a) $\frac{1}{7}$ (b) $\frac{2}{7}$ (c) $\frac{3}{7}$ (d) $\frac{4}{7}$ (e) $\frac{5}{7}$ (f) $\frac{6}{7}$

C Multiplying decimals

Using the 'decimal places' rule for multiplication gives $0.2 \times 0.4 = 0.08$.

If we change the decimals to fractions, $0.2 = \frac{2}{10}$ and $0.4 = \frac{4}{10}$.

- Work out $\frac{2}{10} \times \frac{4}{10}$.
  Use this result to explain why $0.2 \times 0.4 = 0.08$.

C1 (a) Change 0.6 to a fraction.

 (b) Change 0.7 to a fraction.

 (c) Multiply these two fractions together.

 (d) Use your answer to (c) to write down the answer to 0.6×0.7 as a decimal.

C2 Work these out.

(a) 0.2×0.8 (b) 0.3×0.1 (c) 0.9×0.4 (d) 0.2×0.3 (e) 0.8×0.6

C3 Work these out.

(a) 0.2^2 (b) 0.9^2 (c) 0.4^2 (d) 0.7^2 (e) 0.1^2

To multiply numbers involving decimals

Work out 2.45×3.6.

- First count the number of decimal places in the calculation.
  $2.\underline{45} \times 3.\underline{6}$ has **3** decimal places.

- Ignore decimal points and multiply.

	200	40	5
30	6000	1200	150
6	1200	240	30

```
  6000
  1200
   150
  1200
   240
+   30
  8820
```

```
   245
 ×  36
     1
     7
```

- Write the answer with the same number of decimal places as in the calculation.
  $8.\underline{820}$ has **3** decimal places.
  So $2.45 \times 3.6 = 8.820$

  > Check your answer by estimating.
  > 2.45 is about 2 and 3.6 is about 4.
  > $2 \times 4 = 8$

C4 Use the fact that $156 \times 48 = 7488$ to write down the answer to each of these.

(a) 1.56×48 (b) 15.6×4.8 (c) 1.56×4.8 (d) 1.56×0.48 (e) 0.156×0.48

C5 (a) Write down an estimate for 2.8×5.1.

(b) Calculate 2.8×5.1.

C6 Work these out. Check your answers by estimating.

(a) 3.4×5.6 (b) 2.6×5.7 (c) 4.5×5.3 (d) 1.4×3.5 (e) 7.5×3.6

(f) 421×3.8 (g) 3.49×2.1 (h) 0.13×5.6 (i) 6.02×3.4 (j) 78.2×0.25

C7 Find the areas of these rugs in m².

(a)

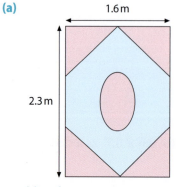

1.6 m
2.3 m

(b)

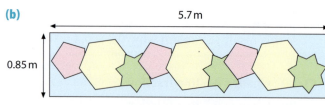

5.7 m
0.85 m

D Dividing by a single-digit decimal

You can change division by a decimal to division by a whole number by multiplying 'top and bottom' by 10 or 100 or …

Examples

× 10

$$\frac{8}{0.2} = \frac{80}{2} = 40$$

× 10

× 100

$$\frac{1.5}{0.03} = \frac{150}{3} = 50$$

× 100

D1 Work these out.

(a) $\dfrac{6}{0.3}$
(b) $\dfrac{12}{0.2}$
(c) $\dfrac{2.4}{0.3}$
(d) $\dfrac{1.4}{0.2}$
(e) $\dfrac{120}{0.4}$

D2 Work these out.

(a) $\dfrac{1.2}{0.03}$
(b) $\dfrac{8}{0.04}$
(c) $\dfrac{16}{0.08}$
(d) $\dfrac{0.15}{0.03}$
(e) $\dfrac{0.8}{0.02}$

D3 Work these out.

(a) $\dfrac{4}{0.2}$
(b) $\dfrac{2}{0.05}$
(c) $\dfrac{2.8}{0.7}$
(d) $\dfrac{3.2}{0.04}$
(e) $\dfrac{0.36}{0.09}$

D4 These three cards | 0.5 | | = 8 | | 4 | can make a division:

Arrange these six cards to make two correct divisions.

| 0.3 | | = 0.5 | | 1.5 | | 30 | | 15 | | = 5 |

D5 Arrange these six cards to make two correct divisions.

| 0.8 | | 24 | | 2.4 | | 0.08 | | = 3 | | = 300 |

D6 Choose two of the four numbers in the loop to go in the boxes to make a correct division.

4 0.4 0.8 8

$$\frac{}{} = 5$$

D7 Do the same as in D6 for each of these.

(a)
$$\frac{}{} = 30$$

12 4 1.2 0.4

(b)
$$\frac{}{} = 5$$

9 4.5 0.45 0.9

(c)
$$\frac{}{} = 2.5$$

10 0.5 5 0.2

(d)
$$\frac{}{} = 20$$

10 0.05 5 1

D8 Work these out.

(a) $\dfrac{4.68}{0.2}$
(b) $\dfrac{0.42}{0.3}$
(c) $\dfrac{0.18}{0.6}$
(d) $\dfrac{0.06}{0.3}$
(e) $\dfrac{0.86}{0.05}$

E Dividing by a two-digit decimal

Here is one way to work out $59.8 \div 0.26$.

- First multiply top and bottom by 100 to get an equivalent whole-number division.

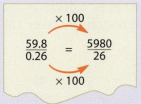

$$\frac{59.8}{0.26} = \frac{5980}{26}$$

- Divide 5980 by 26.

$$
\begin{array}{r}
5980 \\
\mathbf{200} \times 26 \quad -5200 \\
\hline
780 \\
\mathbf{30} \times 26 \quad -780 \\
\hline
0
\end{array}
$$

$\mathbf{200} + \mathbf{30} = 230$

$$
\begin{array}{r}
230 \\
26\overline{)5980} \\
-52 \\
\hline
78 \\
-78 \\
\hline
0
\end{array}
$$

So $59.8 \div 0.26 = 230$.

> Check your answer by estimating.
> 59.8 is about 60 and 0.26 is about 0.3.
> $$\frac{60}{0.3} = \frac{600}{3} = 200$$

E1 Find three matching pairs of divisions.

$\dfrac{32.2}{1.4}$ $\dfrac{322}{0.14}$ $\dfrac{32.2}{0.14}$ $\dfrac{32\,200}{14}$ $\dfrac{3220}{14}$ $\dfrac{322}{14}$

E2 Use the fact that $612 \div 36 = 17$ to write down the answer to each of these.

(a) $\dfrac{61.2}{3.6}$ (b) $\dfrac{6.12}{0.36}$ (c) $\dfrac{612}{3.6}$ (d) $\dfrac{612}{0.36}$ (e) $\dfrac{61.2}{0.36}$

E3 Work these out.

(a) $\dfrac{32.2}{1.4}$ (b) $\dfrac{4.68}{0.36}$ (c) $\dfrac{44.2}{0.26}$ (d) $\dfrac{1.69}{0.13}$ (e) $\dfrac{5.2}{0.65}$

E4 A Smart car is 2.5 metres long.
Bumper to bumper, a line of these cars is 40 metres long.
How many cars are in the line?

E5 You are told that $13 \times 19 = 247$.
Use this fact to work these out.

(a) $\dfrac{247}{19}$ (b) $\dfrac{24.7}{1.3}$ (c) $\dfrac{24.7}{1.9}$ (d) $\dfrac{247}{1.3}$ (e) $\dfrac{247}{0.19}$

E6 Martha buys 0.4 kg of grapes for £1.40.
Work out the cost of 1 kg of grapes.

F Using a calculator to solve problems with decimals

When you solve a problem it is important to set your working out clearly.

Example

Jack bought a pair of trainers in New York for $110.
He saw the same pair of trainers in London for £64.50.

The exchange rate was £1 = $1.94.

How much cheaper were the trainers in New York?

> You can work in either dollars or pounds.
> In this case we will use dollars.

> To change pounds to dollars multiply by 1.94.

> Change both prices to the same currency.
> 64.50 × 1.94 = 125.13
> So £64.50 = $125.13
> Difference in price = $125.13 – $110 = $15.13
> The trainers were $15.13 cheaper in New York.

> Remember to give the correct currency in your answer.

F1 The exchange rate from pounds to US dollars is £1 = $1.94.

    (a) A football shirt costs £34.50. How much is this in dollars?

    (b) A basketball shirt costs $35.99.

        (i) Estimate the cost of the basketball shirt in pounds.

        (ii) Use your calculator to work out the cost in pounds, to the nearest penny.

F2 Parveen buys a digital camera in Birmingham for £122.50.
She sees the same camera on sale in Paris for €192.40.
The exchange rate is £1 = €1.48.

    In which city is the camera cheaper and by how much?

F3 Here are the prices of some items at a fish shop.

> Sea bass £9.40 per kg
>
> Cod £8.20 per kg
>
> Prawns £13.40 per kg

    (a) Find the cost of 1.25 kg of prawns and 1.6 kg of sea bass.

    (b) Nigel bought 0.5 kg of cod and some prawns.
        The total cost was £10.13.
        What weight of prawns did he buy?

F4 Becki bought 0.8 kg of pears at £1.60 per kilogram and 0.5 kg of apples.
The total cost was £1.98.
What was the price per kilogram of the apples?

F5 When Lizzy uses her car on a business trip she is allowed to claim £0.46 per mile
for the first 50 miles travelled and £0.27 per mile for the rest of the journey.
How much can she claim for an 80 mile journey?

G Mixed questions

G1 Given that $17 \times 14 = 238$, write down the answers to these.

(a) 1.7×1.4 (b) 170×140 (c) 17×0.14 (d) $238 \div 14$

(e) $2380 \div 14$ (f) $238 \div 17$ (g) $23.8 \div 1.7$ (h) $23.8 \div 0.14$

G2 This shows a picture in a frame.
Work out

(a) the height of the picture

(b) the width of the picture

(c) the perimeter of the frame

(d) the perimeter of the picture

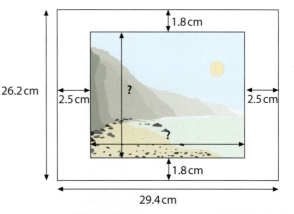

G3 Work out the cost of these purchases.

(a) 1 kg of bananas and 1 kg of grapes

(b) 0.4 kg of grapes

(c) 1.2 kg of apples

(d) 2 kg of pears and 1 kg of bananas

(e) 1.4 kg of apples and 1.5 kg of pears

Apples	Grapes
£0.95 per kilo	£1.90 per kilo

Bananas	Pears
£1.08 per kilo	£1.28 per kilo

G4 Anna keeps copies of her favourite magazine.
Each copy of the magazine is 0.6 cm thick.
She has a magazine file 7.5 cm thick.
Could she keep 12 copies of the magazine in this magazine file?

G5 Gareth worked for 27 hours one week.
He is paid at a rate of £6.40 per hour.
How much was he paid altogether that week?

G6 Jenny buys 2.4 metres of curtain fabric costing £4.75 per metre.
Find the total cost of the fabric.

G7 A rectangular room measures 3.2 m by 4.3 m.

(a) Estimate the area of the room by rounding the measurements to
one significant figure.

(b) Is your estimate bigger or smaller than the actual area?
Explain how you can tell.

(c) Calculate the actual area of the room.

Test yourself

T1 Change each decimal to a fraction in its lowest terms.

(a) 0.45   (b) 0.06   (c) 0.82   (d) 0.225   (e) 0.005

T2 Write each fraction as a recurring decimal.

(a) $\frac{1}{6}$ (b) $\frac{2}{9}$

T3 Work out

(a) $5.4 - 1.28$ (b) $3.64 \times 2 + 13.7$ (c) $0.3 \times 100 + 2.4 \times 10$ AQA

T4 Work these out.

(a) 0.4×0.6 (b) 0.2×0.3 (c) 0.3×0.9 (d) 0.1×0.5 (e) 0.6^2

T5 Work these out.

(a) $\dfrac{2.4}{0.4}$ (b) $\dfrac{9}{0.3}$ (c) $\dfrac{16}{0.02}$ (d) $\dfrac{5}{0.02}$ (e) $\dfrac{1.8}{0.03}$

T6 Using the information that

$$97 \times 123 = 11\,931$$

write down the value of

(a) 9.7×12.3 (b) $0.97 \times 123\,000$ (c) $11.931 \div 9.7$ Edexcel

T7 Work these out.

(a) 1.4×2.3 (b) 260×0.18 (c) 45×0.32 (d) $20.8 \div 0.13$ (e) $64.8 \div 0.27$

T8 You are given that $227.5 \div 35 = 6.5$.
Find the value of

(a) 6.5×3.5 (b) $227.5 \div 350$ (c) $2275 \div 0.35$ AQA

T9 (a) One metre of electric cable weighs 2.8 kg.
How much does 3.5 metres of cable weigh?

(b) Henry pays £1.88 for 0.4 kg of beef.
Calculate the cost of 1 kg of beef.   OCR

T10 A bag of charcoal costs £3.17.
Joe buys 15 of these bags.
Work out the total cost. You must show your working.   OCR

T11 The cost of 4 kg of apples is £3.36.
The total cost of 3 kg of apples and 2.5 kg of pears is £4.12.

Work out the cost of 1 kg of pears.
Give your answer in pence.   Edexcel

Review 2

1 I have a box of 24 chocolates.
   16 of them are milk chocolate and the rest are plain chocolate.

   What fraction of the chocolates are milk?
   Give your answer in its simplest form.

2 Calculate these.

   (a) 2.6×5 **(b)** $2.93 + 5.1$ **(c)** $4.5 - 1.34$ **(d)** $0.83 \div 2$

3 Work out 35% of 120.

4 Jane has n sweets.

   (a) Ayse has 2 more sweets than Jane.
           Write an expression for the number of sweets that Ayse has.

   (b) Fiona has half the number of sweets that Jane has.
           Write an expression for the number of sweets that Fiona has.

5 Write $\frac{3}{8}$ as a decimal.

6 Calculate these.

   (a) 0.6×0.4 **(b)** $(0.3)^2$ **(c)** $\dfrac{12}{0.4}$ **(d)** $\dfrac{0.21}{0.07}$

7 Solve these equations.

   (a) $x - 8 = 4$ **(b)** $3x + 2 = 14$ **(c)** $7x + 1 = 3x + 9$

   (d) $2(x - 5) = 9$ **(e)** $3x + 5 = 5x - 6$ **(f)** $5x - 18 = 3 - 2x$

8 Round 25 638 to one significant figure.

9 Work out the value of each of these when $r = 2$, $s = {}^-3$ and $t = {}^-4$.

   (a) st **(b)** $5r + 3s$ **(c)** $\dfrac{t}{r}$ **(d)** $3r - 2t$

10 Convert these decimals to fractions in their lowest terms.

   (a) 0.4   **(b)** 0.44   **(c)** 0.85   **(d)** 0.12

11 Find a formula for the perimeter
   of this shape that begins $P = \ldots$

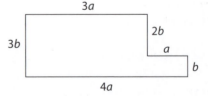

12 Work out $3 + 2 \times 8$.

13 Find all the factors of 24.

14 Calculate these.

(a) 1.3×2.9 (b) 2.3×0.15 (c) $\dfrac{0.84}{0.21}$ (d) $\dfrac{2.85}{0.19}$

15 Simplify each of these.

(a) $4x + 5x - 3x$ (b) $5a + 2b - 3a + 7b$ (c) $5p \times 3$

16 If you convert these fractions to decimals, which one will give a recurring decimal?

$\dfrac{1}{2}$ $\dfrac{1}{3}$ $\dfrac{1}{4}$ $\dfrac{3}{10}$

17 Solve these equations.

(a) $3x + 11 = 2$ (b) $5x + 9 = 3x + 1$

(c) $\dfrac{x}{3} + 1 = 5$ (d) $\dfrac{2x + 7}{5} + 7 = 4$

18 Calculate each of the lettered angles.

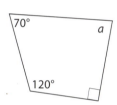 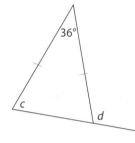

19 This is a sketch of a bedroom.

(a) Draw an accurate scale drawing of the room using a scale of 2 cm to 1 m.

(b) Use your scale drawing to find the length XY in the real room.

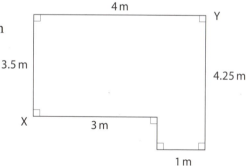

20 A banana costs x pence and an apple costs y pence.
Write down an expression for the total cost of 3 bananas and 5 apples.

21 A shape has been drawn on a grid of centimetre squares.

(a) On centimetre squared paper draw an enlargement with a scale factor of 3 of this shape.

(b) What is the area of the small shape multiplied by to give the area of the enlarged shape?

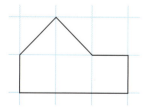

22 Seven sausage rolls and five pies cost £9.30.
The sausage rolls cost 65p each.
Find the cost of a pie.

23 (a) Write and simplify an expression for the sum in degrees of the four angles marked in the shapes below.

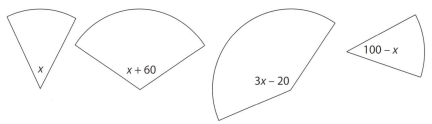

(b) These four shapes fit together to make a complete circle. Form and solve an equation to find the value of x.

24 A train travels at 95 kilometres per hour for 1.2 hours. How far does it go during this time?

25 The value of Mike's car has decreased by 17% over the past year. The car was worth £5600 one year ago. How much is the car worth now?

26 ABC is a tangent to the circle, centre O. B and D are points on the circumference. Angle ODB = 40°.

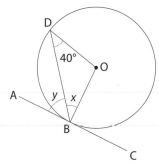

(a) Find angle x. Give a reason for your answer.

(b) Find angle y. Give a reason for your answer.

27 Paula uses this formula to work out how much to charge for a repair job.

$C = 25h + 20$

C is the charge in pounds and h is the number of hours she works.

(a) How much would Paula charge for a job that takes 3 hours?

(b) How much would she charge if the job takes $2\frac{1}{2}$ hours?

(c) Jim pays Paula £145 for a repair job. How long did the job take?

28 (a) In 1994 a pancake 15 m in diameter was flipped in Manchester. What was its circumference?

(b) In 1990 a pizza was cooked in South Africa that had a circumference of 117.5 m. What was the radius of this pizza?

29 You are given the formula $y = 2x + 9$. Find the value of x when $y = 15$.

30 Write down all the prime numbers that are less than 20.

31 Simon walked 6 miles in 1 hour and 30 minutes.
What was his average speed in miles per hour?

32 A car dealer increases his prices by 4%.
A car cost £7500 before the price increase.
What is its new price?

33 Joan is paid £117.88 for 14 hours' work.
How much will she be paid for 25 hours' work at the same rate?

34 The diagram shows two regular pentagons.

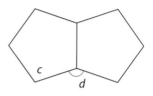

(a) Work out the value of the interior angle c.

(b) Work out the value of d.

35 Match the labelled lines with the equations.

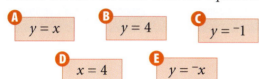

Ⓐ $y = x$ Ⓑ $y = 4$ Ⓒ $y = {}^-1$

Ⓓ $x = 4$ Ⓔ $y = {}^-x$

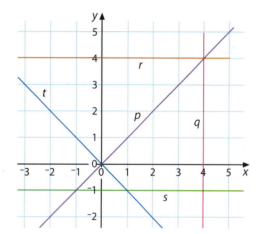

36 The cost of a printer is £250 plus VAT.
The rate of VAT is $17\frac{1}{2}\%$.
Calculate the cost of the printer including VAT.

37 Solve these equations.

(a) $9x + 7 = x - 5$ (b) $4(x + 5) = 10$

(c) $5(2x - 1) = 40$ (d) $2(3x + 1) = x - 9$

38 Each exterior angle of a regular polygon is 15°.

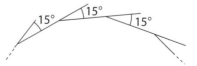

(a) How many sides will this polygon have?

(b) What is the size of each interior angle?

39 The price of a rail ticket goes up from £60 to £63.
What is the percentage increase in the price?

40 Sue and Dave walked 8.5 miles at an average speed of 2 m.p.h.
Calculate how long they took.
Give your answer in hours and minutes.

15 Transformations

You should be able to identify straight lines such as $y = x$ and $x = 3$.

Based mainly on coordinate grids, this work will help you

- reflect a shape using a mirror line such as $y = x$ or $x = 3$
- translate a shape using column notation for vectors
- rotate a shape about any point
- enlarge a shape by a positive scale factor using any point as a centre
- identify congruent shapes
- describe fully how a shape has been transformed

You need sheets F2–2, F2–3, F2–4, F2–5 and F2–6.

A Reflection

A1 Give the shape that is the image after reflecting

(a) shape C in mirror line p **(b)** shape E in line q

(c) shape F in line n **(d)** shape H in line p

(e) shape H in line m **(f)** shape A in line n

A2 Give the mirror line that is used to reflect

(a) F on to E   **(b)** H on to A

(c) A on to F   **(d)** G on to B

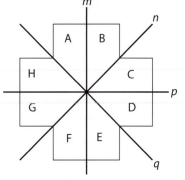

A3 Copy this diagram on to squared paper.

(a) Draw the image of A after reflection in the y-axis. Label this shape C.

(b) Draw the image of A after reflection in the x-axis. Label this shape D.

(c) Describe the reflection that takes shape C to B.

(d) Describe the reflection that takes shape B to D.

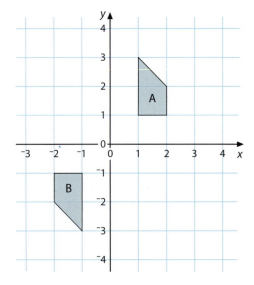

To describe a **reflection** fully you need to describe the position of the mirror line.
On a coordinate grid, you can do this by giving the equation of the line.

The lines with equations $x = 3$ and $y = 1$ are shown on this diagram.

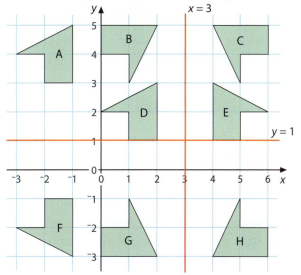

A4 Which shape is the image after reflecting

(a) shape D in the line $x = 3$

(b) shape H in the line $x = 3$

(c) shape A in the line $y = 1$

(d) shape H in the line $y = 1$

A5 Describe the reflection that takes

(a) shape B to shape C

(b) shape G to shape B

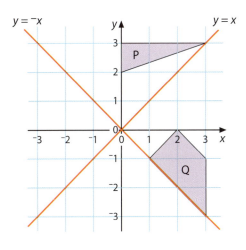

A6 Copy this diagram.

(a) Reflect point $(0, 2)$ in the line $y = x$.
What are the coordinates of the new point?

(b) Reflect shape P in the line $y = x$.
Label the new shape R.

(c) Reflect shape Q in the line $y = {}^-x$.
Label the new shape S.

A7 Copy this diagram on to squared paper.

(a) Describe the reflection that takes shape A to shape B.

(b) Reflect shape A in the line $y = 2$.
Label the new shape C.

(c) Reflect shape A in the line $y = x$.
Label the new shape D.

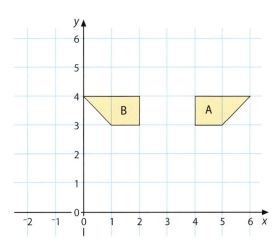

B Translation

Shape A can be taken to shape B by sliding it across and down.

We say shape A has been **translated** to shape B.

Shape B is the image of shape A after a **translation** of 3 units to the right and 1 unit down.

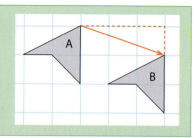

B1 Which shape is the image of

    (a) shape C after translating 6 units to the right and 1 unit up

    (b) shape A after translating 4 units to the left and 2 units up

    (c) shape B after translating 7 units to the left and 6 units down

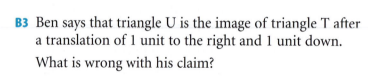

B2 Describe the translation that takes

    (a) A to B   **(b)** C to A

    (c) A to D   **(d)** B to C

B3 Ben says that triangle U is the image of triangle T after a translation of 1 unit to the right and 1 unit down.

What is wrong with his claim?

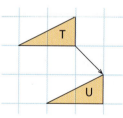

B4 Copy this diagram on to squared paper.

    (a) Draw the image of P after translating it 4 units to the right and 2 units up. Label this shape Q.

    (b) Draw the image of P after translating it 6 units to the right and 3 units down. Label this shape R.

    (c) Describe the translation that takes

        (i) Q to R   **(ii)** R to Q

        (iii) Q to P   **(iv)** R to P

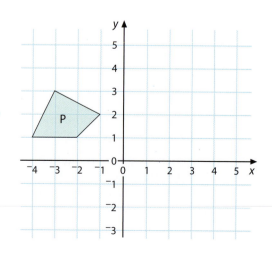

A **column vector** is a convenient way to describe a translation.

The column vector $\begin{bmatrix} 3 \\ -2 \end{bmatrix}$ means 'move 3 units right and 2 units down.'

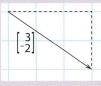

The column vector $\begin{bmatrix} -1 \\ 2 \end{bmatrix}$ means 'move 1 unit left and 2 units up.'

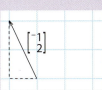

B5 Which column vector below translates shape A to shape B?

$\begin{bmatrix} 5 \\ 1 \end{bmatrix}$ $\quad$ $\begin{bmatrix} 1 \\ -5 \end{bmatrix}$ $\quad$ $\begin{bmatrix} -5 \\ -1 \end{bmatrix}$ $\quad$ $\begin{bmatrix} 1 \\ 5 \end{bmatrix}$ $\quad$ $\begin{bmatrix} 5 \\ -1 \end{bmatrix}$ $\quad$ $\begin{bmatrix} -1 \\ 5 \end{bmatrix}$

B6 Give the shape that is the image of shape A after a translation by

(a) $\begin{bmatrix} 1 \\ 3 \end{bmatrix}$ $\qquad$ (b) $\begin{bmatrix} 3 \\ 1 \end{bmatrix}$

(c) $\begin{bmatrix} -2 \\ -2 \end{bmatrix}$ $\qquad$ (d) $\begin{bmatrix} 3 \\ -1 \end{bmatrix}$

B7 Give the column vector for the translation that takes

(a) E to D $\qquad$ (b) B to D

(c) F to E $\qquad$ (d) F to D

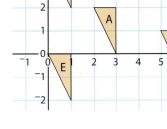

B8 Copy this diagram.

(a) Translate shape P by $\begin{bmatrix} 3 \\ 0 \end{bmatrix}$.

Label the new shape Q.

(b) Translate shape P by $\begin{bmatrix} -3 \\ -2 \end{bmatrix}$.

Label the new shape R.

(c) Write down a column vector for the translation that takes shape R to shape Q.

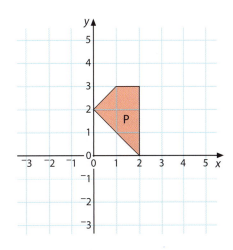

C Rotation

To describe a **rotation** fully you need to include the **angle**, the **direction** (clockwise or anticlockwise) and the **centre of rotation**.

For example, the rotation that takes shape P to shape Q is a rotation of 90° anticlockwise about C.

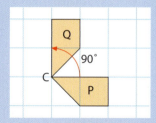

C1 (a) Which shape is the image after rotating

   (i) shape A by 90° clockwise about O

   (ii) shape B by 90° anticlockwise about O

(b) Which shape is the image after rotating

   (i) shape A by 180° clockwise about O

   (ii) shape A by 180° anticlockwise about O

   What do you notice?

(c) 'To get from D to C rotate 90° about centre O.' What is missing from this instruction?

(d) Describe **fully** the rotation that takes

   (i) D on to B   (ii) C on to A

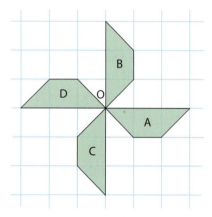

Tracing paper can help you find the image of a shape after a rotation.
Here is how you can use it to rotate a shape through 90° clockwise about the point (0, 0).

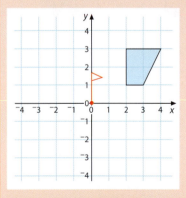

Draw a 'flag' pointing up from the centre of rotation.

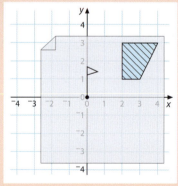

Trace the shape, centre of rotation and flag.

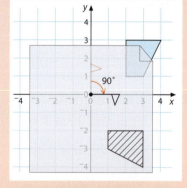

Rotate the shape about (0, 0) until the flag has turned through 90° clockwise.

C2 Use the diagrams above to find the image of the point (4, 3) after a rotation of 90° clockwise about (0, 0).

C3 Copy this diagram on to squared paper.

(a) Draw and label the images produced by the following.

    (i) A 90° anticlockwise rotation about (0, 0) takes triangle T to triangle V.

    (ii) A 90° clockwise rotation about (1, 1) takes triangle T to triangle W.

    (iii) A 180° rotation about (0, 0) takes triangle T to triangle X.

(b) Describe fully the rotation that takes triangle X to triangle V.

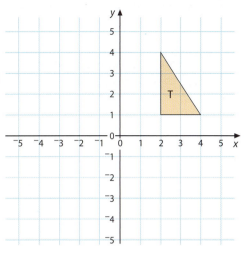

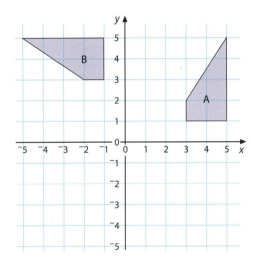

C4 Copy this diagram.

(a) Describe fully the rotation that takes shape A to shape B.

(b) On your grid, rotate shape A 90° clockwise about (0, 0). Label the new shape C.

(c) Describe the rotation that takes shape B to shape C.

(d) On your grid, rotate shape C 180° about (0, ⁻4). Label the new shape D.

C5 (a) Triangle A can be rotated on to triangle B.

    (i) Give the coordinates of the centre of rotation.

    (ii) State the angle and direction of this rotation.

(b) Triangle C can be rotated on to triangle D.

    (i) Give the coordinates of the centre of rotation.

    (ii) State the angle of this rotation.

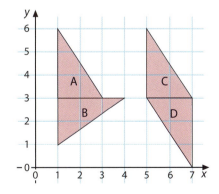

*C6 Triangle A can be rotated on to triangle D.

(a) Give the coordinates of the centre of rotation.

(b) State the angle of this rotation.

D Enlargement

We can enlarge a shape using a **centre of enlargement**.
Here we enlarge a shape using a scale factor of 2 with (2, 1) as the centre of enlargement.

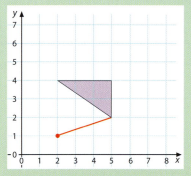 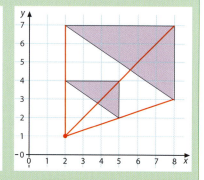

Draw a line from the centre of enlargement to one of the vertices of the shape.

Extend the line so that it becomes 2 times as long from the centre.

Do this with all the vertices. The end points of these 'rays' make the enlarged shape.

To make the length of each side of the shape 2 times as long we extend the rays so they are 2 times as long.

You don't need to measure if you use the grid to help you like this.

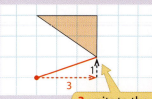

3 units to the right and **1** unit up from the centre of enlargement takes you to this point.

Multiplying these values by 2 gives **6** units to the right and **2** units up from the centre of enlargement to this point.

D1 Copy this diagram on to squared paper.

(a) Enlarge shape A by scale factor 2 from the centre of enlargement (1, 2). Label your new shape B.

(b) Check that the length of each side of triangle A has been multiplied by 2.

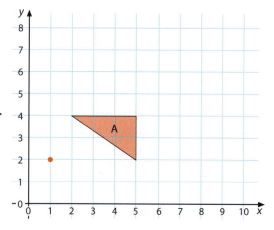

D2 This question is on sheet F2–2.

We can enlarge a shape using a **fractional** scale factor.
If the scale factor is a fraction less than 1, then the image will be a smaller shape.

D3 Copy this diagram.
An enlargement of the triangle has centre (0, 0)
and scale factor $\frac{1}{2}$.

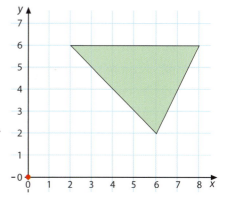

    (a) **(i)** Draw a line from the centre of enlargement
to the vertex with coordinates (6, 2).

        (ii) Plot the point on this line halfway along
from the centre of enlargement to the vertex.

    (b) Do this with all the vertices.
Join the plotted points make the new shape.

D4 This question is on sheet F2–3.

To describe an **enlargement** fully you need to include the **scale factor** and
the **centre of enlargement**.

You can find the centre of an enlargement like this.

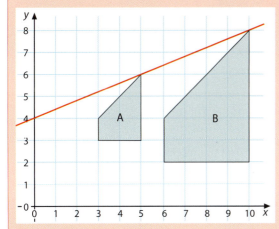

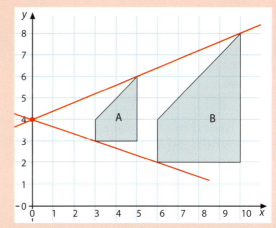

Draw a line through any pair of
corresponding vertices.

Do this with another pair of vertices.
The point where the lines cross
is the centre of enlargement.

From shape A to shape B, the lengths of the sides are multiplied by 2.
So here we have an enlargement with a scale factor of 2 and a centre (0, 4).

From shape B to shape A, the lengths of the sides are multiplied by $\frac{1}{2}$.
So here we have an enlargement with a scale factor of $\frac{1}{2}$ and a centre (0, 4).

D5 This question is on sheet F2–4.

E Reflection, translation, rotation and enlargement

Reflections, translations, rotations and enlargements are all examples of **transformations**. We say that a transformation **maps** a shape on to its image.

E1 Describe fully the single transformation that maps

(a) A on to B

(b) A on to C

(c) A on to D

(d) A on to G

(e) G on to C

(f) A on to F

(g) A on to E

(h) G on to F

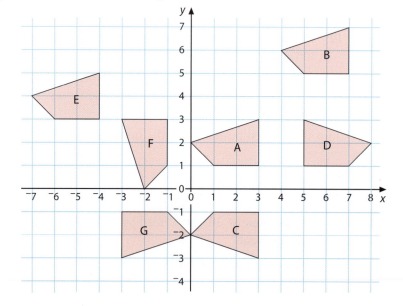

E2 Copy this diagram or use the copy on sheet F2–5.

(a) Reflect shape A in the line $y = 1$. Label the image B.

(b) Write down the vector that translates shape A on to shape C.

(c) Rotate shape A 90° anticlockwise about point (0, 1). Label the image D.

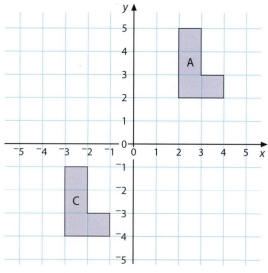

OCR

Two shapes that are identical in shape and size are said to be **congruent**.
A shape and its image after a translation, reflection or rotation are congruent to each other.

E3 Copy shapes A, B and C as shown on to a grid with both axes going from ⁻5 to 10.
Alternatively, use the copy on sheet F2–5.

(a) Describe fully the transformation that maps shape A on to shape B.

(b) Describe fully the transformation that maps shape A on to shape C.

(c) Draw the image of shape A after a translation by $\begin{bmatrix} -3 \\ 5 \end{bmatrix}$.
Label it D.

(d) Draw the image of shape B after a 180° rotation, centre $(0, 0)$.
Label it E.

(e) Draw the image of shape A after an enlargement scale factor 3, centre $(0, 0)$.
Label it F.

(f) List all the shapes on your diagram that are congruent to shape A.

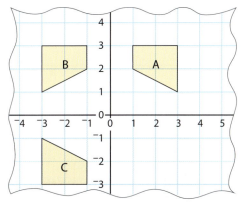

E4 Copy this diagram or use the copy on sheet F2–6.

(a) Reflect shape A in the y-axis. Label the image D.

(b) Describe the single transformation that maps triangle A to triangle B.

(c) Triangle C is an enlargement of triangle A.

(i) Write down the scale factor of the enlargement.

(ii) Find the coordinates of the centre of the enlargement.

(d) (i) Reflect shape B in the line $y = 3$. Label the image E.

(ii) Describe the single transformation that maps triangle A to triangle E.

(e) List all the shapes on your diagram that are congruent to shape A.

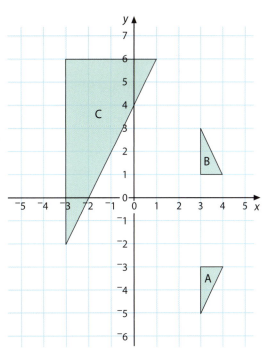

Test yourself

T1 Triangle A is drawn on the grid below.

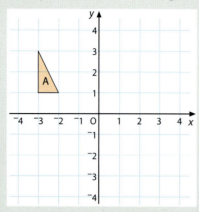

Copy the diagram or use the copy on sheet F2–6.

(a) Reflect triangle A in the *x*-axis.
Label the triangle B.

(b) Rotate triangle A 90° clockwise
about the origin O.
Label the triangle C.

AQA

T2 Copy the diagram or use the copy on
sheet F2–6.

(a) Enlarge triangle P by scale factor 2,
with (0, 0) as the centre.
Label the image Q.

(b) Translate triangle P 5 units right.
Label the image R.

(c) Describe fully the single transformation
that maps triangle Q on to triangle R.

(d) Translate triangle P by $\begin{bmatrix} 3 \\ -2 \end{bmatrix}$.

Label the image S.

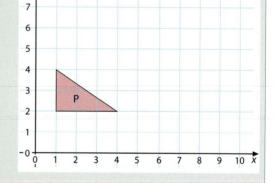

T3 Describe fully the single transformation
that maps

(a) A on to C

(b) A on to B

(c) A on to D

(d) C on to E

(e) E on to D

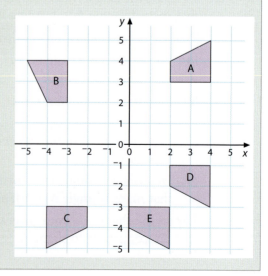

16 Indices

This work will help you

- use index notation
- substitute into expressions that involve indices
- simplify expressions that involve indices

You need sheets F2–7 and F2–8.

A Index notation

Ruth wants to give her nephew Daniel a present to thank him for helping her to lay a patio in her garden.

The patio has been paved with 25 slabs.

Ruth says she will put

> 1p on the first slab,
>
> 2p on the second slab,
>
> 4p on the third slab,
>
> 8p on the fourth slab …

… carry on doubling the amount of money until the last slab …

… and then give him the total amount of money on the patio.

Daniel says that he wants his aunt to put a £1 coin on each slab instead.

She agrees to do what he wants.

- Do you think Daniel did the right thing?

We can write a multiplication such as $2 \times 2 \times 2 \times 2 \times 2$ using **index notation**.

We write $2 \times 2 \times 2 \times 2 \times 2$ as 2^5.

In 2^5, the raised number 5 is called the **index**.
It tells you how many 2s to multiply together.

We say 2^5 as 'two to the power of five'.

A1 Write these using an index each time.

(a) $3 \times 3 \times 3 \times 3$

(b) $5 \times 5 \times 5 \times 5 \times 5 \times 5 \times 5$

(c) $2 \times 2 \times 2 \times 2 \times 2 \times 2 \times 2 \times 2$

(d) $4 \times 4 \times 4 \times 4 \times 4 \times 4 \times 4 \times 4 \times 4 \times 4 \times 4$

A2 Match each expression in the loop with the correct multiplication on the right.

3^4 4^2 2^5 5^5 5^2

$2 \times 2 \times 2 \times 2 \times 2$ 5×5 $3 \times 3 \times 3 \times 3$

$5 \times 5 \times 5 \times 5 \times 5$ 4×4

We can calculate the value of the expression 5^3 by working out the answer to $5 \times 5 \times 5$.
So $5^3 = 5 \times 5 \times 5 = 125$.

A3 Calculate the value of

(a) 2^4 (b) 4^3 (c) 3^3 (d) 7^2

A4 Decide whether each of these statements is true or false.

(a) The value of 3^2 is greater than the value of 2^3.

(b) The value of 2^6 is less than the value of 5^2.

(c) The value of 3^4 is less than the value of 6^2.

(d) The value of 10^3 is greater than the value of 2^{10}.

A5 Choose the correct word, **greater** or **less**, to complete each statement below.

(a) The value of 4^3 is .... than the value of 3^4.

(b) The value of 7^2 is .... than the value of 2^7.

(c) The value of 2^5 is .... than the value of 5^2.

A6 What is the value of 1^{20}?

The value of 5^1 is 5.

We can think of it as following this pattern: $5^4 = 5 \times 5 \times 5 \times 5$
$5^3 = 5 \times 5 \times 5$
$5^2 = 5 \times 5$
$5^1 = 5$

A7 Write down the value of   (a) 3^1 (b) 6^1 (c) 12^1

A8 Choose the correct word, **greater** or **less**, to complete the statement below.

The value of 4^1 is .... than the value of 1^4.

A9 Calculate the value of

(a) 10^1 (b) 10^2 (c) 10^3 (d) 10^4 (e) 10^5

A10 Find the missing number in the statement $10^{\blacksquare} = 1\,000\,000\,000$.

A11 Find the missing numbers in these statements.

(a) $2^{\blacksquare} = 8$ (b) $3^{\blacksquare} = 81$ (c) $9^{\blacksquare} = 81$ (d) $2^{\blacksquare} = 2$

A12 Many calculators have a special key for working with indices.

Find this key on your calculator.

(It might look like x^y or y^x or $\wedge$.)

Use this key on your calculator to work out

(a) 2^5 (b) 10^2 (c) 3^3

A13 Calculate the value of each of these.

(a) 13^6 (b) 2^{12} (c) 3^{10} (d) 5^9 (e) 9^5

A14 Which do you think will be larger, 2^{25} or 25^2?
Check with your calculator.

B Calculating powers

An expression such as 2^4 is sometimes called a **power**.

Work out the value of any power before adding or subtracting, but work out the value of any expressions inside brackets first.

Examples

$$1 + 2^4$$
$$= 1 + (2 \times 2 \times 2 \times 2)$$
$$= 1 + 16$$
$$= 17$$

$$5^2 - 3^2$$
$$= (5 \times 5) - (3 \times 3)$$
$$= 25 - 9$$
$$= 16$$

$$(5 - 2)^3$$
$$= 3^3$$
$$= 3 \times 3 \times 3$$
$$= 27$$

• Check that you can use your calculator to work these out.

B1 Work out the value of each of these.

(a) $6^2 + 1$ (b) $2^3 - 5$ (c) $5^2 - 3$

(d) $4 + 3^2$ (e) $2^2 + 9^2$ (f) $6^2 - 2^4$

(g) $(6 + 1)^2$ (h) $(5 - 3)^4$ (i) $(10 - 7)^3$

B2 Use a calculator to work out the value of each of these.

(a) $5^3 + 12$ (b) $6^3 - 16$ (c) $1 + 15^2$

(d) $200 - 12^2$ (e) $3^5 + 2^8$ (f) $4^5 - 3^1$

(g) $(25 + 13)^2$ (h) $(12 - 5)^4$ (i) $(14 - 11)^9$

(j) $5^6 - 8^3$ (k) $(6 + 5)^5$ (l) $7 + 13^5$

B3 Work out the value of each of these.

(a) $1.5^2 + 8$ (b) $3.25 + 4.5^2$ (c) $2.5^2 + 3.5^2$

(d) $1.2^3 + 3.4^2$ (e) $6.3^2 - 1.8^3$ (f) $1.9^4 - 12$

Work out the value of any power before multiplying or dividing,
but work out the value of any expressions inside brackets first.

Examples

3×2^4

$= 3 \times (2 \times 2 \times 2 \times 2)$

$= 3 \times 16$

$= 48$

$4^3 \div 2$

$= (4 \times 4 \times 4) \div 2$

$= 64 \div 2$

$= 32$

$\left(\dfrac{10}{5}\right)^3$

$= 2^3$

$= 2 \times 2 \times 2$

$= 8$

- Check that you can use your calculator to work these out.

B4 Work out the value of each of these.

(a) 5×3^2

(b) 2×5^3

(c) $3^3 \times 2$

(d) $2^3 \times 5^2$

(e) $6^2 \div 4$

(f) $\dfrac{40}{2^3}$

(g) $(2 \times 5)^2$

(h) $\left(\dfrac{8}{4}\right)^4$

(i) $\left(\dfrac{12}{4}\right)^3$

B5 Work out the value of each of these.

(a) $2^4 \times 3^3$

(b) $(5 + 2)^3 - 5$

(c) $(3 \times 5)^3$

(d) $\dfrac{8^3}{10}$

(e) $\left(\dfrac{8.4}{7}\right)^3$

(f) $(15 - 2)^2 \times 4$

We know that every whole number can be written as the product of prime factors.
One way to find this product is to start with a factor tree.

This is a factor tree for 72.

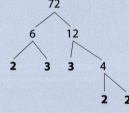

We keep going until each branch ends with a prime factor.

The numbers at the ends of the branches give us the product of prime factors.

$72 = 2 \times 2 \times 2 \times 3 \times 3$

We can use index notation to write this as

$72 = 2^3 \times 3^2$

B6 For each number below, make a factor tree and write the number as
a product of prime factors using index notation.

(a) 45   (b) 56   (c) 36   (d) 96

B7 Work out the value of $2 \times 3^3 \times 5^2$.

C Substituting into expressions containing powers

Examples

$a = 2$, $b = 3$, $c = 5$

$$\begin{aligned} a^4 + b^3 &= (a \times a \times a \times a) + (b \times b \times b) \\ &= (2 \times 2 \times 2 \times 2) + (3 \times 3 \times 3) \\ &= 16 + 27 \\ &= 43 \end{aligned}$$

$$\begin{aligned} 2c^3 - 1 &= 2 \times (c \times c \times c) - 1 \\ &= 2 \times (5 \times 5 \times 5) - 1 \\ &= 2 \times 125 - 1 \\ &= 250 - 1 \\ &= 249 \end{aligned}$$

C1 Evaluate these when $a = 3$ and $b = 4$.

 (a) $a^2 + b^2$ (b) $(a + b)^2$ (c) $5a^2$

C2 Evaluate these when $p = 2$ and $q = 5$.

 (a) $p^3 + q^2$ (b) $2q^2 - 1$ (c) $2p^3 + 5$

 (d) $\dfrac{p^4}{4}$ (e) $q^2 + pq$ (f) $q^3 - p^2$

 (g) $(p + q)^2$ (h) $2(p + q)^2$ (i) $7(q - p)^2$

C3 Evaluate these when $x = 3$.

 (a) $x^2 - 2x$ (b) $x^3 + x^2$ (c) $2x^2 + x$

C4 (a) Copy and complete: $(^-5)^2 = {}^-5 \times {}^-5 = \blacksquare$.

 (b) Find the value of $2x^2$ when $x = {}^-5$.

C5 (a) Copy and complete: $(^-2)^3 = {}^-2 \times {}^-2 \times {}^-2 = \ldots\ldots$

 (b) Find the value of $n^3 + 2$ when $n = {}^-2$.

C6 Evaluate each of these when $k = {}^-2$.

 (a) $3k^2$ (b) $k^2 + 5$ (c) $2k^3$

C7 Evaluate each of these when $x = {}^-3$.

 (a) $5x^2$ (b) $2x^2 + x$ (c) $2x^3 + 1$

C8 Evaluate each of these when $a = {}^-2$ and $b = 5$.

 (a) $a^3 + 1$ (b) $4a^2 - 5$ (c) $a^2 + b$

 (d) $\dfrac{a^3}{4}$ (e) $b^2 + a^2$ (f) $2a^5$

C9 Work out the value of $4(x + 2)^2$ when $x = {}^-5$.

C10 Complete the puzzles on sheet F2–7.

D Multiplying powers

Sometimes multiplications can be simplified.

Examples

$2^4 \times 2^3$
$= (2 \times 2 \times 2 \times 2) \times (2 \times 2 \times 2)$
$= 2 \times 2 \times 2 \times 2 \times 2 \times 2 \times 2$
$= 2^7$

$7^5 \times 7$
$= (7 \times 7 \times 7 \times 7 \times 7) \times 7$
$= 7 \times 7 \times 7 \times 7 \times 7 \times 7$
$= 7^6$

We have written $7^5 \times 7$
as **a single power of 7.**

- Find the missing number in each of these calculations.

  $2^3 \times 2^2 = (2 \times 2 \times 2) \times (2 \times 2) = 2^\blacksquare$

  $5^3 \times 5^6 = (5 \times 5 \times 5) \times (5 \times 5 \times 5 \times 5 \times 5 \times 5) = 5^\blacksquare$

  $7^5 \times 7^4 = (7 \times 7 \times 7 \times 7 \times 7) \times (7 \times 7 \times 7 \times 7) = 7^\blacksquare$

  $3^5 \times 3 = (3 \times 3 \times 3 \times 3 \times 3) \times 3 = 3^\blacksquare$

- Can you find a rule for multiplying powers?

D1 Write down the numbers missing from these calculations.

(a) $3^2 \times 3^3 = 3^\blacksquare$ (b) $4^2 \times 4^4 = 4^\blacksquare$ (c) $8 \times 8^7 = 8^\blacksquare$

(d) $6^3 \times 6^9 = 6^\blacksquare$ (e) $2^6 \times 2^5 = 2^\blacksquare$ (f) $6 \times 6^5 = 6^\blacksquare$

D2 Find three pairs of equivalent expressions.

A $2^5 \times 2^2$ **B** 2^9 **C** $2^9 \times 2$ **D** 2^7 **E** 2^{10} **F** $2^5 \times 2^4$

D3 Write the answers to these using indices.

(a) $3^4 \times 3^3$ (b) $10^5 \times 10^6$ (c) $4^8 \times 4^4$ (d) $8^4 \times 8$

(e) $2^4 \times 2^5$ (f) 7×7^9 (g) $10^2 \times 10^9$ (h) $9^9 \times 9^3$

D4 Write each of these as a single power of 5.

(a) $5^6 \times 5^2$ (b) $5^5 \times 5^5$ (c) $5^3 \times 5$ (d) 5×5^4

D5 Complete the cover-up puzzles on sheet F2–8.

D6 Copy and complete these statements.

(a) $(7^3)^2 = 7^3 \times 7^3 = 7^\blacksquare$ (b) $(2^4)^2 = 2^4 \times 2^4 = 2^\blacksquare$

*D7 Write each of these as a single power of 3.

(a) $3^2 \times 3^3 \times 3^5$ (b) $3^4 \times 3 \times 3^9$ (c) $(3^3)^2$ (d) $(3^4)^2$

*D8 Write $(11^2)^5$ as a power of 11.

E Dividing powers

- Find the answer to each of these calculations.

$$5 \times 6 \div 6 = ?$$ $$7 \times 14 \div 14 = ?$$ $$12 \times 139 \div 139 = ?$$ $$54 \times 72 \div 72 = ?$$

- What happens if you multiply by a number and then divide by the same number?

Sometimes divisions can be simplified.

Examples

$2^5 \div 2^3$

$= (2 \times 2 \times 2 \times 2 \times 2) \div (2 \times 2 \times 2)$

$= (2 \times 2) \times (2 \times 2 \times 2) \div (2 \times 2 \times 2)$

$= 2 \times 2$

$= 2^2$

$\dfrac{5^6}{5^2}$

$= 5^6 \div 5^2$

$= (5 \times 5 \times 5 \times 5 \times 5 \times 5) \div (5 \times 5)$

$= (5 \times 5 \times 5 \times 5) \times (5 \times 5) \div (5 \times 5)$

$= 5 \times 5 \times 5 \times 5$

$= 5^4$

- Can you find a rule for dividing powers?

E1 Write down the numbers missing from these calculations.

(a) $4^6 \div 4^2 = 4^{\blacksquare}$ (b) $8^5 \div 8^2 = 8^{\blacksquare}$ (c) $6^7 \div 6^4 = 6^{\blacksquare}$

(d) $2^9 \div 2^4 = 2^{\blacksquare}$ (e) $7^7 \div 7^2 = 7^{\blacksquare}$ (f) $3^5 \div 3^4 = 3^{\blacksquare}$

E2 Find three pairs of equivalent expressions.

A $\dfrac{2^6}{2^2}$ **B** $\dfrac{2^5}{2^4}$ **C** $\dfrac{2^4}{2}$ **X** 2^3 **Y** 2 **Z** 2^4

E3 Write the answers to these using indices.

(a) $\dfrac{5^6}{5^2}$ (b) $\dfrac{3^7}{3^5}$ (c) $\dfrac{10^8}{10^2}$ (d) $\dfrac{7^5}{7}$ (e) $\dfrac{2^4}{2^3}$

E4 Write each of these as a power of 2.

(a) $\dfrac{2^4 \times 2^3}{2^2}$ (b) $\dfrac{2^7 \times 2^4}{2}$ (c) $\dfrac{2^9}{2^3 \times 2^3}$ (d) $\dfrac{2^6 \times 2^2}{2^8 \div 2^5}$

E5 Simplify $\dfrac{3^{10}}{3^8}$ and hence work out its value.

E6 Find the value of $\dfrac{5^{12}}{5^9}$.

*__E7__ $2^{13} = 8192$ and $2^9 = 512$.
Work out the value of $8192 \div 512$.
Show your method clearly.

These are the rules for multiplying and dividing powers of the same number.

- To **multiply** you can **add** the indices.

$$3^4 \times 3^2 = 3^{4+2} = 3^6$$

- To **divide** you can **subtract** the indices.

$$3^5 \div 3^2 = 3^{5-2} = 3^3$$

F Simplifying expressions containing powers

F1 Find four pairs of equivalent expressions.

 A $a \times a$
 B $a + a$
 C $a + a + a$
 D $a \times a \times a$

 P $2a$
 Q $3a$
 R a^3
 S a^2

F2 Simplify each of these.

(a) $b \times b$ (b) $a \times a \times a \times a$ (c) $x \times x \times x \times x$ (d) $p \times p \times p \times p \times p$

Algebraic additions that involve indices can sometimes be simplified.

For example, $k^2 + k^2 + k^2 + k^2$ can be simplified to $4k^2$.

However $k^2 + h^2$ cannot be simplified.

F3 Simplify each of these.

(a) $p^2 + p^2$ (b) $x^3 + x^3$ (c) $a^2 + a^2 + a^2$ (d) $m^4 + m^4 + m^4 + m^4$

(e) $2a^2 + 3a^2$ (f) $4x^2 + x^2$ (g) $5g^2 - 2g^2$ (h) $2k^3 - k^3$

Algebraic multiplications and divisions can sometimes be simplified too.

Examples

$$a^5 \times a^2 = a^{5+2} = a^7$$

$$\frac{b^7}{b^3} = b^{7-3} = b^4$$

F4 Find three pairs of equivalent expressions.

 A $a^3 \times a^4$
 B $a^3 \times a$
 C $a \times a^2$
 D a^3
 E a^7
 F a^4

F5 Simplify each of these.

(a) $b^3 \times b^2$ (b) $g^4 \times g^2$ (c) $x^3 \times x^5$ (d) $p^2 \times p^2$

(e) $a^3 \times a$ (f) $h \times h^4$ (g) $k^2 \times k^7$ (h) $m \times m^{11}$

F6 Find three pairs of equivalent expressions.

 $\dfrac{a^6}{a}$ $a^7 \div a^3$ $\dfrac{a^3}{a^2}$ a^4 a^5 a

F7 Simplify each of these.

(a) $x^6 \div x^2$ (b) $\dfrac{y^5}{y^2}$ (c) $\dfrac{m^3}{m}$ (d) $\dfrac{n^9}{n^2}$ (e) $\dfrac{p^5}{p^4}$

F8 Simplify each of these.

(a) $h^3 \times h^2$ (b) $\dfrac{k^4}{k^2}$ (c) $n^4 \times n$ (d) $\dfrac{a^3}{a}$ (e) $w^3 \times w \times w^2$

Some examples of more complex multiplications are shown below.

$4a \times 3a$
$= (4 \times a) \times (3 \times a)$
$= 4 \times 3 \times a \times a$ ← Multiplications can be done in any order.
$= 12a^2$

$2p^2 \times 5p$
$= (2 \times p^2) \times (5 \times p)$
$= 2 \times 5 \times p^2 \times p$
$= 10p^3$

F9 Simplify each of these.

(a) $2p \times 5p$ (b) $6a \times 4a$ (c) $3x \times 2x^2$ (d) $2n^3 \times 4n^2$

F10 Find an expression for the area of each rectangle.

(a)    (b) 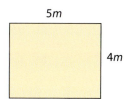   (c)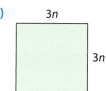

F11 Show that a formula for the area of this triangle is
$A = 12b^2$

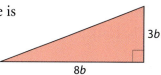

F12 Find an expression for the area of each triangle.

(a) 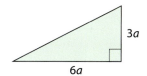   (b)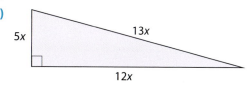

Test yourself

T1 Work out the value of each of these.

   (a) 2^5 **(b)** 10^4 **(c)** $5^2 \times 2^3$ **(d)** $5^3 + 2^2$

T2 Work out the value of $2n^2 - 5$ when

   (a) $n = 4$ **(b)** $n = {}^-3$ **(c)** $n = 1$

T3 Write each of these as a single power of 3.

   (a) $3^4 \times 3^2$ **(b)** $3^9 \div 3^4$ **(c)** $\dfrac{3^6 \times 3^5}{3^7}$

T4 Work out the value of each of these when $a = 2$ and $b = {}^-3$.

   (a) $a^2 + b^2$ **(b)** $a^3 - a$ **(c)** $b^2 - a^2$ **(d)** $b^2 + ab$

T5 The diagram shows a right-angled triangle.
Write, as simply as possible, expressions for

   (a) the perimeter of this triangle

   (b) the area of this triangle

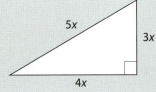

Not to scale

OCR

T6 Simplify these.

   (a) $m \times m \times m \times m$ **(b)** $g^2 \times g^7$ **(c)** $h^8 \div h^3$

T7 Simplify $\dfrac{k^6}{k^2}$.

T8 Simplify   **(a)** $7p^2 - 5p^2$ **(b)** $n^2 + n^2 + n^2$

T9 Simplify   **(a)** $5n \times 3n$ **(b)** $4p^2 \times 3p$

T10 This diagram shows a square inside another square.
The smaller square is made by joining
the mid-points of the larger square.

Show that the black area is given by the formula

   $A = 8n^2$

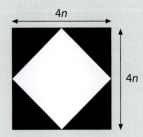

T11 Work out the value of $\dfrac{3^{10}}{3^7}$.

T12 Work out the value of each of these.

   (a) $(11 - 5)^3 \times 3$ **(b)** $8 + 1.3^2$ **(c)** $(8 + 1.3)^2$

17 Ratio

You will revise using ratios written in the form $a:b$.

This work will help you

- divide a quantity in a given ratio
- use ratios written in the form $a:b:c$

A Review: ratio

A1 Rose pink paint is made by mixing red and white in the ratio $1:3$.
Which of these mixtures would make rose pink paint?

A For every 100 ml of red, use 300 ml of white.

B Use 6 parts white to 3 parts red.

C Mix 0.5 litres of red with 1.5 litres of white.

D Mix white and red in the ratio $6:2$.

E Use 3 litres of white and 1 litre of red.

F Mix 1 tin of white with 3 tins of red.

A2 On a school trip, the ratio of adults to children is $1:8$.

(a) If 5 adults are going on the trip, how many children can go?

(b) If 200 children want to go on the trip, how many adults will be needed?

A3 A recipe requires 250 g flour and 100 g sugar.

(a) Write the ratio of flour to sugar in its simplest form.

(b) Write the ratio of sugar to flour in its simplest form.

A4 To make dark grey paint, Tom mixes black and white paint in the ratio $4:1$.

(a) How much white paint would he need to go with 1 litre of black?

(b) How much black paint would he need to go with 500 ml of white?

A5 A tea blender mixes Indian and African teas in the ratio $3:5$.

(a) How much African tea does she mix with 15 kg Indian tea?

(b) How much Indian tea does she mix with 20 kg African tea?

(c) How much tea will she make altogether if she uses 10 kg of African tea?

A6 When choosing tiles for a bathroom floor, Pat wants
2 patterned tiles for every 15 plain tiles.

(a) If she buys 150 plain tiles, how many patterned tiles will she need?

(b) If she buys 120 plain tiles, how many patterned tiles will she need?

Fair shares

Martin and David have been earning money by washing windows.

They have earned £40 altogether.

They are discussing, with Mum's and Dad's help, how to share the money.

Martin is 15. David is 9.

- What ratios are being suggested?

- How much money would they get with each suggestion?

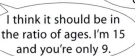

Well, I did 14 windows. You only did 6.

I think it should be in the ratio of ages. I'm 15 and you're only 9.

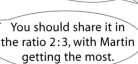

I don't see why you can't just share it equally.

You should share it in the ratio 2:3, with Martin getting the most.

To share something in a given ratio you first have to work out how many 'shares' there are.

Examples

Share £20 in the ratio 2:3.

> Altogether there are 2 + 3 = 5 shares.
> So 1 share is worth £20 ÷ 5 = £4.
>
> The first person gets 2 × £4 = £8.
> The second person gets 3 × £4 = £12.
>
> Check:
> £8 + £12 = £20 so all the money is shared.

Share £20 in the ratio 3:1.

> Altogether there are 3 + 1 = 4 shares.
> So 1 share is worth £20 ÷ 4 = £5.
>
> The first person gets 3 × £5 = £15.
> The second person gets 1 × £5 = £5.
>
> Check:
> £15 + £5 = £20 so all the money is shared.

B1 (a) Share £50 in the ratio 3:2.   (b) Divide £12 in the ratio 1:3.

(c) Divide 48 kg in the ratio 5:3.   (d) Share 200 kg in the ratio 4:1.

(e) Share £1.50 in the ratio 2:1.   (f) Divide £35 in the ratio 2:5.

B2 A farmer has 24 sheep.
He decides to give them to his sons in the ratio of their ages.
Geraint is 5. Idris is 3.
How many sheep do they each get?

B3 A fruit crumble contains blackberries and apples in the ratio 2:5.
The weight of fruit altogether must weigh 350 g.

(a) What weight of blackberries should be used?

(b) What weight of apples should be used?

B4 The ratio of boys to girls in a sports club is 3:2.
If there are 60 members, how many are boys?

B5 Maize porridge is a popular food in Africa.
It is made from maize flour and water in the ratio $1:4$.
How much maize flour and water is needed to make 750 g of porridge?

B6 A judge rules that Yukon Developments and Skelly Council are
jointly responsible for a pollution disaster.
She orders that the £14 million compensation be paid by Yukon and
Skelly in the ratio $4:3$.
How much do they each pay?

B7 A simple mixture of salt and sugar is added to water for use by
aid workers in countries where there is a drought.
It is made from 1 part of salt and 8 parts of sugar.
How much salt and sugar are needed to make 450 kg of the mixture?

C Ratios in the form $a:b:c$

A recipe for blackberry and apple jam needs 8 kg blackberries, 2 kg apples and 6 kg sugar.

The ratio **blackberries : apples : sugar** is $8:2:6$.

This can be simplified (by dividing by 2) to **4:1:3**.

C1 A recipe for marmalade needs 15 kg oranges, 5 kg grapefruit and 10 kg sugar.
Write the ratio oranges : grapefruit : sugar in its simplest form.

C2 Write each of these ratios in its simplest form.

    (a) $3:12:18$ **(b)** $10:15:25$ **(c)** $40:60:100$ **(d)** $48:36:24$

C3 Joan mixes 2 litres of white paint with 500 ml of blue and 200 ml of yellow.

    (a) How much white and blue should she mix with 100 ml of yellow paint?

    (b) Which of the following shows the correct ratio of white : blue : yellow?

         $1:250:100$ $20:5:2$ $2:5:2$

C4 Steve is making cakes.
He mixes 1.5 kg sultanas with 250 g cherries and 100 g candied peel.
Write the ratio sultanas : cherries : candied peel in its simplest form.

C5 This is an ancient Chinese recipe for gunpowder.

Use this recipe to find what weights would be needed

    (a) of saltpetre and charcoal with 50 g of sulphur

    (b) of sulphur and charcoal with 100 g of saltpetre

> 5 parts saltpetre
> 1 part sulphur
> 2 parts charcoal

C6 John, Stella and Naomi share £60 in the ratio 3:2:1.

(a) Copy and complete this working to show how much John should get.

> Altogether there are 3 + 2 + 1 = ⬤ shares.
> So 1 share is worth £60 ÷ ⬤ = £⬤.
> John gets 3 × £⬤ = £⬤.

(b) How much should Stella and Naomi each get?

C7 To make cheese straws you need flour, margarine and cheese in the ratio 4:3:3.

(a) Write out a recipe to make 500 g of cheese straw mix.

(b) How much margarine and cheese would you need if you used 100 g of flour?

C8 A box contains milk, plain and white chocolates in the ratio 5:3:2.
If there are 40 chocolates altogether, how many of each type are there?

D Converting between ratios, fractions and percentages

Example

A packet contains round balloons and long balloons in the ratio 3:1.
What fraction of all the balloons are round?

> Drawing a picture helps.
>
> There are 3 round balloons for every 1 long balloon.
>
> Out of every 4 balloons, 3 are round. So $\frac{3}{4}$ of all the balloons are round.

D1 A bag of chocolates contains milk and dark chocolates in the ratio 4 milk to 1 dark.
What fraction of all the chocolates are dark chocolates?

D2 The ratio of male fish to female fish in a tank is 1:7.
What fraction of the fish are (a) male (b) female

D3 At a party, the ratio of children to adults is 5:1.
What fraction of the people are (a) children (b) adults

D4 A box of chocolates contains soft centres and hard centres in the ratio 1:3.

(a) What fraction of the chocolates are hard centres?

(b) What percentage of the chocolates are hard centres?

D5 The ratio of girls to boys in a choir is 3:2.

(a) What fraction of the choir are girls?

(b) What percentage are girls?

D6 In a box of 40 biscuits, $\frac{1}{4}$ are chocolate and the rest are plain.

    (a) How many of each type of biscuit are there?

    (b) What is the ratio of chocolate to plain biscuits?

D7 In a primary school class, $\frac{1}{2}$ the children are boys.
Is the ratio of boys to girls 1:2, 2:1, 1:1, or none of these?

D8 In a pet shop, $\frac{1}{3}$ of the kittens are male.
What is the ratio of male to female kittens?

    M   F   F

D9 In the pet shop, $\frac{3}{5}$ of the puppies are male.

    (a) What is the ratio of male to female puppies?

    (b) What is the ratio of female to male puppies?

    M   M   M   F   F

Test yourself

T1 Bob and Mary win £250 on the Premium Bonds.
They share the money in the ratio 1:4.

    (a) How much money does each person receive?

    (b) What percentage of the £250 does Mary receive?   AQA

T2 Divide £30 in the ratio 3:2.

T3 **(a)** In Belgium the ratio of people who can speak at least two languages
to those who can speak only one language is 1:8.
Belgium has a population of 10.8 million.
How many of them can speak at least two languages?

    (b) In a Swiss school 360 students speak German and 90 students speak
French as their first language.
Write these numbers as a ratio in its simplest terms.   OCR

T4 Chocolate butter icing uses caster sugar, butter and
cocoa powder in the ratio 5:3:1.

    (a) How much of each ingredient would you need to make 450 g of icing?

    (b) If you used 100 g of caster sugar, how much butter would you need?

T5 There are twice as many boys as girls in a swimming club.

    (a) What is the ratio of boys to girls in the club?

    (b) What fraction of the club are girls?

18 Area of a circle and related shapes

This work will help you

- find the area of a circle from its radius or diameter
- find the area of a shape involving part of a circle
- distinguish between area and circumference calculations
- express an area or circumference as an exact value with π in it

You need a pair of compasses.

A Area of a circle

This diagram is drawn on centimetre squared paper.
The circle has a radius of 3 cm.
The yellow square's sides are same length as this radius.

- What is the area of the yellow square in cm²?

- Why must the area of the circle be less than four times the area of the yellow square?

To estimate the area of the circle, the grid squares inside the circle have been marked as follows.

Whole square or nearly a whole square: **marked 1**

Roughly half a square: **marked $\frac{1}{2}$**

Small part of a square: **left blank**

- What is the estimated area of the circle?

On centimetre squared paper, draw circles with radii 4 cm, 5 cm and 8 cm.
For each circle, draw a square with its sides the same length as the radius, as above.
Mark the grid squares inside each circle with 1s and $\frac{1}{2}$s as above.

Copy and complete this table.

Radius	Area of square	Estimated area of circle
3 cm		
4 cm		
5 cm		

- What rough rule connects the area of a circle with the area of square that has sides the same length as the radius?

A1 Use the rough rule to find the approximate areas of these circles.

(a)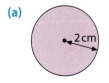

(b)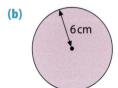

(c)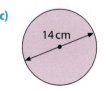

(d)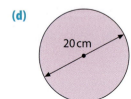

The previous activity shows that the area of a circle is roughly **three** times the area of a square that has sides the length of the radius.

You may have noticed that the area of a circle tends to be a bit more than three times the area of the square. In fact it is π times the area, where π is the number $3.14159...$, which you met in chapter 7.

So this is the rule for getting the area of a circle:

radius → square it → × π → area

You can write this as the formula $A = \pi r^2$, where A is the area of the circle and r is the radius.

If you only have a basic calculator, you can do πr^2 by keying in $3.142 \times r \times r$.

If your calculator has its own value for π and a squaring key, use them.

To work out 7^2, for example, press $\boxed{7}$ $\boxed{x^2}$.

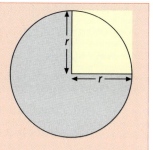

A2 Find the areas of these circles giving answers to 1 d.p.

(a)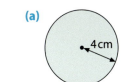
4 cm

(b)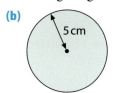
5 cm

(c)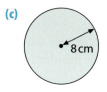
8 cm

(d)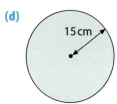
15 cm

A3 For each of these circles, find   **(i)** the radius   **(ii)** the area to 1 d.p.

(a)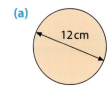
12 cm

(b)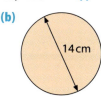
14 cm

(c)
20 cm

(d)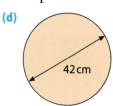
42 cm

After you have used your calculator to find the area of a circle, always do a rough check mentally.

For example, if the radius is 4 cm …

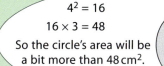

$4^2 = 16$
$16 \times 3 = 48$
So the circle's area will be a bit more than $48\,cm^2$.

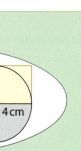
4 cm
4 cm

A4 Find the areas of circles with these radii.
Do a rough mental check for each answer.

(a) 9 cm   (b) 20 cm   (c) 2.5 cm   (d) 6.4 cm

A5 For each circle with diameter given below,

    (i) find the radius   **(ii)** find the area and check the answer for the area

    (a) 60 cm   **(b)** 22 cm   **(c)** 15 cm   **(d)** 3.6 cm

A6 Here are pictures of some euro coins. For each coin,

    (i) measure its diameter to the nearest 0.1 cm

    (ii) work out its radius

    (iii) calculate the area of one side of the coin

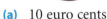

    (a) 10 euro cents   **(b)** 1 euro   **(c)** 2 euros

A7 A landing pad for a helicopter is a white circle with radius 4.5 m.
What is its area?

A8 A certain cricket pitch is circular with diameter 110 metres.
Find its area to the nearest hundred square metres.

A9 Paolo's pizzas come in two sizes – large with diameter 30 cm and
small with diameter 20 cm.
Which has the greater surface area, one large pizza or two small ones?

B Area of a shape that involves part of a circle

B1 This is a circle divided into two semicircles (half circles).

    (a) What value does your calculator show for the area of
the whole circle? Keep this value on your calculator.

    (b) What is the area of one semicircle to 1 d.p.?

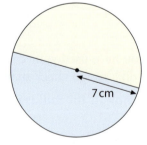

        7 cm

B2 This circle is divided into six equal sectors.

    (a) What value does your calculator show for the area of
the whole circle? Keep this value on your calculator.

    (b) What is the area of one sector to 1 d.p.?

    A **sector** is a 'slice' of a circle.

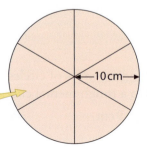

        10 cm

B3 This quarter circle is on a grid of centimetre squares.

  (a) Find the area of the quarter circle, to 1 d.p.

  (b) Check your answer using square counting.

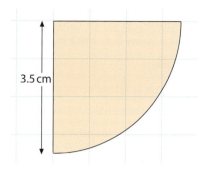

3.5 cm

In problems like these, keep each calculator result on your calculator and use it for the next stage. Don't round until you get your final answer.

Example

This shape consists of a semicircle joined to a square.
Find the total area of the shape, rounding your answer to 1 d.p.

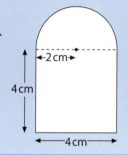

2 cm

4 cm

4 cm

Area of the whole circle would be $\pi r^2 = \pi \times 2^2 = 12.566...$ cm^2

So area of semicircle = $12.566... \div 2 = 6.283...$ cm^2
Area of square = $4 \times 4 = 16$ cm^2

So total area = $6.283... + 16 = 22.3$ cm^2 (to 1 d.p.)

B4 Draw the shape in the example above on centimetre squared paper, then estimate the area from the number of squares as a check of the answer.

B5 This shape consists of a quarter of a circle joined to a square.
Find the total area of the shape, to 1 d.p., showing full working.
Check your answer by drawing the shape on
centimetre squared paper and estimating the area
from the number of squares.

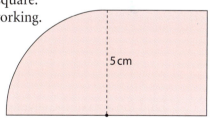

5 cm

B6 This shape consists of three-quarters of a circle joined
to a square.
Find the total area of the shape, to the nearest cm^2.
Check that your answer is sensible.

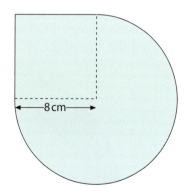

8 cm

Sometimes you can find the area of a shape by **subtracting** one area from another.
Always show full working and check that your answer makes sense.

Example

The shaded shape is a rectangle with a circular hole cut out of it.
Find the area of the shaded shape.

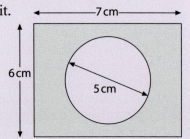

Area of shaded shape is area of rectangle minus area of circle.
Area of rectangle = $6 \times 7 = 42$ cm^2
Diameter = 5 cm so $r = 2.5$ cm
Area of circle = $\pi r^2 = \pi \times 2.5^2 = 19.634\ldots$ cm^2
So area of shaded shape = $42 - 19.634\ldots = 22.4$ cm^2 (to 1 d.p.)

B7 The blue shape consists of a circle with a square hole cut out of it.
Find the area of the blue shape to the nearest cm^2.
Show full working.

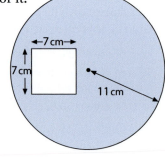

B8 The orange shape consists of a rectangle with
two circles cut out of it.
Find the area of the orange shape to 1 d.p.

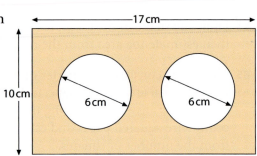

B9 Find the area of the silver part of a CD or DVD.

B10 This blue segment of a circle consists of a quarter circle
with the triangle PQR subtracted from it.
Find the area of the blue segment, to 1 d.p.

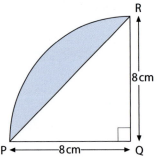

A **segment** is a piece cut off
from a circle by a straight line.

A straight line joining two points
on a circle is called a **chord**.

In circle work be sure you choose the correct formula:

$$\text{circumference} = 2\pi r \quad (r \text{ is the radius.})$$
$$\text{circumference} = \pi d \quad (d \text{ is the diameter.})$$
$$\text{area} = \pi r^2$$

To avoid making mistakes …

• Think of the experiment with the can and the strip of paper (page 52). The circumference was 3-and-a-bit times the diameter.

• Think of how you related the area of a circle to the area of a square with sides of length r (page 146): that is why the area formula has r^2 (not r).

• Be careful about whether you substitute the diameter or the radius into the formula you are using.

• Check every answer. Use the estimation methods on pages 57 and 147 or look at a sketch with lengths marked or a drawing on centimetre squared paper to decide whether your answer makes sense.

In the following questions, give your answers to an appropriate degree of accuracy. For example, if a radius is given to one decimal place then give the circumference to one decimal place.

C1 For each of these circles, find **(i)** the circumference **(ii)** the area

(a)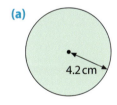
4.2 cm

(b)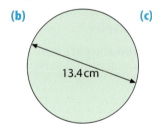
13.4 cm

(c)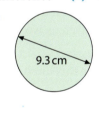
9.3 cm

(d)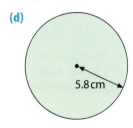
5.8 cm

C2 For each coin, measure and calculate to find

   (i) the circumference

   (ii) the area you can see

(a) Hong Kong **(b)** Tunisia **(c)** Canada **(d)** Indonesia **(e)** Hungary

C3 A circular pond has a circumference of 16 metres.

   (a) Calculate the radius of the pond to 2 d.p.

   (b) Calculate the area of the pond to 1 d.p.

C4 A lawn is made up of a rectangle with a semicircle at each end. Calculate

    (a) the lawn's area   **(b)** the lawn's perimeter

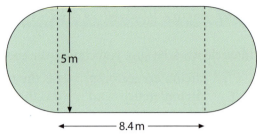

C5 A rectangular piece of metal is curved to make a tube.

    (a) What is the diameter of the tube?

    (b) What is the radius of the tube?

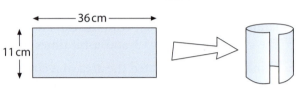

C6 A farmer has some fencing 80 metres long. She wants to form it into a circular sheep pen. What will be the area of the sheep pen?

D Exact values involving π

Suppose we have a circle with radius 7 units (the 'units' could be centimetres, metres and so on.)

The circle's circumference will be $2 \times \pi \times 7$ units, which works out as 43.982... units.

We cannot write this value out exactly because it is a multiple of π, and the decimal for π goes on forever, as we saw in chapter 7.

Instead we can take the expression $2 \times \pi \times 7$ and simplify it to 14π. We call 14π an **exact** value for this circumference, because we have not used a rounded value of π.

D1 Show that the exact value for the area of a circle with radius 7 units is 49π.

D2 Match each circumference or area to an exact expression.

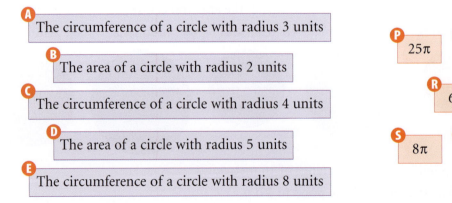

A   The circumference of a circle with radius 3 units

B   The area of a circle with radius 2 units

C   The circumference of a circle with radius 4 units

D   The area of a circle with radius 5 units

E   The circumference of a circle with radius 8 units

P   25π   Q   4π

R   6π

S   8π   T   16π

D3 Give each of these as an exact value.

(a) The circumference of a circle with radius 15 units

(b) The area of a circle with radius 6 units

(c) The circumference of a circle with **diameter** 10 units

(d) The area of a circle with diameter 18 units

Test yourself

T1 Find the area of each of these circles.

(a) 2.8 cm

(b) 4.5 cm

T2 This circle has been divided into 5 sectors the same size. Find the area of one sector.

13 cm

T3 The diagram shows the plan of a room.
The plan consists of a rectangle and a semicircle.
Calculate the total area of the floor.

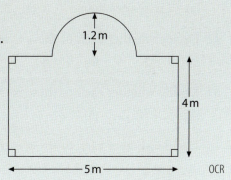

1.2 m

4 m

5 m

OCR

T4 Calculate the area coloured blue.

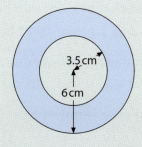

3.5 cm

6 cm

T5 Show that the exact value for the circumference of a circle with radius 5 units is 10π.

19 Inequalities

This work will help you

- understand the notation for inequalities
- solve a simple inequality, showing the solution on a number line

A Basic notation

The symbol $<$ means **is less than**.

$2 < 3$ means '2 is less than 3' so the statement is true.

$3.5 < 1$ means '3.5 is less than 1' so the statement is false.

The symbol $>$ means **is greater than**.

$4 > 3$ means '4 is greater than 3' so the statement is true.

$5 > 10$ means '5 is greater than 10' so the statement is false.

A1 Rewrite each statement, using either $<$ or $>$.

    (a) 6 is greater than 5   **(b)** 3.5 is less than 4   **(c)** ⁻2 is less than 1

A2 Decide whether each of these is true or false.

    (a) $9 > 3$ **(b)** $4 < 8$ **(c)** $4.5 > 5$ **(d)** $1.2 < 3$ **(e)** $0.9 < 1$

A3 Decide whether each of these is true or false.

    (a) $3 > {}^{-}4$ **(b)** ${}^{-}2 > 1$ **(c)** ${}^{-}10 < 0$ **(d)** ${}^{-}2 < {}^{-}7$ **(e)** ${}^{-}5 > {}^{-}1$

A4 Decide whether each of these is true or false.

    (a) $\frac{1}{2} < \frac{1}{4}$ **(b)** $\frac{1}{3} > \frac{1}{2}$ **(c)** $\frac{1}{4} > \frac{1}{8}$ **(d)** $\frac{2}{3} > \frac{1}{2}$ **(e)** $\frac{3}{8} < \frac{3}{4}$

A5 Choose the correct symbol, $<$ or $>$, for each box below.

    (a) $0.5 \,\blacksquare\, 0.3$ **(b)** $1.8 \,\blacksquare\, 2.1$ **(c)** $0.25 \,\blacksquare\, 0.4$ **(d)** $2.7 \,\blacksquare\, 2.34$

A6 Decide whether each of these is true or false.

    (a) $0.3 > \frac{1}{2}$ **(b)** $0.2 < \frac{1}{2}$ **(c)** $0.5 < \frac{1}{4}$ **(d)** $0.4 < \frac{3}{4}$ **(e)** $\frac{1}{2} > 0.5$

A7 Decide whether each of these is true or false.

    (a) $2^3 > 6$ **(b)** $4^2 < 10$ **(c)** $3^2 < 2^3$ **(d)** $2^5 > 5^2$ **(e)** $9^2 > 3^4$

A8 Choose the correct symbol, $<$ or $>$, for each box below.

    (a) $\sqrt{7} \,\blacksquare\, 2$ **(b)** $\sqrt{26} \,\blacksquare\, 5$ **(c)** $\sqrt{8} \,\blacksquare\, 3$ **(d)** $\sqrt{12} \,\blacksquare\, 4$

B Extending the notation and using a number line

The symbol ≤ means **is less than or equal to**.

The symbol ≥ means **is greater than or equal to**.

$x \geq 3$ represents the set of numbers that are greater than or equal to 3.

• Which of the numbers in the bubble are in this set?

The whole set of numbers can be shown on a diagram like this.

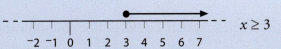

The circle is filled in to show that the number 3 is included.

$x < 2$ represents the set of numbers that are less than 2.

• Which of the numbers in the bubble are in this set?

The whole set of numbers can be shown on a diagram like this.

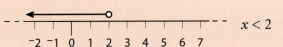

The circle is empty to show that the number 2 is not included.

B1 (a) Which of the numbers in the bubble are in the set $x \leq 1$?

(b) Which are values of x for the set $x > 5$?

Statements such as $4 > 2$ and $x \leq 5$ are called **inequalities**.

B2 (a) Match each diagram A to C with its inequality W, X, Y or Z.

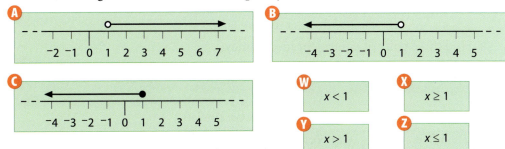

(b) Draw a diagram for the unmatched inequality.

B3 Write an inequality for each of these diagrams.

(a)

(b)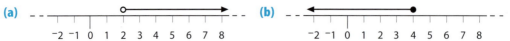

(c)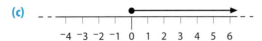

(d)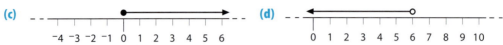

(e)

(f)

B4 For each of these, sketch a number line and show the inequality on it.

(a) $x < 5$ (b) $x \geq 4$ (c) $x \leq 2$ (d) $x > 0$

(e) $x > 1\frac{1}{2}$ (f) $x \leq {}^{-}1$ (g) $x > {}^{-}3$ (h) $x \geq {}^{-}4$

Whole numbers such as $^{-}5$, $^{-}3$, 0, 1 and 12 are called **integers**.

Fractions and decimals such as $\frac{1}{2}$, 1.5 and $^{-}0.75$ are not integers.

B5 Write down five different integers in the set of numbers given by $x > 3$.

B6 Write down five different integers in the set of numbers given by $x \leq 4$.

We say that the values of x that make an inequality true **satisfy** the inequality.

B7 Write down five different integers that satisfy each of these inequalities.

(a) $x < 4$ (b) $x \leq 2$ (c) $x \geq {}^{-}2$ (d) $x > {}^{-}5$

'10 is greater than 6'
means the same as
'6 is less than 10'
so $\mathbf{10 > 6}$ is equivalent to $\mathbf{6 < 10}$.

'x is less than 3'
means the same as
'3 is greater than x'
so $\boldsymbol{x < 3}$ is equivalent to $\boldsymbol{3 > x}$.

B8 Find three pairs of equivalent inequalities.

| $x < 4$ | $4 < x$ | $x \leq 4$ | $x > 4$ | $4 \geq x$ | $4 > x$ |

B9 Write each of these inequalities with x on the left.

(a) $5 < x$ (b) $6 > x$ (c) $0 < x$ (d) $^{-}2 < x$

C Combined inequalities

If x is greater than or equal to 1 ... $\quad x \geq 1$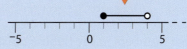

... **and** x is less than 4 ... $\quad x < 4$

... then x lies between 1 and 4 (including 1 but not 4).

We can write this as $1 \leq x$ and $x < 4$ or as the combined inequality $\mathbf{1 \leq x < 4}$.

C1 Which of these diagrams shows the inequality $0 < x \leq 5$?

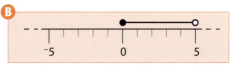
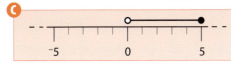
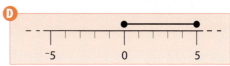

C2 For each of these, sketch a number line to represent the inequality.

(a) $2 \leq x \leq 4$ (b) $1 \leq x < 10$ (c) $0 < x < 6$ (d) $^-3 < x \leq 1$

C3 (a) Which numbers in the loop are in the set $0 < x \leq 5$?

(b) Which are in the set given by $^-3 \leq x \leq 2$?

(c) Which satisfy the inequality $^-2 < x < 3$?

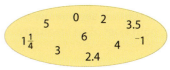

C4 Write a combined inequality for each of these diagrams.

(a)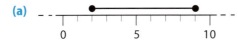
(b)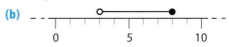
(c)
(d)

C5 List five different numbers that satisfy $1 \leq x < 4$.

C6 $^-2 \leq n \leq 5$

n is an **integer**.

Write down all eight possible values of n.

C7 Write down all the integer values of x that satisfy each inequality.

(a) $3 < x \leq 7$ (b) $2 < x < 5$ (c) $^-2 \leq x < 3$ (d) $^-4 < x \leq 1$

D Solving simple inequalities

- Which numbers in the bubble satisfy $2x \geq 6$?

  1   5 $2\frac{1}{2}$ 3.5   4   3 $^-4$ 5.8

- Which of these describes **all** the numbers that satisfy $2x \geq 6$?

$x > 3$	$x < 3$	$x \leq 3$	$x \geq 3$	$x \geq 6$

- Which numbers in the bubble satisfy $x + 2 < 6$?

  1   5   4   4.5 $3\frac{1}{2}$ 3 $^-1$ 3.7

- Which of these describes **all** the numbers that satisfy $x + 2 < 6$?

$x \leq 3$	$x < 4$	$x < 8$	$x \leq 4$	$x < 3$	$x \leq 8$

To solve an inequality is to find, in its simplest form, the set of all numbers that satisfy the inequality. This set is sometimes called the **solution**.

Examples

Solve $x - 8 \geq 2$.

$$x - 8 \geq 2 \quad [+ 8]$$
$$x \geq 10$$

We can add any number to, or subtract any number from, both sides of an inequality.

Solve $3x < 12$.

$$3x < 12 \quad [\div 3]$$
$$x < 4$$

We can divide both sides of an inequality by any positive number.

Solve $2x + 17 > 25$.

$$2x + 17 > 25 \quad [- 17]$$
$$2x > 8 \quad [\div 2]$$
$$x > 4$$

D1 (a) Solve the inequality $x + 4 > 6$.

(b) Which of these represents the solution on a number line?

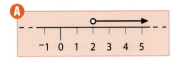
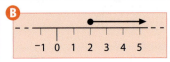
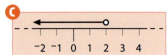

D2 (a) Solve the inequality $4x \leq 20$.

(b) Show the solution on a number line.

D3 Solve each of these inequalities.

(a) $x + 5 \leq 11$ (b) $x + 3 < 10$ (c) $x - 5 \geq 11$ (d) $x - 1 > 6$

(e) $2x \leq 12$ (f) $3x > 24$ (g) $4x < 20$ (h) $2x \geq 7$

D4 (a) Solve the inequality $2x + 3 > 11$.

(b) Show the solution on a number line.

D5 Solve each of these inequalities.

(a) $4x + 1 \geq 17$ (b) $2x - 1 \leq 13$ (c) $3x + 5 < 11$ (d) $3x - 2 \leq 10$

(e) $2x + 1 > 10$ (f) $4x - 3 \leq 7$ (g) $1 + 2x > 11$ (h) $2x - 6 \geq 5$

D6 Solve each of these inequalities.

(a) $x + 5 < 3$ (b) $x + 7 \geq 3$ (c) $3x \leq {}^-3$ (d) $2x > {}^-8$

D7 Solve $3x + 8 > 2$ and show the solution on a number line.

D8 Solve each of these inequalities.

(a) $3x + 7 > 4$ (b) $4x - 3 < 8$ (c) $4x + 9 \geq 1$ (d) $2x + 9 \leq 2$

D9 Solve each of these inequalities.

(a) $5n + 6 < 1$ (b) $4k - 1 \geq 8$ (c) $3m + 10 \leq 1$ (d) $2y + 1 > {}^-8$

Test yourself

T1 Write down an inequality for each of these diagrams.

(a) 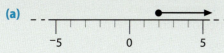   (b)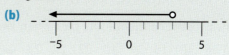

T2 Write an inequality for the range of values represented on this number line.

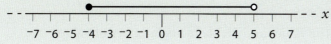

OCR

T3 ${}^-1 \leq z < 5$
z is an integer.
Write down all the possible values of z.

T4 Write down the integer values of n that satisfy the inequality ${}^-3 < n \leq 4$.

T5 (a) Solve $2x - 1 \geq 5$.

(b) Represent your solution to part (a) on a copy of this number line.

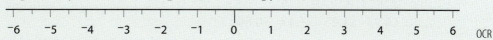

OCR

T6 Solve each inequality.

(a) $x + 2 > 7$ (b) $x - 3 < 10$ (c) $5x \geq 15$ (d) $2x \leq 7$

T7 Solve each inequality and show each solution on a number line.

(a) $4x + 1 \leq 9$ (b) $7x - 3 < 18$ (c) $3x + 2 \geq 14$ (d) $2x - 4 > 5$

T8 Solve each inequality.

(a) $n + 7 < 1$ (b) $3k + 10 \geq 4$ (c) $4m + 1 \leq 8$ (d) $2y + 9 > 2$

20 Interpreting data

You will revise how to find the mean, median and range of a set of ungrouped data.

For grouped data, you will learn how to

- find the class interval that contains the median
- estimate the mean
- draw a frequency polygon

A Ungrouped data: median, mean and range

Median

When a set of data is written in order of size, the **median** is

- the middle value when the number of values is odd:

  4 6 6 9 (12) 13 16 17 20

- halfway between the middle pair when the number of values is even:

  5 8 10 13 17 (18 22) 22 24 24 26 29

                                       20

Mean

To find the mean, you add up all the values and divide by the number of values.

$$23 \quad 31 \quad 17 \quad 22 \quad 64 \qquad \text{Mean} = \frac{23 + 31 + 17 + 22 + 64}{5} = \frac{157}{5} = 31.4$$

Range

The range is the difference between the highest and lowest values.

$$(17) \quad 22 \quad 23 \quad 31 \quad (64) \qquad \text{Range} = 64 - 17 = 47$$

A1 A student doing a shop survey noted down the price of a 500 g packet of cornflakes in each of six shops. Here are her results.

      £1.39 £0.95 £1.25 £1.45 £0.89 £1.15

(a) Write the list of prices in order, lowest to highest, and find the median price.

(b) Find the mean price.

(c) Find the range of the prices.

A2 A group of five friends took part in a sponsored swim. The number of completed lengths each person swam is given below.

      13 10 19 20 18

For these numbers find

(a) the mean   (b) the median   (c) the range   OCR

A3 A group of boys and girls took a French test. These are the boys' marks.

3 4 4 0 7 2 8 1 4 3 5

(a) Find the range of the boys' marks.

(b) Calculate, to one decimal place, the mean of the boys' marks.

(c) The mean mark for the girls was 3.2 and the girls' marks had a range of 5. Make two statements about the differences between the boys' and girls' marks in the French test.

A4 A greengrocer sold bags of apples from different countries.

A bag contained 9 French apples.
The weight of each apple is given below, in grams.

101 107 98 109 115 103 96 112 104

(a) Calculate the mean weight of a French apple.

(b) Find the range of the weights of the French apples.

Another bag contained 9 South African apples.
Their mean weight was 107 g and their range was 19 g.

(c) Make two comments on the weights of the apples in the two bags.   OCR

A5 When 17 values are put in order, the median is the 9th value:

1st 2nd 3rd 4th 5th 6th 7th 8th **9th** 10th 11th 12th 13th 14th 15th 16th 17th

Copy and complete these statements.

(a) When 23 values are put in order, the median is the __th value.

(b) When 31 values are put in order, the median is the __th value.

A6 When 14 values are put in order, the median is halfway between the 7th and 8th values:

1st 2nd 3rd 4th 5th 6th **7th** | **8th** 9th 10th 11th 12th 13th 14th

Copy and complete these statements.

(a) When 20 values are put in order, the median is halfway between the __th and __th values.

(b) When 26 values are put in order, the median is halfway between the __th and __th values.

*A7 You have this set of cards.   3 4 5 6 6 7 8

Find

(a) four cards whose mean is 5

(b) five cards with median 6 and range 4

(c) four cards with median 5 and range 5

(d) six cards whose mean and median are the same

B Frequency tables: mode, median, range and mean

A class of 17 children were given a test.
Their marks are shown in this frequency table.

Mark	Frequency
12	1
13	2
14	4
15	4
16	6
Total	17

- The **mode** is the mark with the highest frequency.
  It is 16.

- With 17 children, the **median** mark is the 9th in order of size.

  Going down the table, you can see that the lowest mark is 12.
  Then come two marks of 13, then four of 14:

  12   13   13   14   14   14   14   ...

  That's seven children's marks so far.
  The 9th mark will be in the next group of four, which are all 15:

  12   13   13   14   14   14   14   15   (15)   15   15   ...

  median

- The highest mark is 16 and the lowest 12, so the **range** is $16 - 12 = 4$.

B1 A student doing a traffic survey counted the number of people in each car that passed him.
He made this frequency table.

Number of people	Frequency
1	6
2	7
3	9
4	2
5	1

  (a) What is the modal number of people in a car?

  (b) How many cars did the student count altogether?

  (c) What is the median number of people in a car?

B2 In a memory experiment, children were given twenty words to learn in a minute.
Ten minutes later, they were asked how many they could remember.

The results are shown in this frequency table.

Number of words remembered	Frequency
10	4
11	6
12	6
13	8
14	4
15	2

  (a) How many children took part in the experiment?

  (b) What is the median number of words remembered?

  (c) What is the modal number of words remembered?

  (d) What is the range of the number of words remembered?

B3 The children in a village school are aged from 3 to 7.
This table shows the number of children of each age.

Age	Frequency
3	5
4	2
5	4
6	7
7	9

  (a) What age is the mode?

  (b) How many children are in the school?

  (c) What is the median age of the children?

Mean

Look again at the frequency table of marks at the top of the opposite page.

To find the mean mark, you first work out the total of all the marks.
There is one mark of 12, then two marks of 13, then four of 14, and so on.
So the total of all the marks is

$$12 \times 1 + 13 \times 2 + 14 \times 4 + 15 \times 4 + 16 \times 6 = 250$$

There are 17 children, so the mean mark is $\frac{250}{17} = 14.705\ldots = \mathbf{14.7}$ to 1 d.p.

B4 In question B1, find the mean number of people in a car.

B5 In question B2, find the mean number of words remembered.

B6 In a household survey, people were asked how many TVs they had in their home. The results are shown in this table.

Find the mean number of TVs in a home.

Number of TVs	Frequency
0	2
1	12
2	10
3	3
4	1

C Grouped data: modal interval and median

The frequency table of students' marks in an exam is shown here.

The marks have been grouped into class intervals:

0–9   10–19   20–29   …

The **modal interval** is the one with the highest frequency, 30–39.

The individual marks are not known, so we can't find the median. But we can find which class interval it is in.

Marks	Frequency
0–9	3
10–19	6
20–29	10
30–39	12
40–49	2

The total number of students is $3 + 6 + 10 + 12 + 2 = 33$.

So the median mark is the 17th in order of size.

Going down the table, we have 3 students with marks in the interval 0–9, then 6 in the interval 10–19 (that's 9 students' marks so far), then 10 in the interval 20–29 (that's 19 so far).

So the 17th mark, the median, must be in the interval **20–29**.

C1 This frequency table shows the numbers of goals scored by the teams taking part in a competition.

(a) What is the modal interval?

(b) How many teams took part?

(c) In which class interval is the median number of goals?

Goals	Frequency
0–4	1
5–9	10
10–14	20
15–19	15

C2 This table gives information about the ages of the people living in a nursing home.

Age	Frequency
65–69	3
70–74	4
75–79	6
80–84	7
85–89	8

(a) Which is the modal class interval?

(b) In which class interval does the median age lie?

C3 This table shows the distribution of the weights of babies born in a hospital during one week.

Weight (kg)	2.00–2.25	2.25–2.50	2.50–2.75	2.75–3.00	3.00–3.25	3.25–3.50
Frequency	3	7	4	8	6	3

In which class interval does the median weight lie?

D Grouped data: estimating the mean

Here again is the frequency table of students' marks in an exam.

We don't know the individual marks, so we can't find the mean mark.

Marks	Frequency
0–9	3
10–19	6
20–29	10
30–39	12
40–49	2

But we can **estimate** it, like this.

- There are 3 students with marks in the interval 0–9.
  Give each student the mark that is halfway between 0 and 9.

  To find this **mid-interval value**, we add 0 and 9 and divide by 2: $\frac{0 + 9}{2} = 4.5$

- Similarly, the mid-interval value for 10–19 is $\frac{10 + 19}{2} = 14.5$, and so on.

Here is the table with the mid-interval values included.

We can estimate the mean mark by using the mid-interval values.

Marks	Mid-interval value	Frequency
0–9	4.5	3
10–19	14.5	6
20–29	24.5	10
30–39	34.5	12
40–49	44.5	2

- There are 3 students given a mark of 4.5,
  6 given a mark of 14.5, and so on.

  So an estimate of the total of all their marks is

  $$4.5 \times 3 + 14.5 \times 6 + 24.5 \times 10 + 34.5 \times 12 + 44.5 \times 2 = 848.5$$

- The number of students is $3 + 6 + 10 + 12 + 2 = 33$

  so the estimated mean mark is $\frac{848.5}{33} = 25.7$ to 1 d.p.

Here is the calculation set out with an extra column 'mid-interval value × frequency'.

Marks	Mid-interval value	Frequency	Mid-interval value × frequency
0–9	4.5	3	13.5
10–19	14.5	6	87.0
20–29	24.5	10	245.0
30–39	34.5	12	414.0
40–49	44.5	2	89.0
Total		33	848.5

Estimated mean
$$= \frac{848.5}{33}$$
$$= 25.7 \text{ to 1 d.p.}$$

D1 Here again is the frequency table of goals scored in a competition.

(a) Explain why the mid-interval value for 0–4 is 2.

(b) What is the mid-interval value for 5–9?

(c) Calculate an estimate of the mean number of goals scored.

Goals	Frequency
0–4	1
5–9	10
10–14	20
15–19	15

D2 Some students were entered for an exam which was marked out of 100.

This table shows the distribution of the marks they got.

(a) Explain why the mid-interval value for 1–20 is 10.5.

(b) What is the mid-interval value for 21–40?

(c) How many students entered the exam?

(d) Calculate an estimate of the mean mark.

Marks	Frequency
1–20	6
21–40	10
41–60	8
61–80	7
81–100	4

D3 A survey of dairy farms in a part of England resulted in the frequency table shown here.

The farms were grouped according to the number of cows they had.

(a) How many farms were included in the survey?

(b) Calculate an estimate of the mean number of cows on a farm.

Number of cows	Number of farms
1–25	2
26–50	5
51–75	7
76–100	10
101–125	2
126–150	1

D4 A student is surveying blocks of flats in her area. She records how many flats there are in each block. A frequency table of her results is shown here.

(a) How many blocks of flats were included in the survey?

(b) Calculate an estimate of the mean number of flats in a block.

Number of flats in block	Frequency
1–5	7
6–10	9
11–15	4
16–20	6
21–25	3
26–30	1

E Continuous data, frequency polygon

A student is doing a project on the size of people's handwriting.
He asks each person to write 'The quick brown fox jumps over the lazy dog'.
He then measures the length of the written sentence, in millimetres.

Here is an example.

The length of this sentence is between 96 mm and 97 mm. It is about 96.3 mm.
The length does not have to be a whole number of millimetres.

Some of the sentence lengths recorded by the student are shown below.

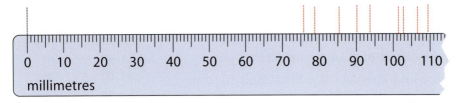

The student wants to group his data.

- If he uses class intervals like 70–79, 80–89, 90–99, … he has a problem, because he won't know where to put, for example, 89.3.
- But if he uses intervals like 70–80, 80–90, 90–100, … he also has a problem, because 90.0, for example would be in two intervals, 80–90 **and** 90–100.

He can use the second method if he makes it clear where to put lengths of exactly 70, 80, 90, … .

A good way to do this is to write the interval 80–90 as

either $80 \leq l < 90$ or $80 < l \leq 90$

        (includes 80 but not 90)   (includes 90 but not 80)

l stands for 'length in mm'.

Discrete and continuous data

The number of children in a family is an example of **discrete** data.
It can only be 0, 1, 2, 3, … It can't be in between these values.

The length in mm of a written sentence is an example of **continuous** data.
It does not have to be a whole number.

When the student had finished the handwriting project, he made this frequency table of the results.

Length of sentence (l mm)	Frequency
$70 \leq l < 80$	6
$80 \leq l < 90$	5
$90 \leq l < 100$	12
$100 \leq l < 110$	19
$110 \leq l < 120$	7

On the frequency diagram for the lengths there are no gaps between the bars.

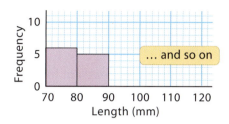

E1 Look at the frequency table above.

  (a) In which interval does a length of exactly 110 mm go?

  (b) Which is the modal interval?

  (c) How many sentences were measured altogether?

  (d) In which interval does the median length lie?

  (e) Copy and complete the frequency diagram for the data.

E2 The maximum daily temperature for the month of October was recorded at a Sussex weather station as follows.

Max. temp. (°C)   16.7 13.9 15.4 14.6 14.1 14.2 12.5 14.6 12.2 12.9 12.2 13.0 14.7
                  12.7 13.9 12.7 13.9 14.4 14.0 14.5 14.7 14.1 14.7 12.9 14.4 13.1
                  13.6 14.6 12.8 13.3 12.4

  (a) Copy and complete this grouped frequency table to record the temperatures.

Max. temp. (°C)	Frequency
$12.0 \leq t < 13.0$	
$13.0 \leq t < 14.0$	
$14.0 \leq t < 15.0$	
$15.0 \leq t < 16.0$	
$16.0 \leq t < 17.0$	
Total	

  (b) What is the modal group of temperatures in Sussex during October?

  (c) On how many days in October was the maximum temperature below 14 °C?

  (d) Draw a frequency diagram for the data.

Estimating the mean

Mid-interval values can be used as before to calculate an estimate of the mean.

E3 This table shows the distribution of the weights of the children in a sports club. The mid-interval values are shown.

(a) How many children are there in the club?

(b) Calculate an estimate of the mean weight of the children.

(c) Draw a frequency diagram for the data.

Weight (w kg)	Mid-interval value	Frequency
$20 < w \leq 25$	22.5	3
$25 < w \leq 30$	27.5	8
$30 < w \leq 35$	32.5	10
$35 < w \leq 40$	37.5	9
$40 < w \leq 45$	42.5	4

E4 Here again is the handwriting data.

(a) What is the mid-interval value for the interval $70 \leq l < 80$?

(b) Calculate an estimate of the mean length of the sentences.

Length of sentence (l mm)	Frequency
$70 \leq l < 80$	6
$80 \leq l < 90$	5
$90 \leq l < 100$	12
$100 \leq l < 110$	19
$110 \leq l < 120$	7

Frequency polygon

A **frequency polygon** is another type of frequency diagram. At each mid-interval value you plot the frequency, and join the points with straight lines.

The frequency polygon shown here is drawn from the data in question E3.

E5 Draw a frequency polygon for the data in question E4.

E6 Draw a frequency polygon for the data in question E2.

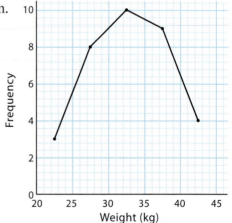

*E7 This is the frequency polygon of the height, h cm, of the children in a year group.

(a) What is the mid-interval value for the interval $120 < h \leq 125$?

(b) How many children are there altogether in the year group?

(c) Calculate an estimate of the mean height of the children.

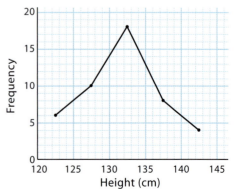

F Mixed questions

F1 This stem-and-leaf table shows the scores of an under-14 cricket team during a season.

7	8 9
8	3 3 7 7
9	1 4 6 6 8
10	4 5 5 8 9 9 9
11	6 6 7
12	0 1

Key: **9** | 1 means 91

(a) How many matches did the team play?

(b) What is the median score?

(c) What is the range of the scores?

(d) It is discovered later that in one of the matches some of the players were over the age of 14.
The score for this match, 108, is removed from the record.
What is the new median score?

F2 The age distribution of the people living in a street is shown in this frequency table.

Age in years	Frequency
0–19	6
20–39	20
40–59	14
60–79	9
80–99	2

(a) What is the modal class interval?

(b) How many people live in the street?

(c) In which class interval is the median age?

(d) A new house is built in the street and 3 people aged 45, 48 and 76 come to live in it.
In which class interval is the new median age?

F3 Sam is working on a project to compare girls' and boys' handwriting.
She asks some girls and boys to write a particular sentence.
Then she measures its length in cm.

Her results are shown in the table below.

Length (l cm)	Frequency (girls)	Frequency (boys)
$8 < l \leq 9$	2	5
$9 < l \leq 10$	10	18
$10 < l \leq 11$	19	11
$11 < l \leq 12$	6	4
$12 < l \leq 13$	3	2

(a) How many girls and how many boys took part in the project?

(b) In which class interval is the median length for

    (i) the girls   (ii) the boys

(c) Calculate an estimate of the mean length for

    (i) the girls   (ii) the boys

(d) On the same set of axes, draw two frequency polygons, one for the girls and one for the boys.

(e) Describe briefly what the data shows about the girls' and boys' handwriting.

Test yourself

T1 Paul found the playing time of 60 tracks from his CD collection.
His results are summarised in the table below.

Time (t minutes)	$1 < t \leq 2$	$2 < t \leq 3$	$3 < t \leq 4$	$4 < t \leq 5$	$5 < t \leq 6$	$6 < t \leq 7$
Frequency	3	12	17	19	6	3

(a) Write down the modal class.

(b) Which class interval contains the median?
Explain how you know this.

(c) Draw a frequency diagram to represent the information in the table. OCR

T2 The table below shows the selling price of 120 sofas in a shop.

Amount (£x)	Frequency
$0 < x \leq 100$	12
$100 < x \leq 200$	40
$200 < x \leq 300$	36
$300 < x \leq 400$	24
$400 < x \leq 500$	8

(a) Write down the modal class.

(b) Calculate an estimate of the mean selling price. OCR

T3 A group of people are going on holiday.
This table shows the distribution of the
weights of their luggage.

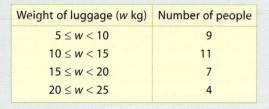

Weight of luggage (w kg)	Number of people
$5 \leq w < 10$	9
$10 \leq w < 15$	11
$15 \leq w < 20$	7
$20 \leq w < 25$	4

(a) Draw a frequency polygon for the data.

(b) Calculate an estimate of the mean
weight of the luggage.

T4 This frequency polygon shows the distribution
of the weights of the fish caught in a weekend
fishing competition.

(a) How many fish were caught altogether?

(b) Calculate an estimate of the mean
weight of the fish.

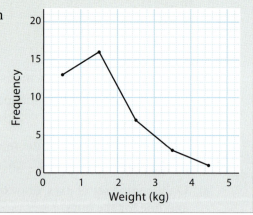

21 Map scale

You should know how to use ratios.

This work will help you use a scale on a map or plan given as a ratio.

A Using a scale given as a ratio

This map is part of an Ordnance Survey map.

The scale of the map is 1 : 50 000.
This means that 1 cm on the map represents
50 000 cm in real life.

- What is 50 000 cm in metres?
- What is 50 000 cm in kilometres?
- The gridlines on the map are 2 cm apart.
  What distance, in kilometres, does
  this represent in real life?
- Complete this statement:

  On the map, ... cm represents 1 km.

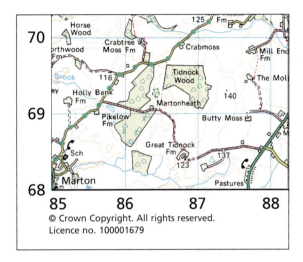

A1 (a) On the map above, measure the straight-line distance between
Holly Bank Farm and Butty Moss.

(b) What is the real distance, in kilometres, between Holly Bank Farm and Butty Moss?

A2 A map uses a scale of 1 : 250 000.

(a) What does 1 cm on the map represent in real life in centimetres?

(b) What does 1 cm on the map represent in real life in metres?

(c) What does 1 cm on the map represent in real life in kilometres?

(d) Copy and complete this statement.

On the map, 1 cm represents ... km.

(e) On the map, the distance between two schools is 6 cm.
How far apart are the actual schools, in km?

A3 The scale on a map is given as 5 cm represents 1 kilometre.

(a) What does 1 cm on the map represent in real life in metres?

(b) What does 1 cm on the map represent in real life in centimetres?

(c) Which of these ratios is the correct scale for the map?

| 5 : 1 | 1 : 200 | 5 : 100 000 | 1 : 20 000 | 5 : 1000 |

Examples

A map uses a scale of $1:100\,000$.
A footpath measures 4 cm on the map.
How long is the actual footpath in kilometres?

> 1 cm on the map represents 100 000 cm.
> So 4 cm represents 4 × 100 000 cm = 400 000 cm
> 400 000 cm = 4000 m = 4 km
> So the actual footpath is 4 km long.

A plan of a garden is drawn to a scale of $1:25$.
The diameter of the actual pond is 1.6 m.
What is the diameter of the pond on the plan?

> 1.6 m = 160 cm
> 1 cm on the plan represents 25 cm.
> So diameter of pond on plan = 160 ÷ 25
> = 6.4 cm

A4 The plan of a house is drawn to a scale of $1:50$.

(a) The length of the living room is 9.5 cm on the plan.
How long, in metres, is it in real life?

(b) The actual width of the front door is 85 cm.
How wide is the front door on the plan?

(c) The actual kitchen is 2.8 m long.
How long, in centimetres, is the kitchen on the plan?

A5 A map uses a scale of $1:25\,000$.

(a) The distance between two farmhouses is measured on the map as 5 cm.
How far apart are the actual farmhouses, in km?

(b) How long, in cm, will a 10 km walk be on the map?

A6 Emma measures the distance from her home to school as 7 cm on a map.
The scale of the map is $1:50\,000$.
What is the actual distance, in kilometres, from Emma's home to school?

Test yourself

T1 The scale of a map is given as $1:50\,000$.
Geoff plans the route for a walk on the map.
The route measures 15 cm.
What is the real length of the route in kilometres?

T2 The length of a coach is 15 metres.
Jonathan makes a model of the coach.
He uses a scale of $1:24$.
Work out the length, in centimetres,
of the model coach.

Edexcel

Review 3

You need sheet F2–9 and an angle measurer.

1 There are 24 women and 6 men in a Spanish class.

    (a) What is the ratio of women to men in its simplest form?

    (b) What percentage of the class are men?

2 Work out the value of each of these.

    (a) 2^5 **(b)** 7^1 **(c)** $3^2 \times 2^3$ **(d)** $2^4 + 5^2$

3 $^-5 < k \le 2$
k is an integer.
Write down all the possible values of k.

4 Use the map on sheet F2–9.

    (a) How far apart in kilometres are the two lighthouses?

    (b) What is the bearing of

        (i) Needle Rock from lighthouse A   **(ii)** Needle Rock from lighthouse B

    (c) A boat is on a bearing of 105° from lighthouse A and on a bearing of 230° from lighthouse B.

        (i) Mark the position of the boat.

        (ii) How far, in kilometres, is the boat from Needle Rock?

5 What is the value of $n^2 + 5$ when

    (a) $n = 3$ **(b)** $n = 6$ **(c)** $n = 1$ **(d)** $n = {}^-4$

6 (a) Describe fully the transformation that maps shape A on to

        (i) shape B

        (ii) shape C

        (iii) shape D

    (b) Describe the reflection that maps shape B on to shape D.

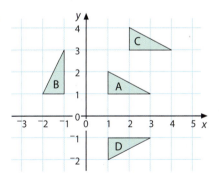

7 Write inequalities to describe the following number line diagrams.

    (a)

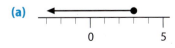

    (b)

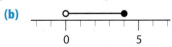

8 (a) Find the value of $2k^2$ when $k = 5$.

    (b) Find the value of $x^3 - x$ when $x = 3$.

9 Write the ratio $36:12$ in its simplest form.

10 Solve each of these inequalities and show each solution on a number line.

    (a) $7x + 5 \geq 19$ **(b)** $2a - 7 \leq 4$ **(c)** $3n + 5 > 2$

11 This stem-and-leaf table shows the typing speeds in words per minute of some people who took an audio-typing test.

2	9
3	2 2 4 7 8
4	0 1 1 3 4 5 5 9
5	1 3 4 4 6 7
6	2

Stem: 10 words per minute

    (a) How many people took the test?

    (b) What was the range of the typing speeds?

    (c) What was the median speed?

    (d) People with speeds of 38 words per minute or more had their work checked for accuracy. How many people was this?

12 Jenny makes lime fizz by mixing lemonade and lime juice in the ratio $9:1$. How much lime juice would she need to make 300 ml of lime fizz?

13 Draw a set of axes, each numbered from ⁻6 to 6.
Plot and join the points $(1, 1)$, $(1, 3)$, $(2, 2)$ and $(2, 1)$. Label the shape A.

    (a) **(i)** Draw the image of A after an enlargement with centre $(0, 0)$ and scale factor 2. Label it B.

       (ii) Draw the image of A after the translation $\begin{bmatrix} 1 \\ -2 \end{bmatrix}$. Label it C.

      (iii) Describe fully the single transformation that maps shape B to shape C.

    (b) **(i)** Draw the image of shape A after a reflection in the y-axis. Label it D.

       (ii) Draw the image of shape D after a reflection in the x-axis. Label it E.

      (iii) Describe fully the single transformation that maps shape A to shape E.

14

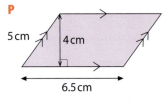

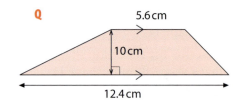

    (a) Calculate the area of each shape.

    (b) Find the perimeter of the parallelogram.

15 Holly, Ivy and Noel share £60 in the ratio $3:2:1$. Calculate Holly's share.

16 Write 144 as the product of its prime factors using index notation.

17 The table shows the results of a survey into the number of TV sets in people's homes.

Number of sets	Number of homes
0	1
1	5
2	10
3	12
4	3

  (a) How many of these homes contain more than two TV sets?

  (b) Calculate the mean number of sets in a home, correct to one decimal place.

  (c) Find the median number of sets.

  (d) What is the mode?

18 A circle has a radius of 3.2 m.

  (a) Find the area of the circle.

  (b) Find its circumference.

3.2 m

19 Write each of these as a single power of 2.

  (a) $2^4 \times 2^5$ **(b)** $2^3 \times 2$ **(c)** $2^9 \div 2^3$ **(d)** $2^8 \div 2$

20 The table shows the time, in minutes, that some children spent on a computer game.

Time (minutes)	Frequency
$0 \leq t < 20$	6
$20 \leq t < 40$	12
$40 \leq t < 60$	15
$60 \leq t < 80$	7

  (a) What is the modal class interval of time spent?

  (b) Calculate an estimate of the mean time spent on this computer game.

21 Simplify each of these.

  (a) $m^2 \times m^3$ **(b)** $2n \times 6n$ **(c)** $2k \times 3k^2$ **(d)** $a^2 + a^2 + a^2$

22 A circle has a radius of 5 cm.
Find the area of the circle as an exact value in terms of π.

23 Sue's recipe for dry martinis mixes vermouth and gin in the ratio $1:6$.

  (a) How much gin would Sue mix with 50 ml of vermouth?

  (b) How much vermouth would she mix with 180 ml of gin?

24 This shape consists of the square ABCD and a semicircle.
AD = 12 cm.

Calculate the total area of the shape.
Give your answer to the nearest 0.1 cm².

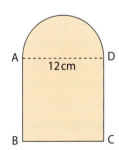

A - - - - - - - - - - D
12 cm
B ⌐_____⌐ C

22 Changing the subject

You should know

- how to solve equations like $3a + 2 = 17$ or $4a - 2 = 10$
- that an expression like $\dfrac{b-6}{10}$ means 'take 6 off b and divide the result by 10'

This work will help you change the subject of a formula with letters and numbers in it, for example $a = 4d + 5$ and $h = 2k + g$.

A Review: using formulas

Stella is a garden designer who plants ornamental vegetable beds.
To keep away pests, she plants rows of artichokes with marigolds by them in this pattern.

marigold

artichoke

This pattern has 5 artichokes and 14 marigolds.

- Look at the pattern carefully.
  Show how Stella would plant a row of 6 artichokes.
  (You don't need to draw the plants: use Ⓐ for an artichoke and Ⓜ for a marigold.)

- How many marigold plants does she need for 6 artichokes?
  How many marigold plants does she need for 3 artichokes planted like this?

- Which of these is a formula that links the numbers of artichokes and marigolds?
  a stands for the number of artichokes and m stands for the number of marigolds.

  | $m = a + 2$ | $m = 4a + 2$ | $m = 2a + 4$ | $m = a + 10$ |

- Use the formula to find the number of marigolds needed for 10 artichokes.

- Stella plants a row of artichokes and surrounds them with 40 marigolds.
  Form and solve an equation to find the number of artichokes she had planted.

A1 (a) How many marigolds would Stella need for 8 artichokes in a row like this?

(b) Stella is planting a row of artichokes.
She has 80 marigold plants.
What is the maximum number of artichokes that she can plant in a row like this?

A2

Stella also plants rows of broccoli.
She puts ornamental cabbages above and below each row of broccoli
and at the ends in the pattern shown above.

(a) Look at the pattern carefully.

   (i)   Show how Stella would plant a row of 3 broccoli plants.
         (Use Ⓑ for a broccoli plant and Ⓒ for a cabbage plant.)

   (ii) How many cabbage plants does she need for 3 broccoli plants?

(b) How many cabbage plants does she need for a row of

   (i)   10 broccoli plants   (ii) 100 broccoli plants

(c) Given that *b* stands for the number of broccoli plants in a row and
     c stands for the number of cabbage plants, write a formula connecting *b* and *c*.

This is an order for one row of broccoli plants.
We need to find the number of broccoli plants to order.

Order from Brown's
Broccoli plants
Cabbage plants   90

(d) (i)   Put $c = 90$ in your formula.
           Solve the equation you get to find *b*.

   (ii) How many broccoli plants does Stella need?

A3 Stella grows Spanish onions and garlic in patterns like this.

Suppose *s* stands for the number of Spanish onions in a row
and *g* stands for the number of garlic bulbs.

(a) Explain why the formula connecting *s* and *g* is $g = 6s + 4$.

(b) For one row of onions, Stella plants 40 garlic bulbs.
     Form and solve an equation to find how many Spanish onions are in the row.

(c) For one row of onions, Stella plants 100 garlic bulbs.
     How many Spanish onions are in the row?

For Stella's onion and garlic rows, the formula $g = 6s + 4$ connects the letters g and s.

We can find s when $g = 100$
like this:

We can work with the letters
themselves instead of numbers.

$100 = 6s + 4$

Take 4 from both sides.

$96 = 6s$

Divide both sides by 6.

$16 = s$

$g = 6s + 4$

$g - 4 = 6s$

$\dfrac{g - 4}{6} = s$

So $s = \dfrac{g - 4}{6}$

It is usual to write a formula
with the subject on the left.

Each time, we do the same thing to both sides of the formula.
We call this 'rearranging the formula to make s the subject' or
'making s the subject of the formula'.

Now we can find the value of s more easily for different values of g.

For example, when $g = 64$, $s = \dfrac{64 - 4}{6} = \dfrac{60}{6} = 10$.

B1 Stella plants red and white onions in rows like this.

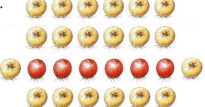

Using r for the number of red onions and w for the number of white onions,

$w = 3r + 2$

is the formula for this pattern.

(a) Copy and complete this working
to make r the subject of this formula.

$w = 3r + 2$

$w - \blacklozenge = 3r$

$\dfrac{w - \blacklozenge}{\blacklozenge} = r$

(b) Find the value of r when $w = 14$.
Check your result by drawing a diagram for a planting of
red and white onions that uses 14 white onions.

(c) How many red onions are there in a planting that has 68 white onions in it?

(d) What is the value of r when $w = 302$?

B2 The formula for this pattern of red and white onions is $w = 2r + 4$.

(a) Rearrange the formula $w = 2r + 4$ to make r the subject.

(b) Work out r when $w = 88$.

(c) How many red onions are there in a planting like this with 126 white onions?

B3 Make g the subject of the formula $f = 3g + 2$.

B4 Make the bold letter the subject of each of these formulas.

(a) $b = 8\mathbf{w} + 7$ (b) $u = 5\mathbf{v} + 2$ (c) $g = 6\mathbf{d}$ (d) $y = 12 + 3\mathbf{x}$

(e) $t = 9\mathbf{b} + 5$ (f) $f = 8 + 3\mathbf{d}$ (g) $h = \mathbf{k} + 5$ (h) $w = 7\mathbf{z} + 1$

When a formula involves a subtraction, it is often best to add to both sides to remove it first.

Example

Rearrange $y = 5x - 6$ to make x the subject.

$y = 5x - 6$

$\qquad [+ 6]$

$y + 6 = 5x$

$\qquad [\div 5]$

$\dfrac{y + 6}{5} = x$

So $\quad x = \dfrac{y + 6}{5}$

Each operation in brackets shows what is done to both sides to get the next line.

B5 Which of the following is a correct rearrangement of $a = 2b - 10$?

A $\quad b = \dfrac{a - 10}{2}$ **B** $\quad b = \dfrac{a + 10}{2}$ **C** $\quad b = \dfrac{a + 2}{10}$ **D** $\quad b = \dfrac{a - 2}{10}$

B6 Make the bold letter the subject of each of these formulas.

(a) $a = 8\mathbf{w} - 6$ (b) $b = 4\mathbf{h} - 1$ (c) $h = 2\mathbf{f} - 2$ (d) $y = \mathbf{x} - 7$

(e) $z = 3\mathbf{r} - 15$ (f) $k = 5\mathbf{d} - 3$ (g) $b = \mathbf{g} - 5$ (h) $l = 6\mathbf{m} - 1$

B7 Rearrange each of these formulas to make the bold letter the subject.

(a) $a = 30 + 3\mathbf{b}$ (b) $s = 2\mathbf{t} - 40$ (c) $t = 12\mathbf{g} - 60$ (d) $f = 7\mathbf{g} + 12$

(e) $y = 12 + 8\mathbf{x}$ (f) $r = 5\mathbf{s} - 20$ (g) $a = 9\mathbf{b}$ (h) $v = 7\mathbf{u} - 10$

(i) $y = 35 + \mathbf{x}$ (j) $8 + 4\mathbf{j} = d$ (k) $k = 8\mathbf{j} - 45$ (l) $7\mathbf{z} - 1 = w$

Sometimes formulas use more than two letters.

For example, the perimeter P of this isosceles triangle is given by the formula

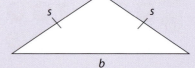

$$P = b + 2s$$

We can rearrange the formula to make s the subject like this.

$$P = b + 2s$$
$$\qquad\qquad [- b]$$
$$P - b = 2s$$
$$\qquad\qquad [\div 2]$$
$$\frac{P - b}{2} = s$$

So $\quad s = \dfrac{P - b}{2}$

C1 Make the bold letter the subject of each of these formulas.

    (a) $w = 3\boldsymbol{u} + v$ (b) $b = 2\boldsymbol{m} + n$ (c) $h = 5\boldsymbol{f} + g$ (d) $P = \boldsymbol{y} + x$

    (e) $y = x + 2\boldsymbol{z}$ (f) $k = c + 4\boldsymbol{b}$ (g) $P = b + 7\boldsymbol{s}$ (h) $H = c + \boldsymbol{d}$

*C2 Make the bold letter the subject of each of these formulas.

    (a) $A = \boldsymbol{p} - q$ (b) $y = 2\boldsymbol{x} - z$ (c) $P = 2\boldsymbol{L} + 2W$ (d) $h = 3\boldsymbol{f} + 2g$

Test yourself

T1 Rearrange this formula to make x the subject.

    $y = 12 + 10x$ OCR

T2 (a) Which of these rearrangements of $y = 2x - 3$ is correct?

  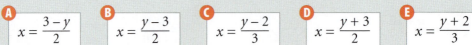

    A $x = \dfrac{3 - y}{2}$ **B** $x = \dfrac{y - 3}{2}$ **C** $x = \dfrac{y - 2}{3}$ **D** $x = \dfrac{y + 3}{2}$ **E** $x = \dfrac{y + 2}{3}$

    (b) Use the correct rearrangement to find the value of x when $y = 15$.

T3 Rearrange each of these formulas to make the bold letter the subject.

    (a) $e = 4\boldsymbol{v} - 12$ (b) $f = 2\boldsymbol{w} + 15$ (c) $g = \boldsymbol{x} - 12$ (d) $h = 5\boldsymbol{y}$

    (e) $y = 2\boldsymbol{x} + 9$ (f) $s = 4\boldsymbol{t} - 7$ (g) $n = 8 + 5\boldsymbol{t}$ (h) $m = 3\boldsymbol{u} - 5$

T4 Make the bold letter the subject of each formula.

    (a) $j = 5\boldsymbol{k} + l$ (b) $f = g + 8\boldsymbol{h}$ (c) $P = Q + \boldsymbol{R}$

23 Coordinates in three dimensions

This work will help you identify points in three-dimensional space using coordinates.

You will need scissors, adhesive and sheets F2–10 and F2–11.

A Identifying points

To give the position of a point in 3-D space, a third axis is needed called the **z-axis**.
So each point has three coordinates, written in the form (x, y, z).

Making your own grid

- Cut out the 3-D grid from sheet F2–10 and stick it together.
  Place it on the desk with the x-axis and the y-axis on the desk
  and the z-axis pointing upwards.

- Here a rod 3 units long has been placed on the grid.
  The bottom of the rod has coordinates $(2, 4, 0)$.
  What are the coordinates of the top of the rod?

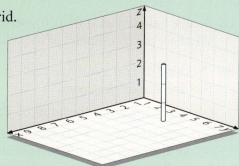

- Cut out the rectangle from sheet F2–11.
  Place it on the bottom of the 3-D grid with its x-axis and y-axis matching the grid.
  What are the 3-D coordinates of P, Q, R and S?

- Lift the rectangle up 3 units. What are the coordinates of P, Q, R and S now?

- Cut out the net for the cuboid from sheet F2–11 and glue it together.
  Place the cuboid on the 3-D grid like this
  (vertex B is at $(0, 0, 0)$ and face P is at the bottom).
  What are the coordinates of each corner
  that you can see?

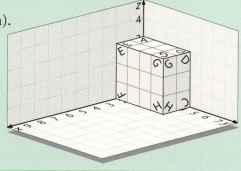

A1 Place the cuboid on the 3-D grid with corner A at $(0, 0, 0)$ and face M at the bottom.
Write down the coordinates of these vertices.

   (a) F   **(b)** C   **(c)** E   **(d)** H

A2 Place the cuboid with corner C at $(0, 0, 0)$ and face N at the bottom.
Write down the coordinates of these vertices.

(a) B (b) G (c) E (d) A

A3 Place the cuboid with face M at the bottom, corner A at $(5, 2, 0)$ and corner D at $(1, 2, 0)$.
Write down the coordinates of these vertices.

(a) G (b) B (c) F (d) H

A4 Place the cuboid so that face P is at the bottom, B is at $(1, 3, 0)$ and C is at $(1, 7, 0)$.
Write down the coordinates of these points.

(a) H (b) A (c) D (d) G

*A5 If the cuboid is placed so that C is at $(3, 2, 1)$, E is at $(1, 6, 4)$ and face P is facing downwards, what are the coordinates of these points?

(a) F (b) B (c) G (d) A

A6 A cube has vertices at $(0, 0, 0)$, $(4, 0, 0)$ and $(0, 4, 0)$.
What are the coordinates of the other five vertices?

A7 On this 3-D grid is a shape made from five one-centimetre cubes.

(a) What letter is at the point $(2, 2, 1)$?

(b) Write down the 3-D coordinates of the other four labelled points.

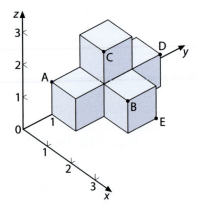

Test yourself

T1 The diagram shows eight one-centimetre cubes fixed together.

Corner A has coordinates $(1, 1, 0)$.

Write down the coordinates of points B and C.

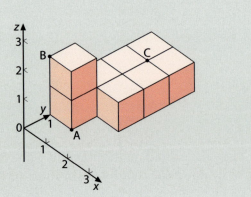

OCR

24 Drawing and using quadratic graphs

You will revise drawing and using linear graphs.

This work will help you draw quadratic graphs and use them to solve equations.

A Review: linear graphs

Part of the graph of $y = 3x - 2$ is shown.

It crosses the x-axis at about 0.7.
At this point the value of y is 0.

So $x = 0.7$ is the approximate solution
of the equation $3x - 2 = 0$.

> Give values from a graph to an
> appropriate degree of accuracy.
> Here, you can give values correct
> to one decimal place.

• Use the graph to solve $3x - 2 = 3$.

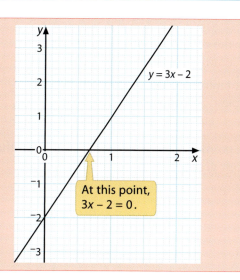

At this point,
$3x - 2 = 0$.

A1 (a) Copy and complete this table
for the equation $y = 2x + 1$.

x	$^-1$	0	1	2	3
y	$^-1$				

(b) On axes like those on the right,
draw the graph of $y = 2x + 1$.
Label the line with its equation.

(c) Use your graph to solve the
equation $2x + 1 = 0$.

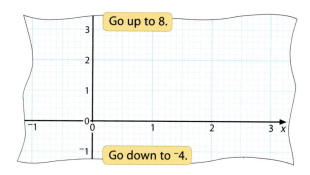

Go up to 8.

Go down to $^-4$.

A2 (a) Copy and complete this table
for the equation $y = 3x - 1$.

x	$^-1$	0	1	2	3
y	$^-4$				

(b) On axes exactly like the ones used in A1, draw and label the graph of $y = 3x - 1$.

(c) Use your graph to solve the equation $3x - 1 = 0$.

(d) Use your graph to solve the equation $3x - 1 = 7$.

B Simple quadratic graphs

A **quadratic** rule involves x^2.

Examples of quadratic rules are $y = x^2 - 3$, $y = 2x^2 + x$ and $y = 8 - x^2$.

The graph of any quadratic rule is a curve that has a vertical line of symmetry.

It will look like this or like this.

To draw the graph of a quadratic rule, first draw up a table of values.
Include a range of positive and negative values for x.

This is a table of values for $y = x^2$, the simplest quadratic rule.

x	-3	-2	-1	0	1	2	3
x^2	9	4	1	0	1	4	9

Plot the points shown by your table and join them with a **smooth** curve.
Label your graph with its equation.

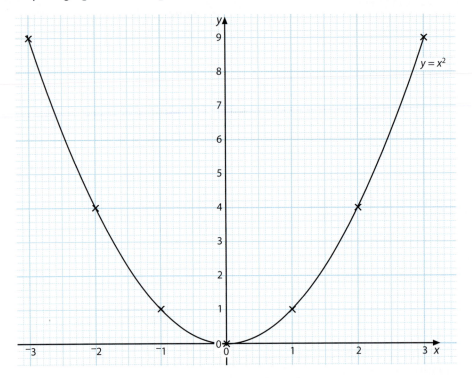

Use the graph of $y = x^2$ above to

- find approximate values for 1.2^2 and $(^-1.9)^2$

- solve the equation $x^2 = 3$ to an appropriate degree of accuracy

Each of the graphs below is an attempt to draw $y = x^2$.
What is wrong with each one?

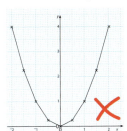 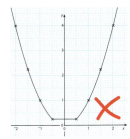 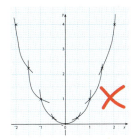 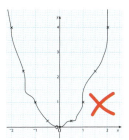

B1 (a) Copy and complete this calculation.

> When $x = 4$, $x^2 + 3$
> $= 4^2 + 3$
> $= 4 \times 4 + 3$
> $= \blacksquare + 3$
> $= \blacktriangledown$

(b) Work out the value of $x^2 + 3$ when $x = 3$.

(c) Copy and complete this table of values for $y = x^2 + 3$.

x	⁻4	⁻3	⁻2	⁻1	0	1	2	3	4
y	19	12	7	4					

(d) On graph paper draw a pair of axes with x from ⁻4 to 4, and y from 0 to 20. Draw and label the graph of $y = x^2 + 3$.

B2 (a) Copy and complete this calculation.

> When $x = {}^-3$, $x^2 - 2$
> $= (^-3)^2 - 2$
> $= {}^-3 \times {}^-3 - 2$
> $= \blacklozenge - 2$
> $= \blacklozenge$

(b) Work out the value of $x^2 - 2$ when $x = 4$.

(c) Copy and complete this table of values for $y = x^2 - 2$.

x	⁻4	⁻3	⁻2	⁻1	0	1	2	3	4
y	14			⁻1	⁻2				

(d) On graph paper draw a pair of axes with x from ⁻4 to 4, and y from ⁻2 to 14. Draw the graph of $y = x^2 - 2$.

(e) Use your graph to find the two solutions to the equation $x^2 - 2 = 0$.

C More complex quadratic graphs

An example of a more complex rule is $y = x^2 + 2x$.

When $x = 3$, $x^2 + 2x$

$$= 3^2 + 2 \times 3$$
$$= 3 \times 3 + 2 \times 3$$
$$= 9 + 6$$
$$= 15$$

- Copy and complete this table for $y = x^2 + 2x$.

x	-3	-2	-1	0	1	2	3
y		0	-1				15

- Draw the graph of $y = x^2 + 2x$ for values of x from $^-3$ to 3.
- Use your graph to solve $x^2 + 2x = 1$.

C1 (a) Copy and complete this calculation.

When $x = 3$, $x^2 + x$

$$= 3^2 + 3$$
$$= 3 \times 3 + 3$$
$$= \blacksquare + 3$$
$$= \blacksquare$$

(b) Copy and complete this table of values for $y = x^2 + x$.

x	-3	-2	-1	0	1	2	3
y	6		0		2		

(c) On graph paper draw a pair of axes with x from $^-3$ to 3, and y from $^-2$ to 12. Draw and label the graph of $y = x^2 + x$.

(d) Solve the equation $x^2 + x = 0$.

(e) Use your graph to solve the equation $x^2 + x = 1$.

C2 (a) Work out the value of $x^2 - 3x$ when $x = 4$.

(b) Show that $x^2 - 3x = 10$ when $x = ^-2$.

(c) Copy and complete this table of values for $y = x^2 - 3x$.

x	-2	-1	0	1	2	3	4
y	10	4	0	-2			

(d) On graph paper draw a pair of axes with x from $^-2$ to 4, and y from $^-4$ to 10. Draw and label the graph of $y = x^2 - 3x$.

(e) Use your graph to solve the equation $x^2 - 3x = 3$.

C3 (a) Work out the value of $2x^2 - 3$ when $x = 1$.

(b) Copy and complete this table of values for $y = 2x^2 - 3$.

x	-2	-1	0	1	2
y		-1	-3		5

(c) On graph paper draw a pair of axes with x from -2 to 2, and y from -4 to 6. Draw and label the graph of $y = 2x^2 - 3$.

(d) Use your graph to solve the equation $2x^2 - 3 = 0$.

D Using a calculator

A calculator is useful when dealing with more complex quadratic expressions.

To find the value of $x^2 - 2x + 5$ when $x = 3$, Ross used this key sequence on his calculator.

| 3 | x^2 | − | 2 | × | 3 | + | 5 |

- Use your calculator to find the value of $x^2 - 2x + 5$ when $x = 3$.

To find the value of $x^2 - 5x$ when $x = {}^-4$, Ross used this key sequence on his calculator.

| (| − | 4 |) | x^2 | − | 5 | × | − | 4 |

- Why do you think Ross needed to use brackets here?
- Use your calculator to find the value of $x^2 - 5x$ when $x = {}^-4$. You may need to use the 'change sign' key instead of the subtract key (see page 44).

D1 (a) Find the value of $x^2 - 5x$ when $x = 1$.

(b) Copy and complete this table for $y = x^2 - 5x$.

x	-2	-1	0	1	2	3	4	5	6
y		6	0		-6		-4		

(c) On axes with scales like these, draw and label the graph of $y = x^2 - 5x$.

(d) Write down the two solutions to the equation $x^2 - 5x = 0$.

(e) Use your graph to solve $x^2 - 5x = 4$.

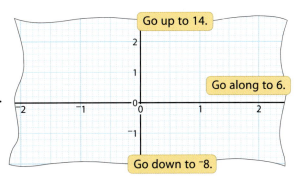

Go up to 14.

Go along to 6.

Go down to -8.

For each question on this page, use axes with scales like these.

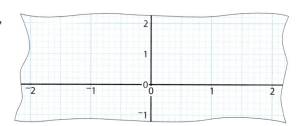

D2 (a) Copy and complete this table of values for $y = 8 - x^2$.

x	⁻3	⁻2	⁻1	0	1	2	3
y	⁻1			7	8		4

(b) Draw and label the graph of $y = 8 - x^2$.
Use a pair of axes with x from ⁻3 to 3, and y from ⁻2 to 9.

(c) Use your graph to solve the equation $8 - x^2 = 0$.

D3 (a) Copy and complete this table of values for $y = x^2 - 4x + 2$.

x	⁻2	⁻1	0	1	2	3	4	5
y	14			⁻1	⁻2		2	

(b) Draw and label the graph of $y = x^2 - 4x + 2$.
Use a pair of axes with x from ⁻2 to 5, and y from ⁻4 to 14.

(c) Use your graph to solve these equations.

(i) $x^2 - 4x + 2 = 0$ **(ii)** $x^2 - 4x + 2 = 6$

Test yourself

T1 (a) Copy and complete this table of values for $y = x^2 - 5$.

x	⁻3	⁻2	⁻1	0	1	2	3
y		⁻1	⁻4	⁻5	⁻4		

(b) Draw and label the graph of $y = x^2 - 5$.
Use a pair of axes with x from ⁻3 to 3, and y from ⁻5 to 4.

(c) Use your graph to solve the equation $x^2 - 5 = 0$.

T2 (a) Copy and complete this table of values for $y = x^2 - 3x - 1$.

x	⁻2	⁻1	0	1	2	3	4
y	9		⁻1	⁻3		⁻1	

(b) Draw and label the graph of $y = x^2 - 3x - 1$.
Use a pair of axes with x from ⁻2 to 4, and y from ⁻4 to 10.

(c) Use your graph to solve $x^2 - 3x - 1 = 0$.

25 Units of area and volume

You should know how to find
- the area of a simple two-dimensional shape
- the volume of a cuboid

This work will help you convert between different units for area and volume.

A Units of area

A1 (a) Calculate the area of this rectangle in m².

(b) Sketch the rectangle, showing the length and width in centimetres.

(c) Calculate the area of the rectangle in cm².

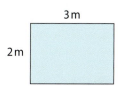

A2 (a) Calculate the area of this rectangle in cm².

(b) Sketch the rectangle, showing the length and width in metres.

(c) Calculate the area of the rectangle in m².

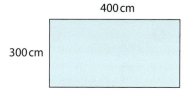

A3 For each of these shapes

(i) calculate the area in m²

(ii) sketch the shape, showing the dimensions in centimetres

(iii) calculate the area in cm²

(a) 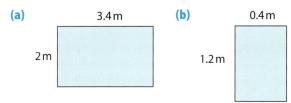 **(b)** **(c)**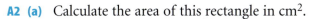

A4 (a) Calculate the area of this rectangle in cm².

(b) Sketch the rectangle, showing the length and width in millimetres.

(c) Calculate the area of the rectangle in mm².

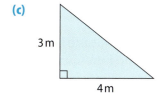

A5 (a) Calculate the area of this rectangle in mm².

(b) Sketch the rectangle, showing the length and width in centimetres.

(c) Calculate the area of the rectangle in cm².

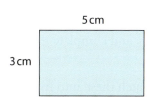

B Converting units of area

This picture shows part of a square measuring 1 metre by 1 metre drawn on a very large piece of centimetre squared paper.

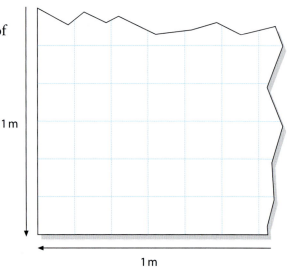

- How many centimetre squares are there along each edge?

- How many centimetre squares are there altogether in one square metre?

- Copy and complete this.

    area in m² — [× ?] → area in cm²

B1 Match these into five pairs of equivalent areas.
Write each pair as a statement, for example 20 000 cm² = 2 m².

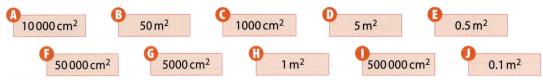

A   10 000 cm²   B   50 m²   C   1000 cm²   D   5 m²   E   0.5 m²

F   50 000 cm²   G   5000 cm²   H   1 m²   I   500 000 cm²   J   0.1 m²

B2 Change these areas in m² into cm².

(a) 4 m²   (b) 25 m²   (c) 4.8 m²   (d) 0.6 m²   (e) 0.35 m²

B3 Change these areas in cm² into m².

(a) 70 000 cm²   (b) 300 000 cm²   (c) 45 000 cm²   (d) 9000 cm²   (e) 7500 cm²

Here is a square measuring 1 centimetre by 1 centimetre.
It is divided up into square millimetres.

1 cm
1 cm

- How many millimetre squares are there along each edge?

- How many millimetre squares are there altogether in one square centimetre?

- Copy and complete this.   area in cm² — [× ?] → area in mm²

B4 Match these into five pairs of equivalent areas.
Write each pair as a statement.

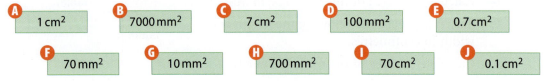

A   1 cm²   B   7000 mm²   C   7 cm²   D   100 mm²   E   0.7 cm²

F   70 mm²   G   10 mm²   H   700 mm²   I   70 cm²   J   0.1 cm²

B5 Change these areas in cm² into mm².

(a) 4 cm²   (b) 12 cm²   (c) 6.5 cm²   (d) 0.5 cm²   (e) 0.38 cm²

B6 Change these areas in mm² into cm².

(a) 300 mm²   (b) 2000 mm²   (c) 850 mm²   (d) 74 mm²   (e) 40 mm²

B7 For each of the shapes below

(i) calculate the area in cm²   (ii) write down the area in m²

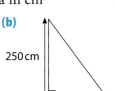

(a)   150 cm   200 cm

(b)   250 cm   160 cm

(c)   150 cm   800 cm

(d)   500 cm   300 cm   500 cm

C Converting units of volume

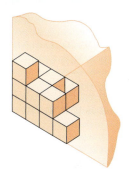

This picture shows part of a box that is a cube measuring
1 metre by 1 metre by 1 metre.
Imagine that the box is filled with 1 cm cubes.

- How many centimetre cubes would it take to make a layer
  to cover the bottom of the box?

- How many layers would it take to fill the box to the top?

- How many centimetre cubes are there altogether
  in one cubic metre?

- Copy and complete this.

  volume in m³ — [× ?]→ volume in cm³

C1 Match these into five pairs of equivalent volumes.
Write each pair as a statement, for example 2 000 000 cm³ = 2 m³.

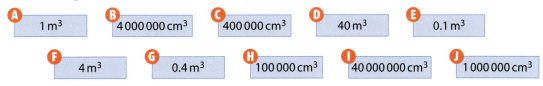

A 1 m³   B 4 000 000 cm³   C 400 000 cm³   D 40 m³   E 0.1 m³

F 4 m³   G 0.4 m³   H 100 000 cm³   I 40 000 000 cm³   J 1 000 000 cm³

C2 Change these volumes in m³ into cm³.

(a) 2 m³   (b) 34 m³   (c) 0.2 m³   (d) 0.04 m³

C3 Change these volumes in cm³ into m³.

(a) 7 000 000 cm³   (b) 90 000 000 cm³   (c) 1 500 000 cm³   (d) 600 000 cm³

The measurement system for the volume of solids is related to the system for liquids and the capacity of containers.

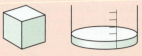

$1\,cm^3 = 1\,ml$ (millilitre)

C4 (a) Calculate the volume of this fish tank in cm^3.

(b) Write down the capacity of the tank in millilitres.

(c) Using the fact that 1 litre = 1000 ml, find the capacity of the tank in litres.

(d) Copy and complete this.

1 litre = ... cm^3

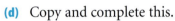

C5 Calculate the capacity in litres of each tank.

(a)

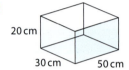

(b)

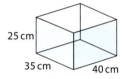

C6 A carton contains 1.5 litres of orange juice. What is this in cm^3?

C7 A pot contains 150 ml of yoghurt. What is this in cm^3?

Test yourself

T1 (a) Change $8\,m^2$ into cm^2. **(b)** Change $40\,000\,cm^2$ into m^2.

T2 (a) Change $12\,cm^2$ into mm^2. **(b)** Change $250\,mm^2$ into cm^2.

T3 (a) Change $5\,m^3$ into cm^3. **(b)** Change $6\,000\,000\,cm^3$ into m^3.

T4 Calculate the area of this rectangle. Give your answer in cm^2.

75 mm

52 mm

T5 (a) Calculate the volume of this tank in cm^3.

(b) How many litres of water does the tank hold when it is completely full?

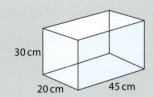

26 Trial and improvement

You should be able to substitute into expressions such as $x^3 + x$ and $x^3 - 2x$.

This work will help you solve equations using trial and improvement.

A Searching for an exact solution to an equation

Natasha and Pete are solving number puzzles.

I think of a positive number. I square it and then multiply by 3. The result is 675. What was my number?

I can write this as the equation $3x^2 = 675$ and then solve it by doing the same thing to each side.

Pete solves the equation $3x^2 = 675$ like this.

$$3x^2 = 675 \qquad [\div 3]$$
$$x^2 = 225 \qquad [\text{square root}]$$
$$x = \sqrt{225}$$
$$= 15$$

I think of a positive number. I cube it and then add it to itself. The result is 738. What was my number?

I can write this as the equation $x^3 + x = 738$ and then solve it by trial and improvement.

This table shows Natasha's first few trials.

- Carry on to find the number that Pete is thinking of.

x	$x^3 + x$	Comment
10	1010	Too high
5	130	Too low

- Why did Natasha use trial and improvement to solve the equation $x^3 + x = 738$?

Natasha used this key sequence to find the value of $x^3 + x$ when $x = 5$.

| 5 | x^y | 3 | + | 5 | = |

A1 (a) Find the value of $x^3 - x$ when (i) $x = 6$ (ii) $x = 15$

(b) Use trial and improvement to solve the equation $x^3 - x = 1716$.
Show all your trials in a table like this.

x	$x^3 - x$	Comment
6		

A2 Solve each of these equations by trial and improvement.

(a) $x^3 = 2197$ (b) $x^3 + x = 1740$ (c) $x^3 - x = 7980$ (d) $x^2 + 5x = 300$

(e) $2x^2 + 3x = 20$ (f) $x^3 + 7x = 160$ (g) $2x^2 - x = 36$ (h) $x + \dfrac{1}{x} = 10.1$

B Searching for an approximate solution to an equation

Sometimes an equation does not have an exact solution.
You can use trial and improvement to find an **approximate** solution.

Example

Use trial and improvement to find a solution to $x^3 + 5x = 100$.
Give the solution correct to one decimal place.

4 is too low.
5 is too high.
So try decimals in between.

4.3 is too high.
4.2 is too low.

We need to know which
value is closer to the
solution of the equation.

So try decimals in between.

x	$x^3 + 5x$	Comment
4	84	Too low
5	150	Too high
4.5	113.625	Too high
4.3	101.007	Too high
4.2	95.088	Too low
4.28	99.802 752	Too low
4.29	100.403 589	Too high

You can set up a
spreadsheet to solve
a problem like this.

4.28 is too low and 4.29 is too high so the decimal value for x begins 4.28…

So $x = 4.3$ to 1 d.p.

B1 Suneet is using trial and improvement to find a solution to the equation

$x^3 + x = 15$

This table shows his first two trials.

Copy and continue the table to find
a solution to the equation.
Give your answer to one decimal place.

x	$x^3 + x$	Comment
2	10	Too low
3	30	Too high

B2 Dean is using trial and improvement to find a solution to the equation

$x^3 + 3x = 200$

This table shows his first two trials.

Copy and continue the table to find
a solution to the equation.
Give your answer to one decimal place.

x	$x^3 + 3x$	Comment
5	140	Too low
6	234	Too high

B3 Karly is using trial and improvement to find a solution to the equation

$x^3 - 9x = 10$

This table shows her first two trials.

Copy and continue the table to find
a solution to the equation.
Give your answer to one decimal place.

x	$x^3 - 9x$	Comment
4	28	Too high
3	0	Too low

When solving an equation using trial and improvement, it often helps to show your working clearly in a table.

B4 The equation $x^3 + 2x = 25$ has a solution between 2 and 3.
Use trial and improvement to find this solution.
Give your answer to one decimal place.

B5 The equation $x^3 - 6x = 50$ has a solution between 4 and 5.
Use trial and improvement to find this solution, correct to one decimal place.

B6 The equation $x + \dfrac{1}{x} = 9$ has a solution between 8 and 9.
Use trial and improvement to find this solution, correct to one decimal place.

B7 **(a)** Find the value of $x^3 + 6x$ when   **(i)** $x = 3$ **(ii)** $x = 4$

    (b) **(i)**   Show that the equation $x^3 + 6x = 50$ has a solution between 3 and 4.

        (ii)   Use trial and improvement to find this solution, correct to one decimal place.

B8 The equation $x^3 - 5x = 30$ has a solution which is a positive number.
Use trial and improvement to find this solution, correct to one decimal place.

B9 Use trial and improvement to find the positive solution of $x^3 - 4x - 1 = 0$.
Give this solution correct to one decimal place.

B10 Use trial and improvement to find the value of x, correct to 1 d.p., when
$$x^3 + x^2 = 5$$

*B11 Use trial and improvement to solve $x^3 - 9x = 100$, giving the value of x to **2 d.p.**

Test yourself

T1 Parveen is using trial and improvement to find a solution to the equation
$$x^3 + 7x = 30$$
This table shows her first two trials.

Copy and continue the table to find a solution to the equation.
Give your answer to one decimal place.

x	$x^3 + 7x$	Comment
2	22	Too small
3	48	Too big

AQA

T2 The equation $x^3 - 2x = 67$ has a solution between 4 and 5.

Use trial and improvement to find this solution.
Give your answer correct to one decimal place.
You must show **all** your working.

Edexcel

T3 Use a trial and improvement method to find the value of x correct to **one** decimal place when $x^3 - 3x = 38$.

Show clearly your trials and their outcomes.

OCR

27 Pythagoras's theorem

This work will help you

- find the length of one side of a right-angled triangle if you know the lengths of the other two sides
- solve simple problems involving the lengths of the sides of a right-angled triangle
- find the distance between two points on a coordinate grid

You need a set square.

A Squares on right-angled triangles

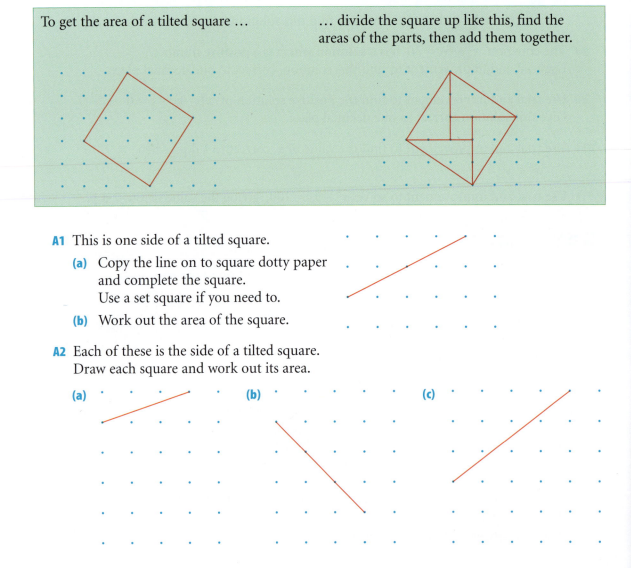

To get the area of a tilted square …

… divide the square up like this, find the areas of the parts, then add them together.

A1 This is one side of a tilted square.

   (a) Copy the line on to square dotty paper and complete the square.
Use a set square if you need to.

   (b) Work out the area of the square.

A2 Each of these is the side of a tilted square.
Draw each square and work out its area.

   (a)   **(b)**   **(c)**

The three squares Q, R and S are drawn on the sides of a right-angled triangle.

Copy the drawing on to dotty paper.
Find and record the area of each square.

Repeat this process for different right-angled triangles.
You could do this in a group, sharing out the work.

Square S must be on the side opposite the right angle.
Record your results in a table.

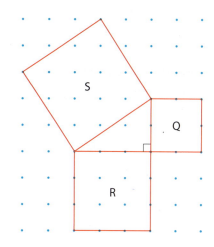

Area of square Q	Area of square R	Area of square S

What do you notice about the areas?

A3 Find the area of the largest square on each of these right-angled triangles.

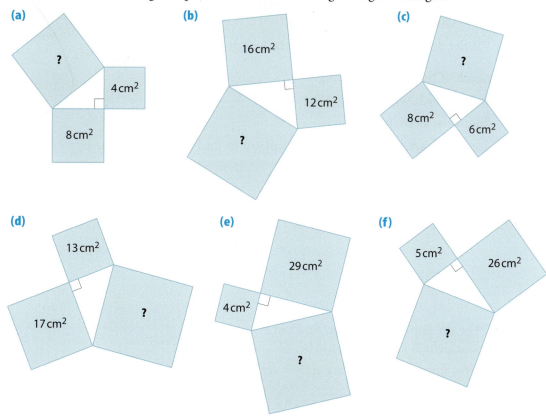

(a) ?   4 cm²   8 cm²

(b) 16 cm²   12 cm²   ?

(c) ?   8 cm²   6 cm²

(d) 13 cm²   17 cm²   ?

(e) 29 cm²   4 cm²   ?

(f) 5 cm²   26 cm²   ?

B Using Pythagoras to find the hypotenuse

In a right-angled triangle, the side opposite the right angle is called the **hypotenuse**.

You have found that the area of the square on the hypotenuse equals the total of the areas of the squares on the other two sides.

Here, area C = area A + area B

This is known as **Pythagoras's theorem** (or 'Pythagoras' for short). Pythagoras was a Greek mathematician and mystic. A theorem is a statement that can be proved true.

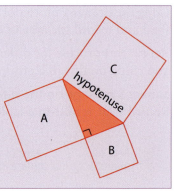

B1 (a) Sketch this triangle. Include the label 'hypotenuse'.

(b) Sketch a square on each side of the triangle.

(c) Work out the area of each of the smaller squares and write each area in the correct square.

(d) Calculate the area of the square on the hypotenuse and write it in.

(e) What do you need to do to find the length of the hypotenuse?

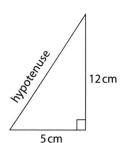

B2 For each of the following triangles,

- decide which side is the hypotenuse

- follow the steps in B1

- use the square root key on your calculator to find the length of the hypotenuse

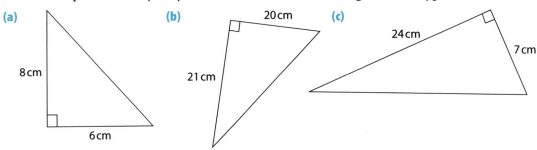

(a) 8 cm, 6 cm

(b) 20 cm, 21 cm

(c) 24 cm, 7 cm

B3 (a) Use the approach of B2 to find out what length side LN should be.

(b) Now draw the triangle accurately with a ruler and set square.
Measure the length of LN and check whether it agrees with the length you calculated.

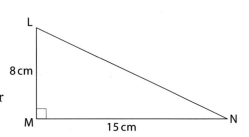

You don't have to draw squares on the sides of a right-angled triangle to use Pythagoras's theorem so long as you set your working out clearly.

Example

Find the length of the hypotenuse in this triangle.

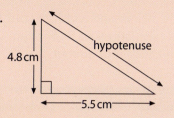

Calculate the area of the square on one of the smaller sides … $4.8 \times 4.8 = 23.04$

… then calculate the area of the square on the other smaller side. $5.5 \times 5.5 = 30.25$

Add these areas to find the area of the square on the hypotenuse. $23.04 + 30.25 = 53.29$

$\sqrt{53.29} = 7.3$

So the hypotenuse is 7.3 cm long.

Always check your answer is sensible: the hypotenuse should be the longest side; but it should not be longer than the sum of the other two sides.

B4 Find the length of the hypotenuse in each of these triangles.

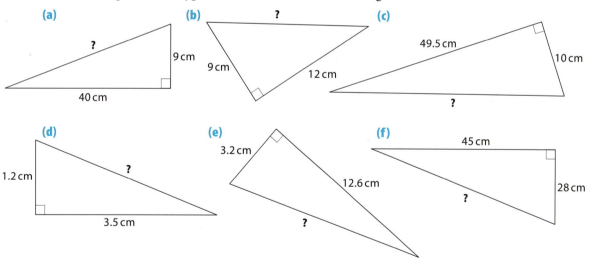

B5 Find the length of the hypotenuse in each of these triangles, rounding each answer to one decimal place.

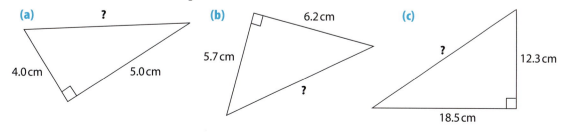

B6 A certain exercise book is 14.0 cm wide by 20.0 cm high.

  (a) How long is the longest straight line you can draw on a single page of the book?

  (b) How long is the longest straight line you can draw on a double page?

B7 Measure the height and width of your own exercise book.
Repeat the calculations in B6 for your own book.
Measure to check your answers.

C Distance between two points on a coordinate grid

T Points A and B are plotted on a coordinate grid that has centimetre squares.

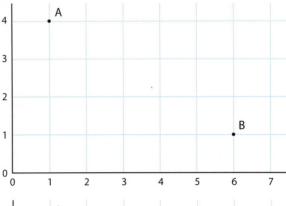

We can add a right-angled triangle to the diagram like this. Line segment AB is the hypotenuse of this triangle.

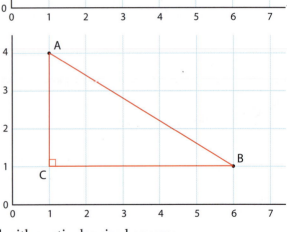

- What length is AC?
- What length is CB?
- Use Pythagoras to find length AB to 1 d.p.
- Check by measuring.

If the coordinates we are given are not for a grid with particular sized squares,
we can give distances in 'units' – for example '5 units' instead of '5 centimetres'.

C1 (a) Copy these axes on to squared paper and plot points P and Q carefully.

  (b) Add a right-angled triangle that has line segment PQ as its hypotenuse. Label the lengths of the two shorter sides of the triangle.

  (c) Calculate the length of PQ to 1 d.p.

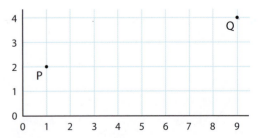

C2 Plot the points (6, 1) and (10, 7) on a coordinate grid.
Use the method of C1 to find the distance between the two points, to 1 d.p.

C3 Calculate the distance between each of these pairs of points, to 1 d.p.
Either draw on squared paper or make a sketch, labelling lengths you need.

(a) $(5, 2)$ and $(2, 5)$ (b) $(3, 0)$ and $(5, 7)$ (c) $(6, 5)$ and $(7, 2)$

***C4** Find the distance between each of these pairs of points, to 1 d.p.

(a) $(^-1, 2)$ and $(2, 1)$ (b) $(3, 2)$ and $(1, ^-1)$ (c) $(^-2, 1)$ and $(2, ^-4)$

D Using Pythagoras to find one of the shorter sides of the triangle

D1 In these diagrams, the area of one of the **smaller** squares is missing.
Find the area marked ? in each case.

(a)
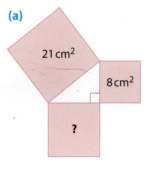

(b)
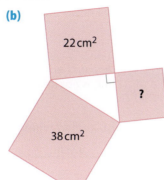

(c)
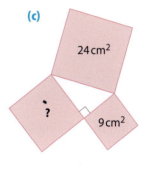

(d)
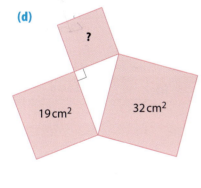

(e)
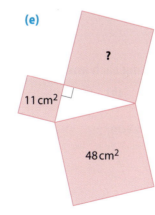

(f)
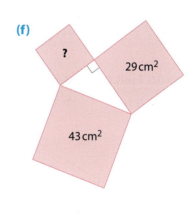

D2 In this right-angled triangle, the length of one of
the shorter sides is missing.

(a) What is the area of square A (the square on
the hypotenuse)?

(b) What is the area of square B?

(c) So what is the area of square C?

(d) Use the square root key on your calculator to
find the missing length.

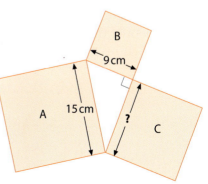

You can use Pythagoras to find one of the shorter sides of a right-angled triangle.

Example

Find the length marked ? in this triangle.

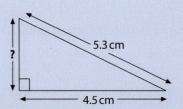

Calculate the area of the square on the hypotenuse … $5.3 \times 5.3 = 28.09$

… then find the area of the square on the smaller side that's given. $4.5 \times 4.5 = 20.25$

Subtract to find the area of the square on the unknown smaller side. $28.09 - 20.25 = 7.84$

$\sqrt{7.84} = 2.8$

So the side is 2.8 cm long.

Again, check that the hypotenuse is the longest side, but is not longer than the sum of the other two sides.

D3 Find the missing lengths in these right-angled triangles.

(a)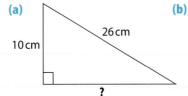

(b)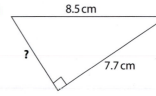

(c)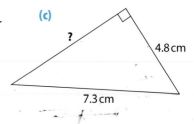

D4 Find the missing lengths, giving each answer to 1 d.p.

(a)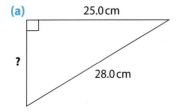

(b)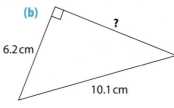

(c)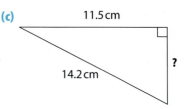

D5 A ladder 3.6 m long rests against a vertical wall. The foot of the ladder is 1.4 m away from the bottom of the wall, on horizontal ground. How far up the wall is the top of the ladder?

D6 The sloping section of this escalator is 12.0 metres long.
It rises by 6.9 metres.
Calculate a, the horizontal distance travelled.

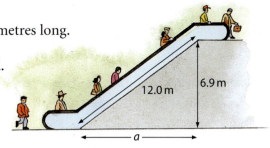

12.0 m

6.9 m

a

Test yourself

T1 Find the length of the hypotenuse in each of these right-angled triangles.
Round to one decimal place where necessary.

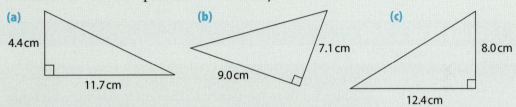

(a) 4.4 cm   11.7 cm

(b) 7.1 cm   9.0 cm

(c) 8.0 cm   12.4 cm

T2 Find the missing side in each of these right-angled triangles.
Round to one decimal place where necessary.

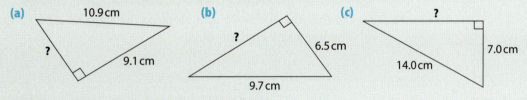

(a) 10.9 cm   ?   9.1 cm

(b) ?   6.5 cm   9.7 cm

(c) ?   14.0 cm   7.0 cm

T3 Points P and Q are on a coordinate grid of
centimetre squares.
Calculate the distance in a straight line
between P and Q. Show your working and
give your answer to two decimal places.

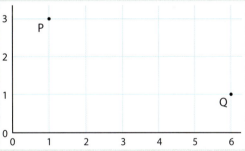

T4 Find the distance between points $(1, 0)$ and $(6, 4)$, to 1 d.p.

T5 A kite string is fixed to horizontal ground at point P.
The length of the string from P to the kite is 32 metres.
The kite is 19 metres above the ground.
Naomi is exactly under the kite.
How far is Naomi from point P?

P   Naomi

T6 Cheryl walks 77 metres due north, then 36 metres due west.
How far is she from where she started?

28 Gradients and straight-line graphs

You should know how to draw the graph of a linear equation such as $y = 2x - 5$.

This work will help you find

- the gradient of a straight line that you have been given
- the gradient of a straight-line graph from its equation
- where a straight line crosses the y-axis from its equation
- the equation of a straight-line graph that you have been given

You need sheets F2–12, F2–13 and F2–14.

A Gradient of a line

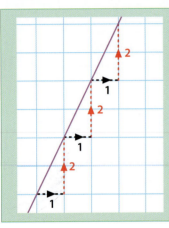

We can make 'steps' along a straight line by
going **1** unit to the right and then up to the line each time.

We call the height of these steps the **gradient** of the line.
It is a measure of how steep the line is.

> On this line, for every unit along to the right we go up **2** units.
> The line has a gradient of **2**.

A1 (a) Find the gradient of each line in the diagram below.

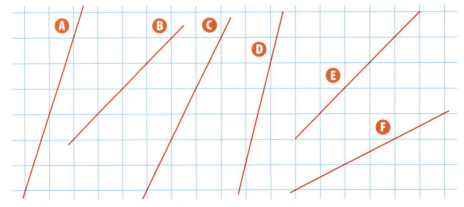

(b) Which is the steepest line?

(c) Which two lines are parallel?

You need sheet F2–12 for questions A2 to A5.

A2 (a) Copy and complete this table for the equation $y = 2x$.

x	-1	0	1	2	3	4
y	-2					8

(b) Draw the graph of $y = 2x$ on diagram A.

(c) What is the gradient of this line?

A3 (a) Copy and complete this table for the equation $y = 3x$.

x	-1	0	1	2	3	4
y				6		

(b) Draw the graph of $y = 3x$ on diagram B.

(c) What is the gradient of this line?

A4 (a) Draw the graph of $y = x$ on diagram C.

(b) What is the gradient of this line?

A5 (a) Copy and complete this table for the equation $y = \frac{1}{2}x$.

x	-1	0	1	2	3	4
y	$-\frac{1}{2}$	0	$\frac{1}{2}$			

(b) Draw the graph of $y = \frac{1}{2}x$ on diagram D.

(c) What is the gradient of this line?

A6 What is the equation of this line?

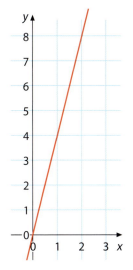

*A7 What is the equation of this line?

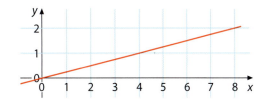

The line $y = 2x - 1$ is shown on the right.

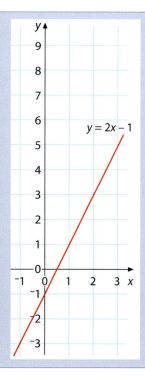

- Copy the diagram.

- Add the lines with equations $y = 2x$ and $y = 2x + 3$ to your diagram. Label each line with its equation.

- What is the gradient of each line?

- Where does each line cross the y-axis?

- What do you notice? Can you explain it?

B1 On squared paper, draw axes with x going from $^-1$ to 3 and y going from $^-4$ to 14. Use the same scale on each axis.

Draw all three graphs in this question on these axes.

x	$^-1$	0	1	2	3
y					

(a) **(i)** Copy and complete the table above for the equation $y = 3x + 5$.

  (ii) Draw and label the graph of $y = 3x + 5$.

(b) Copy and complete the table above for $y = 3x + 2$. Draw and label its graph.

(c) Copy and complete the table above for $y = 3x - 1$. Draw and label its graph.

(d) What is the gradient of each line?

(e) Where does each line cross the y-axis?

(f) What do you notice?

B2 On squared paper, draw axes with x going from $^-1$ to 3 and y going from $^-4$ to 9. Use the same scale on each axis.

Draw all three graphs in this question on these axes.

x	$^-1$	0	1	2	3
y					

- **(a)** **(i)** Copy and complete the table above for the equation $y = x + 6$.
  - **(ii)** Draw the graph of $y = x + 6$.
- **(b)** Copy and complete the table above for $y = x + 2$ and draw its graph.
- **(c)** Copy and complete the table above for $y = x - 3$ and draw its graph.
- **(d)** What is the gradient of each line?
- **(e)** Where does each line cross the y-axis?
- **(f)** What do you notice?

The equation of any straight line can be written in the form

$$y = \blacksquare x + \blacksquare \quad \text{or} \quad y = \blacksquare x - \blacksquare$$

where the boxes contain any numbers.

- The number in the first box is the gradient of the line.

  For example, the line with equation $y = 4x + 5$ has a gradient of 4.

- The number in the second box and the sign next to it tell you where the line crosses the y-axis.

  For example, the line with equation $y = 6x - 3$ crosses the y-axis at $^-3$.

B3 What is the gradient of the line with equation $y = 6x + 1$?

B4 **(a)** Where does the line with equation $y = 2x + 9$ cross the y-axis?
- **(b)** Where does the line with equation $y = x - 10$ cross the y-axis?

B5 Which of these lines is parallel to $y = 2x$?

A $y = x + 2$ **B** $y = x - 2$ **C** $y = 3x + 2$ **D** $y = 2x + 5$

B6 A straight line has the equation $y = 3x - 8$.
- **(a)** What is its gradient?
- **(b)** Where does it cross the y-axis?

*B7 A straight line has the equation $y = 1 + 7x$.
- **(a)** What is its gradient?
- **(b)** Where does it cross the y-axis?

C Finding the equation of a straight-line graph

We can use the connection between the equation of a line, its gradient and where it crosses the y-axis to work out the equation of a line we have been given.

Examples

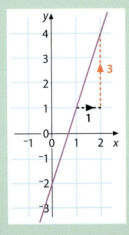

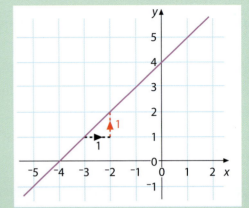

The gradient is 3.
The line crosses the y-axis at $^-2$.
So the equation of the line is $y = 3x - 2$.

The gradient is 1.
The line crosses the y-axis at 4.
So the equation of the line is $y = 1x + 4$.
We usually write this as $y = x + 4$.

C1 Find the equation of each line below.

(a)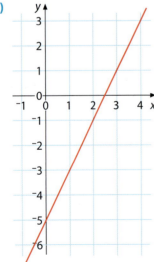

(b)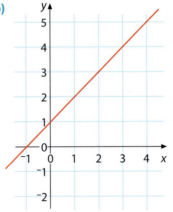

(c)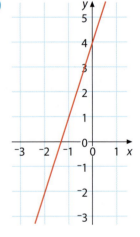

Sometimes the scales on the axes are not the same.

For this graph, for each unit to the right we go up 2 units each time.

This line has a gradient of 2.
It crosses the y-axis at 4.

The equation of the line is $y = 2x + 4$.

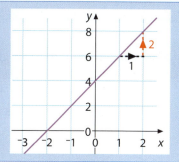

C2 (a) Where does this line cross the y-axis?

(b) Find its gradient.

(c) Which of these is its equation?

$$y = 2x + 1 \qquad y = 10x + 2$$

$$y = x + 2 \qquad y = 4x + 2$$

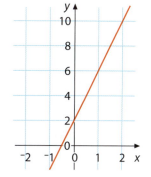

C3 Find the equation of this line.

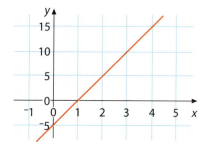

One way to find the gradient of this line is to

- pick two suitable points and use them to draw a triangle as shown
- divide the height by the length of the base to get $\frac{12}{4} = 3$

So the gradient of the line is 3.

The line crosses the y-axis at 2.

Hence the equation of the line is $y = 3x + 2$.

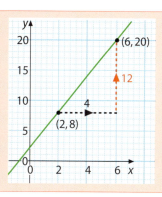

C4 This question is on sheet F2–13.

C5 This question is on sheet F2–14.

*C6 Find the equation of the straight line that passes through the points ($^-4$, 0) and (2, 12).

T

A line that slopes **down** from left to right has a **negative** gradient.

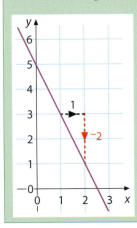

On this line, for each unit to the right, we go **down** 2 units.
This line has a gradient of $^-2$.

The line crosses the y-axis at 5.

So the equation of the line is $y = {}^-2x + 5$.
This can be written as $y = 5 - 2x$.

• Pick a point on the line.
  Check that its coordinates fit the equations
  $y = {}^-2x + 5$ and $y = 5 - 2x$.

D1 Find the equation of each line below.

(a)

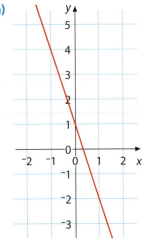

(b)

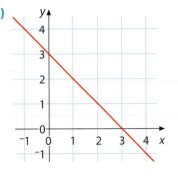

(c)

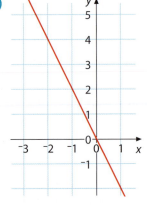

D2 A straight line has the equation $y = {}^-4x + 6$.

    (a) What is its gradient?   **(b)** Where does it cross the y-axis?

D3 A straight line has the equation $y = 9 - 5x$.

    (a) What is its gradient?   **(b)** Where does it cross the y-axis?

*D4 What is the gradient of the straight line with equation $y + 2x = 5$?

*D5 Find the equation of the straight line that passes through
    the points $(^-2, 4)$ and $(8, ^-1)$.

Test yourself

T1 Find the equation of each line below.

(a)
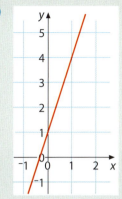

(b)
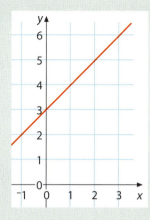

(c)
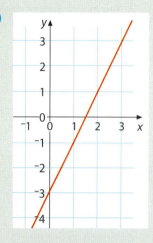

T2 A straight line has the equation $y = 5x - 2$.

    (a) What is its gradient?   **(b)** Where does it cross the y-axis?

T3 Give the equation of any straight line parallel to $y = 7x + 1$.

T4 Find the equation of this line.

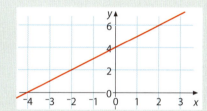

T5 Here are four equations of straight lines.

$$y = {}^-2x + 3 \qquad y = {}^-3x + 2 \qquad y = 2x - 3 \qquad y = 3x + 2$$

The graphs below show two of these lines.
Write the correct equation for each graph.

(a)
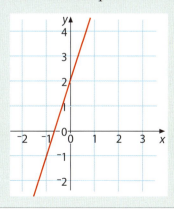

(b)
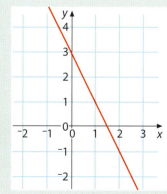

OCR

Review 4

You need a pair of compasses and an angle measurer.

1 Convert $2\frac{3}{4}$ kilograms into grams.

2 (a) Write down the next two numbers in this sequence.

   4, 7, 10, 13, …

(b) Another sequence of numbers begins 4, 7, 13, …
   The rule for continuing the sequence is

   Multiply by 2 and then subtract 1

   What are the next two numbers in the sequence?

3 Work out 15% of £60.

4 Which is greater, 2^3 or $\sqrt{50}$? Show your working clearly.

5 Here is a rough sketch of a triangle.

(a) Use a ruler and compasses to construct
   the triangle accurately.

(b) Calculate the area of the triangle.
   Show clearly the measurements you use.
   Remember to include the units in your answer.

(c) Measure the size of angle PQR in degrees.

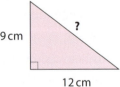

6 Rearrange the formula $v = 7h - 9$ to make h the subject.

7 Find the missing length in this right-angled triangle.

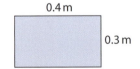

8 Find the area of this rectangle
   (a) in m^2 **(b)** in cm^2

9 For each of these sequences,

   • describe a rule to go from one term to the next

   • find the next term

   (a) 2, 9, 16, 23, …   **(b)** 2, 6, 18, 54, …   **(c)** 64, 32, 16, 8, …

10 Find the cube root of 343.

11 This graph shows Karen's journey to school. She walks to a bus stop, waits for a bus, then a bus takes her the rest of the way to school.

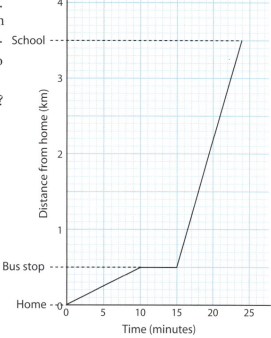

   (a) How far does Karen walk from home to the bus stop?

   (b) How long does she wait at the bus stop?

   (c) How far does the bus take her?

   (d) How long does the bus journey take?

   (e) Karen left home at 08:10.
   What time did she arrive at school?

12 Calculate the length AB.
Give your answer to one decimal place.

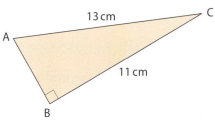

13 (a) Copy and complete the formula below for the perimeter of this triangle.

$$P = \ldots$$

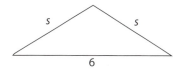

   (b) Rearrange the formula to make s the subject.

   (c) Use your rearranged formula to find the length s when the perimeter is 15 cm.

14 The diagram shows 5 cubes.
Vertex O is at the origin.
Vertex P has coordinates (0, 2, 1).

Write down the coordinates of vertices A, B and C.

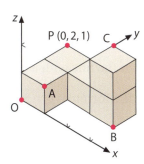

15 A box in the shape of a cuboid measures 30 cm by 50 cm by 90 cm.
Work out the volume of the box in

    (a) cm^3 **(b)** m^3

16 (a) Complete the table of values for $y = x^2 - 6$.

x	⁻3	⁻2	⁻1	0	1	2	3
y		⁻2	⁻5	⁻6	⁻5		3

    (b) On a set of axes like this, draw the graph of $y = x^2 - 6$ for values of x from ⁻3 to 3.

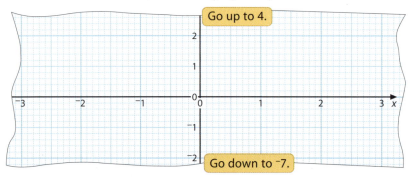

    (c) Use the graph to solve $x^2 - 6 = 0$.

17 P is the point $(5, 6)$.
Q is the point $(⁻3, 2)$.
Find the coordinates of the mid-point of the line PQ.

18 A line has equation $y = 4x - 7$.

    (a) Write down the gradient of this line.

    (b) Where does the line cross the y-axis?

19 Use trial and improvement to complete
the table to find a solution to the equation

    $x^3 - 5x = 30$

Give your answer to one decimal place.

x	$x^3 - 5x$	Comment
3	12	Too low
4	44	Too high

20 (a) Change $60\,000\,cm^2$ to m^2.

    (b) Change $2.5\,m^3$ to cm^3.

21 What is the equation of the line with a gradient of 2 that crosses the y-axis at $(0, 5)$?

22 Make t the subject of the formula $p = 5t + q$.

23 A carton in the shape of a cuboid measures 5 cm by 10 cm by 30 cm.
Find the capacity of the carton in litres.

29 Statements about different types of number

You should

- be able to substitute into expressions such as $p + q$ and $\frac{p}{q}$

- know about different types of number (integers, odds, evens, multiples, primes …)

This work will help you decide when general statements about numbers are true.

A Integers

If a and b can be any integers, which of these are

- always an integer
- sometimes an integer
- never an integer

A $a + b$ **B** $a - b$ **C** $2a$ **D** $\frac{a}{2}$ **E** ab

F a^2 **G** $\frac{a}{b}$ **H** $\sqrt{a}$ **I** $\frac{1}{a}$

A1 Which of these statements are true?

 A If you add 5 to an integer, you always get another integer.

 B If you take 5 from an integer, you always get another integer.

 C If you multiply an integer by 5, you always get another integer.

 D If you divide an integer by 5, you always get another integer.

A2 If n can be each any positive integer, decide which of these are always a positive integer.

 A $n + 3$ **B** $n - 10$ **C** $4n$ **D** $\frac{n}{4}$ **E** n^2

A3 If a and b can each be any positive integer, decide whether each of these is

- always a positive integer
- sometimes a positive integer
- never a positive integer

 (a) $a + b$ **(b)** $a - b$ **(c)** ab **(d)** $\frac{a}{b}$ **(e)** $3(a + b)$

A4 If N can be any negative integer, decide whether each of these is

- always a negative integer
- sometimes a negative integer
- never a negative integer

 (a) $N - 1$ **(b)** $N + 3$ **(c)** N^2 **(d)** $3N$ **(e)** $\frac{N}{2}$

*A5 If x is a negative integer, will $10 - x$ be negative or positive?

B Evens and odds

Which word, **even** or **odd**, completes each statement?

- Any two even numbers always add to give an .... number.
- Any two odd numbers always multiply to give an .... number.
- An even and an odd number always multiply to give an .... number.

B1 Which word, **even** or **odd**, completes each statement to make it true?

    (a) Any two odd numbers always add to give an .... number.

    (b) Any even number added to any odd number always gives an .... number.

    (c) Any two even numbers always multiply to give an .... number.

B2 Peter thinks of an odd number.
He multiplies it by 7 and adds 1.
Is his answer odd or even?

B3 E is an even number.
Decide whether each of these is

- always even
- always odd
- sometimes even and sometimes odd

    (a) $E + 4$ **(b)** $E - 1$ **(c)** $\frac{1}{2}E$ **(d)** E^2 **(e)** $3E + 1$

B4 Donna thinks of an even number.
She squares it and adds 1.
Is her answer odd or even?

B5 O is an odd number.
Is it true that $O + 1$ is even?

B6 P is an odd number.
Q is an even number.

Decide whether these statements are true or false.

    (a) $P + Q$ is odd.   **(b)** $P^2 - 1$ is odd.

    (c) $P + Q + 1$ is odd.   **(d)** $2P + Q$ is odd.

B7 Rory says, 'If P is an odd number then $\dfrac{P + 1}{2}$ is always even.'
Give an example to show that he is wrong.

B8 Preeti says, 'If N is an even number then $\dfrac{N + 1}{3}$ is always an integer.'
Give an example to show that she is wrong.

C Multiples and primes

N is a positive integer.

Which word, **always**, **sometimes** or **never**, completes each statement?

- $3N$ is .... a multiple of 3.
- $2N - 1$ is .... a prime number.
- $3N + 5$ is .... a multiple of 4.
- N^2 is .... a prime number.

C1 N is a positive integer.
Which word, **always**, **sometimes** or **never**, completes each statement?

(a) $6N$ is .... odd.

(b) $10N$ is .... a multiple of 5.

(c) $4N$ is .... a prime number.

(d) $N^2 + 1$ is .... a prime number.

C2 Stacey says, 'Any two even numbers added together always give a multiple of 4.'
Give an example to show that Stacey is wrong.

C3 Kim says, 'All prime numbers are odd.'
Show that she is wrong.

C4 For each statement, give an example to show that it is wrong.

(a) Any even number added to any odd number always gives a prime number.

(b) For any whole number n, the value of $4n - 1$ is always a prime number.

(c) For all whole numbers n, the value of $2n$ is never a prime number.

*C5 E is an even number.
Is it true that $5E$ is always a multiple of 10?

Test yourself

T1 N is a negative number.
Is N^2 positive or negative? Explain your answer. OCR

T2 Sophie says, 'For any whole number, n, the value of $6n - 1$ is always a prime number.'
Sophie is wrong.
Give an example to show that Sophie is wrong. Edexcel

T3 (a) k is an even number.
Jo says that $\frac{1}{2}k + 1$ is always even.
Give an example to show that Jo is wrong.

(b) The letters a and b represent prime numbers.
Give an example to show that $a + b$ is **not** always an even number. AQA

30 Loci and constructions

This work will help you

- understand and use the idea of a locus (a set of points that follow some rule)
- do formal constructions using a straight edge and compasses only

You need coloured counters, a pair of compasses, an angle measurer and a set square.

You need sheet F2–15.

A Points a given distance from a point or from a line

T Put a red counter near the centre of a table.

Now put a different-coloured counter 15 cm from the red counter.

- Put more counters in other positions 15 cm from the red counter. What shape do they make?
- If you had to put a coin **less than 15 cm** from the red counter, what area would the coin need to go in?
- If you had to put a coin **more than 15 cm** from the red counter, where could the coin go?

Take the counters off the table.

Choose one edge of the table.

Put one counter 20 cm from this edge.

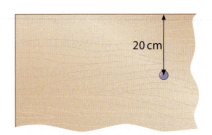

20 cm

- Put more counters in other positions 20 cm from this edge. What do they make?
- If you had to put a coin **less than 20 cm** from this edge, what area would the coin need to go in?
- If you had to put a coin **more than 20 cm** from this edge, where could the coin go?

Keep the counters on the table.

Choose a corner at one end of the edge you have been using.

Put a counter 30 cm from this corner.

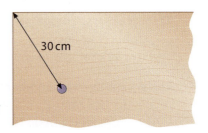

30 cm

- Put more counters in other positions 30 cm from this corner. What shape do they make?
- You are told that a counter has to be 30 cm from this corner **and** 20 cm from the edge you have been using. Where must the counter go?

A1 Sheet F2–15 has a plan of a field, drawn to a scale of 1 cm to 1 metre.

(a) A spy has left a message giving clues about where he has buried a radio transmitter in the field.

> The transmitter is 9 metres from corner B.
>
> It is 5 metres from the fence AD.

(i) Use a pair of compasses to show all the possible places given by this clue.

(ii) Use a ruler and set square to show all the possible places given by this clue.

(iii) Put a cross where the transmitter is buried and label it 'transmitter'.

(iv) How far in metres is the transmitter from corner A?

(b)
> A DVD containing plans of a secret installation is buried 2 metres from fence DC and 6 metres from fence BC.

Use a ruler and set square to find where the DVD is buried. Label it. Leave your pencil marks to show how you found the place.

(c)
> A microchip that encrypts messages is buried 12 metres from corner B and 13 metres from corner D. That should be enough information to find it.

Well no, actually. Use compasses to find **two** possible places where the microchip could be. Label them. Do not rub out the marks you made with your compasses.

(d)
> To be honest, I've forgotten exactly where I buried the truth drug but I know it was not more than 2.5 metres from fence AB.

Shade the area where the truth drug could be.

A set of points that follow a certain rule is called a **locus**. (The plural is **loci**.)

The lines, arcs and area you marked in question A1 are all loci.

A2 Draw this plan of a garden to a suitable scale.

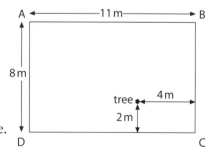

(a) Grass has to be at least 3 metres from the tree. Shade the area of the garden where grass can be.

(b) A bird table will be put in the garden 4 metres from corner A and 3 metres from the wall AD. Show where the bird table must go. Do not rub out the pencil marks you need to make.

A3 Use compasses to draw a triangle with these measurements accurately.

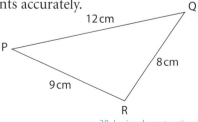

(a) Shade the locus of points in the triangle that are less than 5 cm from P.

(b) Draw the locus of points in the triangle that are 2 cm from QR.

A4 This is a triangular plot of land.
There is an electrical cable running along PQ
and a radio mast at the point R.

It is dangerous for a person to be within 10 m of the cable
or within 20 m of the mast.

Draw the triangle to scale and shade the region where
it is safe to be.

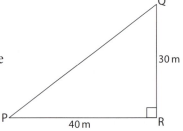

B Points the same distance from two points or from two lines

Put two red counters near the centre of the table, roughly
30 cm apart.

Now place a different-coloured counter so it is the same distance
from each of the red counters.

- Put down more counters that are the same distance from
  both red counters. Describe fully the locus that they lie on.

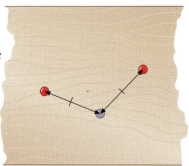

Take the counters off the table.

Choose a corner of the table. Two edges meet there.

Place a counter so it is the same distance from both edges.

- Put down more counters that are the same distance from
  both edges. Describe fully the locus that they lie on.

On a large sheet of paper draw an angle of 70° with long 'arms'.

Place a counter so it is the same distance from both arms
of the angle.

- Put down more counters that are the same distance from
  both arms. Describe fully the locus that they lie on.
- What would the locus be if you had used a 40° angle?
- What would it be if the angle was 120°?

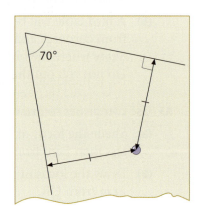

Here are ways of drawing the two types of locus you've met in the previous activities.

The locus of points that are the same distance from two given points A and B

- Draw the line segment AB.
- Measure its length and mark a point halfway along it.
- The required locus is a line drawn through this point at right angles to AB.

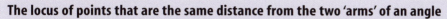

We call this line the **perpendicular bisector** of AB.

The locus of points that are the same distance from the two 'arms' of an angle

- Measure the angle.
- Halve the angle and use an angle measurer to draw a line that goes through the vertex of the angle and divides the angle in half.
- This is the required locus.

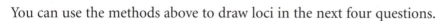

We say this line **bisects** the angle (or that it is the **bisector** of the angle).

You can use the methods above to draw loci in the next four questions.

However, it is possible to draw both types of locus using a straight edge and compasses only, without measuring with a ruler or angle measurer. The methods (called **constructions**) are shown in the first part of the next section. You may be asked to use them in GCSE questions.

B1 This is a plan of a rectangular garden surrounded by fencing. Draw the plan to a suitable scale.

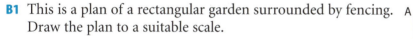

(a) A tree is to be planted in the garden.
Esther wants it planted so it is the same distance from fence AD as it is from fence DC.
Draw the locus of where Esther wants it planted.

(b) Roshan wants the tree planted so it is the same distance from corner A as it is from corner D.
Draw the locus of where Roshan wants it planted.

(c) Where can the tree be planted to satisfy both Esther and Roshan?

B2 Draw this triangle exactly.

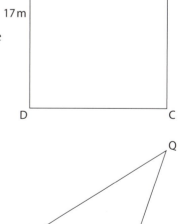

(a) Draw the locus of points that are the same distance from side QP as from side QR.

(b) Draw the locus of points that are the same distance from side PR as from side QR.

(c) Where is the point that is the same distance from all three sides?

B3 This is a plan of a field in the shape of a trapezium.
It has a hedge around it.
Draw the plan to scale.

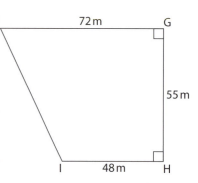

(a) Draw the locus of points that are the same distance from corner F as from corner I.

(b) Draw the locus of points that are the same distance from hedge FG as from hedge FI.

(c) Shade the locus of points that are closer to hedge FG than to hedge FI.

The word **equidistant** means 'the same distance'.

B4 Use a ruler and compasses to draw this triangle exactly.

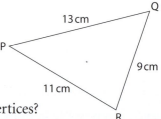

(a) Draw the locus of points that are equidistant from vertex P and vertex Q.

(b) Draw the locus of points that are equidistant from vertices P and R.

(c) Where is the point that is equidistant from all three vertices?

C Formal constructions with straight edge and compasses

In these constructions you are only allowed to use a pair of compasses and a ruler.
And you may only use the ruler to draw lines (as a **straight edge**): you are not
allowed to measure with it. Do not rub out the arcs and lines you draw.

Constructing the perpendicular bisector of a line segment

1 Draw a line segment. Draw an arc about this big with its centre at one end of the segment.

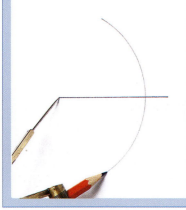

2 Keep your compasses the same radius. Draw an arc with its centre at the other end of the segment.

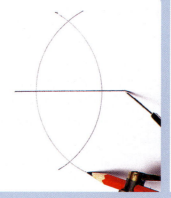

3 Draw a line through the points where the the two arcs cross. This is the perpendicular bisector of the original segment.

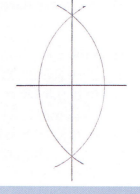

C1 Draw this rectangle accurately.
Construct the perpendicular bisector of the line AC using ruler and compasses only.
Show, by shading, the locus of points within the rectangle that are closer to point A than to point C.

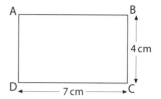

C2 Draw a circle and mark two points U and V inside it.
Show how to find a point on the circle equidistant from U and V.
How many such points are there?

Bisecting an angle

1 Draw an arc with its centre at the vertex of the angle.

2 Draw two arcs with the same radius from the points where your first arc crosses the arms of the angle.

3 Draw the line that bisects the angle.

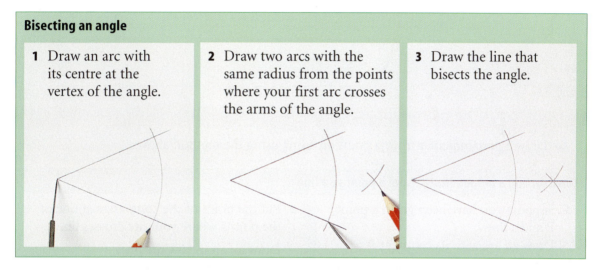

C3 Construct an angle of 45° by

(a) drawing a line segment and constructing its perpendicular bisector

(b) bisecting one of the 90° angles

C4 Construct an angle of 30° by

(a) constructing an equilateral triangle with compasses to get angles of 60°

(b) bisecting one of the 60° angles

C5 Describe how you could construct an angle of 15°.

Constructions using only compasses and the straight edge of a ruler are a kind of challenge, rather than the most efficient way of doing things.

Plainly you can construct a quarter, an eighth, a sixteenth … of any angle by repeated bisection. But people argued for years about whether it was possible to construct a third of any angle (not just a special angle like 90°) using only compasses and straight edge. Eventually this was proved impossible.

Drawing a perpendicular from a point on a line

P is a point on line *l*. Follow this construction to draw a line from P perpendicular to *l*.

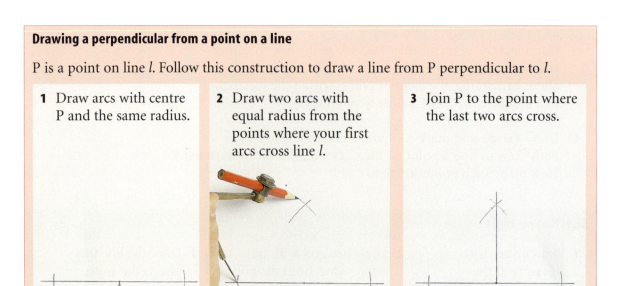

1 Draw arcs with centre P and the same radius.

2 Draw two arcs with equal radius from the points where your first arcs cross line *l*.

3 Join P to the point where the last two arcs cross.

C6 Draw a perpendicular from a point on a line using the method above.

Constructing a perpendicular from a point to a line

1 Suppose you have been given a point P and a line *l*.
Draw an arc with its centre at P, crossing line *l*.

2 Put the point of the compasses at one of the points where your arc crosses line *l*.

Draw an arc below the line.
You need not use the same radius as before.

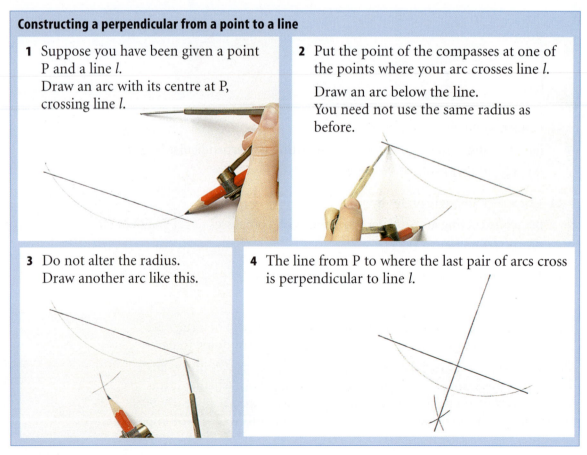

3 Do not alter the radius. Draw another arc like this.

4 The line from P to where the last pair of arcs cross is perpendicular to line *l*.

C7 Draw a perpendicular from a point to a line using the method above.

Test yourself

T1 A goat in a field is attached to a rope 3 metres long. On the other end of the rope is a ring that can slide along a horizontal bar 5 metres long.

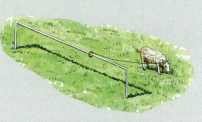

Draw a plan view to a scale of 1 centimetre to 1 metre, representing the bar by a straight line. Shade where the goat can graze, showing the boundary clearly.

T2 Draw this plan of a walled garden to a suitable scale.

(a) A sundial is to be placed 2 m from wall PQ. Draw the locus of where the sundial could go.

(b) The sundial is also required to be the same distance from corner P as it is from corner R. Draw the locus of points that meet this requirement.

(c) Put a cross at the point that meets both requirements.

(d) A bird bath is to be placed not more than 3 m from corner R. Show the locus of where it could go.

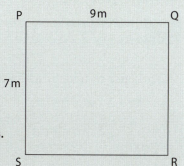

T3 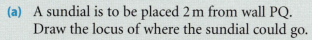 A monkey can reach out 50 cm from the bars that go all round its cage.

Draw the plan of the cage to scale. Shade the ground outside the cage that the monkey can reach.

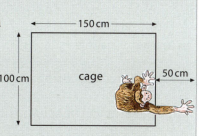

T4 In both parts of this question, do not rub out your construction lines.

(a) Construct accurately triangle ABC when

AB = 8.4 cm, ABC = 74° and AC = 9.7 cm.

(b) Using ruler and compasses only, construct the perpendicular bisector of BC.   OCR

T5 Draw a trapezium with these measurements accurately. Use construction with a straight edge and compasses only to show the following loci. Do not rub out any construction lines or arcs.

(a) The locus of points equidistant from sides KL and KN

(b) The locus of points closer to side LM than to side KL

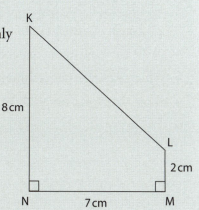

31 Sequences

You should be able to follow a rule to continue a sequence.

This work will help you

- find a rule for the *n*th pattern in a sequence and show it is true by analysing the pattern
- use a rule for the *n*th term to find terms in a sequence
- find a rule for the *n*th term of any linear sequence

A Finding a rule for the *n*th pattern in a sequence

A sequence of matchstick patterns begins like this.

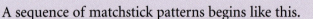

Pattern 1   Pattern 2   Pattern 3   Pattern 4   ......

The number of matches used in each pattern can be shown in a table.

Pattern number	1	2	3	4	5	6
Number of matches	4	7	10			

- What are the missing numbers in the table?

The patterns can be split up like this.

Pattern **1**   Pattern **2**   Pattern **3**   Pattern **4**

      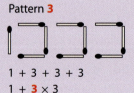   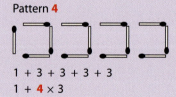

1 + 3   1 + 3 + 3   1 + 3 + 3 + 3   1 + 3 + 3 + 3 + 3
1 + **1** × 3   1 + **2** × 3   1 + **3** × 3   1 + **4** × 3

So the number of matches in pattern *n* is $1 + n \times 3$.
This is usually written as $3n + 1$.

- Work out how many matches you would need for pattern 10.
- Which pattern uses 301 matches?
- Show that you cannot make a pattern in this sequence that uses 60 matches.

A1 Here are some patterns made from matchsticks.

Pattern 1   Pattern 2   Pattern 3   Pattern 4   ......

(a) Copy and complete the table for this sequence.

Pattern number	1	2	3	4	5	6
Number of matches	6	11	16			

(b) Pattern 4 can be split up like this.

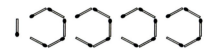

(i) Think about pattern 10 split up in the same way.
How many of these  would there be?

(ii) How many matches would there be altogether in pattern 10?

(c) How many matches are there in pattern 20?

(d) Which of these expressions gives the number of matches in pattern *n*?

$n + 1$	$n + 5$	$5n$	$5n + 1$

A2 Here is a sequence of matchstick diagrams.

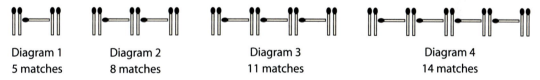

Diagram 1   Diagram 2   Diagram 3   Diagram 4
5 matches   8 matches   11 matches   14 matches

(a) How many matchsticks will there be in diagram 5?

(b) Diagram 4 can be split up like this.

Think about diagram 10 split up in the same way.
How many matches would there be altogether in diagram 10?

(c) How many matches would you need for diagram 100?

(d) (i) Find an expression for the number of matches in diagram *n*.

(ii) Use this expression to show that you would need 152 matches for diagram 50.

(e) A diagram in this sequence uses 62 matches.
Which diagram is this?

A3 Here is a sequence of patterns made from sticks.

Pattern 1   Pattern 2   Pattern 3   Pattern 4   ......

(a) Copy this table and complete the first five rows.

Pattern number	Number of sticks
1	
2	
3	
4	
5	
n	

(b) Find an expression for the number of sticks in pattern n.
Complete the last row in the table.

(c) How many sticks would you need for pattern 100 in this sequence?

(d) Which pattern in this sequence uses 121 sticks?

(e) Show that you cannot make a pattern in this sequence from exactly 50 sticks.

A4 Here is a sequence of dot patterns.

   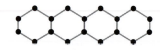

Pattern 1   Pattern 2   Pattern 3   Pattern 4   ......
6 dots   10 dots   14 dots   18 dots

(a) How many dots will there be in pattern 5?

(b) Which of these formulas fits the patterns in this sequence?
D is the number of dots in pattern n.

$D = n + 4$ $D = 2n + 4$ $D = 4n + 2$ $D = 6n + 4$

(c) Which pattern in this sequence has exactly 102 dots?

A5 Here is a sequence of dot patterns.

Pattern 1   Pattern 2   Pattern 3   Pattern 4   ......
4 dots   6 dots   8 dots   10 dots

(a) How many dots will there be in pattern n?

(b) Which pattern in this sequence will have 62 dots?

B Working out terms from the expression for the nth term

We can work out any term in a sequence if we have an expression for its nth term.

For example, the nth term of a sequence is $2n + 5$.

The **1**st term is $2 \times 1 + 5 = 7$

The **2**nd term is $2 \times 2 + 5 = 9$

The **3**rd term is $2 \times 3 + 5 = 11$

The **4**th term is $2 \times 4 + 5 = 13$

The **5**th term is $2 \times 5 + 5 = 15$ ... and so on

So the sequence is $7, 9, 11, 13, 15, \ldots$

B1 The nth term of a sequence is $3n + 4$.
Calculate the 5th term of this sequence.

B2 The nth term of a sequence is $3n - 1$.
Calculate the 10th term of this sequence.

B3 An expression for the nth term of a sequence is $4n - 3$.
Work out the 4th and 5th terms of this sequence.

B4 The nth term of a sequence is $2n + 1$.
(a) Find the first five terms of the sequence.
(b) Calculate the 100th term.

B5 The nth term of a sequence is $5n - 2$.
Find the first six terms of this sequence.

B6 The nth term of a sequence is $5 - n$.
Find the first six terms of this sequence.

B7 The nth term of a sequence is $n^2 + 1$.
Find the first five terms of this sequence.

B8 The nth term of a sequence is $3n + 2$.
(a) Calculate the 30th term.
(b) Which term in the sequence is equal to 152?

B9 The nth term of a sequence is $4n - 2$.
Show that 60 is not a term in this sequence.

*B10 The nth term of a sequence is $n^2 - 1$.
Show that 20 is not a term in this sequence.

The sequence   3, 6, 9, 12, 15, 18, …   is the sequence of all the multiples of 3.

- Show that the *n*th term of this sequence is 3*n*.
  Describe how to get from one term to the next.

- Copy and complete this table.

*n*th term	First six terms					
3*n*	3	6	9	12	15	18
3*n* + 1	4					
3*n* + 2						
3*n* + 5						
3*n* − 1						

- Describe how to get from one term to the next for each sequence in the table.
  Can you explain this?

A **linear** sequence is one where the terms go up or down by the same amount each time. Any linear sequence that

- goes up in 2s has an *n*th term of the form 2*n* + ▪ or 2*n* − ▪ .
- goes up in 3s has an *n*th term of the form 3*n* + ▪ or 3*n* − ▪ .
- goes up in 4s has an *n*th term of the form 4*n* + ▪ or 4*n* − ▪ … and so on.

Example

Find the *n*th term of the linear sequence 7, 12, 17, 22, 27, 32, …

The sequence goes up in 5s so the *n*th term is 5*n* + ? or 5*n* − ?
The sequence with an *n*th term of 5*n* is the sequence of multiples of 5

5, 10, 15, 20, 25, 30, …

The terms in the sequence   7, 12, 17, 22, 27, 32, …
can be found by adding 2 to each term in the sequence of multiples of 5 above.
Hence its *n*th term is 5*n* + 2.

C1 Here are the first five terms of a linear sequence.

5, 7, 9, 11, 13, …

(a) (i)   What do the terms in the sequence go up by each time?

(ii)   Find an expression for the *n*th term of this sequence.

(b)   Use this expression to work out the 50th term in this sequence.

C2 Find the *n*th term of each of these linear sequences.

(a) 9, 11, 13, 15, 17, ...   (b) 7, 11, 15, 19, 23, ...

(c) 6, 11, 16, 21, 26, ...   (d) 1, 4, 7, 10, 13, ...

(e) 4, 9, 14, 19, 24, ...   (f) 2, 9, 16, 23, 30, ...

C3 Here are the first five terms of a sequence.

11, 14, 17, 20, 23, ...

(a) Find an expression for the *n*th term of this sequence.

(b) Use this expression to work out the 10th term in this sequence.

C4 Here are the first five terms of a sequence.

1, 6, 11, 16, 21, ...

(a) Find an expression for the *n*th term of this sequence.

(b) Which term in this sequence is equal to 51?

C5 The *n*th term of a sequence is $15 - 2n$.

(a) Write down the first four terms of this sequence.

(b) Find the *n*th term of the sequence 14, 12, 10, 8, 6, ...

Test yourself

T1 (a) The *n*th term of a sequence is $4n + 1$.

    (i) Write down the first three terms of the sequence.

    (ii) Is 122 a term in this sequence? Explain your answer.

(b) Tom builds fencing from pieces of wood as shown below.

    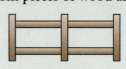   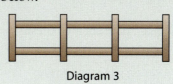

Diagram 1   Diagram 2   Diagram 3

4 pieces of wood   7 pieces of wood   10 pieces of wood

How many pieces of wood will be in diagram *n*?   AQA

T2 The *n*th term of a sequence is $3n - 1$.

(a) Write down the first and second terms of the sequence.

(b) Which term of the sequence is equal to 32?

(c) Explain why 85 is not a term in this sequence.   AQA

T3 Here are the first five terms of a sequence.

9, 13, 17, 21, 25, ...

Find an expression for the *n*th term of this sequence

32 Standard form

You should know

- how to multiply by 10, 100, 1000, …
- how to evaluate powers such as 10^2 and 10^5

This work will help you

- change large numbers to and from standard form
- interpret standard form on a calculator display

A Multiplying by powers of ten

Examples

$2.53 \times 10\,000 = 25\,300$

$\boxed{\times 10\,000}$ 2.53

$25\,300.$

Multiplying by 10 000 moves figures four places to the left.

$6.9 \times 100\,000\,000 = 690\,000\,000$

$\boxed{\times 100\,000\,000}$ 6.9

$690\,000\,000.$

Multiplying by 100 000 000 moves figures eight places to the left.

A1 Calculate each of these.

(a) 2.8945×1000 (b) 24.27×100 (c) $5.4362 \times 10\,000$

(d) 1.904×10 (e) $0.549\,23 \times 1000$ (f) $1.023\,721 \times 100\,000$

A2 Calculate each of these.

(a) $5.38 \times 10\,000$ (b) 6.7×100 (c) $3.56 \times 100\,000$

(d) $0.841 \times 1\,000\,000$ (e) $9 \times 10\,000$ (f) $35.1 \times 100\,000\,000$

(g) $7.4 \times 1\,000\,000\,000$ (h) $6.25 \times 100\,000\,000\,000$ (i) $4.01 \times 10\,000\,000\,000\,000$

A3 Find the missing number in each calculation.

(a) $\blacksquare \times 100 = 2340$ (b) $6 \times \blacksquare = 60\,000$

(c) $\blacksquare \times 100\,000 = 20\,000\,000$ (d) $\blacksquare \times 1\,000\,000 = 4\,500\,000$

(e) $56\,000 \times \blacksquare = 560\,000\,000\,000$ (f) $\blacksquare \times 100\,000\,000 = 2\,400\,000\,000$

(g) $\blacksquare \times 1\,000\,000 = 67\,300\,000$ (h) $1.52 \times \blacksquare = 15\,200\,000\,000$

(i) $\blacksquare \times 1\,000\,000\,000 = 73\,200\,000\,000$ (j) $8.64 \times \blacksquare = 86\,400\,000$

B Index notation for powers of ten

Sometimes index notation is used for powers of 10.

Example

$$1\,000\,000$$
$$= 10 \times 10 \times 10 \times 10 \times 10 \times 10$$
$$= 10^6$$

B1 Write these using index notation.

(a) $10 \times 10 \times 10$

(b) $10 \times 10 \times 10 \times 10 \times 10$

B2 Find the value of

(a) 10^2 (b) 10^5 (c) 10^4 (d) 10^8

B3 What is the value of the letter in each statement?

(a) $1\,000\,000\,000 = 10^x$

(b) $10^y = 100\,000\,000\,000\,000$

B4 Sort these numbers into four matching pairs.

A one thousand   **B** 10^4 **C** ten thousand   **D** 10^6

E 10^5 **F** one million   **G** 10^3 **H** one hundred thousand

B5 Find the result of this calculation.

$$45.6 \times 10^5$$
$$= 45.6 \times 100\,000$$
$$= \ldots\ldots\ldots\ldots$$

B6 Sort these into four matching pairs.

A 47×10^5 **B** 4.7×10^5 **C** 470×10^5 **D** 0.47×10^5

E $47\,000$ **F** $470\,000$ **G** $4\,700\,000$ **H** $47\,000\,000$

B7 Evaluate these.

(a) 13×10^6 (b) 207×10^8 (c) 400×10^3

(d) 6.3×10^4 (e) 29.4×10^7 (f) 7.62×10^9

B8 Find the missing number in each calculation.

(a) $\blacksquare \times 10^3 = 23\,000$

(b) $5 \times 10^{\blacksquare} = 50\,000$

(c) $4.9 \times 10^{\blacksquare} = 4900$

(d) $\blacksquare \times 10^2 = 560$

(e) $71.2 \times 10^{\blacksquare} = 7\,120\,000$

(f) $\blacksquare \times 10^4 = 945\,000$

(g) $1.39 \times 10^{\blacksquare} = 1\,390\,000$

(h) $430 \times 10^{\blacksquare} = 43\,000\,000$

In 2006, the assets of Queen Beatrix of Holland, Europe's richest royal, were £2 600 000 000. We say 2 600 000 000 is written in **ordinary form**.

All of these are ways to write this number …

- $26 \times 100\,000\,000$
- $2.6 \times 1\,000\,000\,000$
- $2\,600\,000 \times 1000$
- 26×10^8
- 2.6×10^9

… but only 2.6×10^9 is in **standard form** (or **standard index form**).

2.6×10^9

In standard form, this number is between 1 and 10 …

… and this number is written in the form 10^n.

C1 Which of these numbers are written in standard form?

A 1.8×10^9 **B** 56×10^2 **C** $4.5 \times 100\,000$ **D** 6×10^5 **E** 2.3×2^4

C2 Write these numbers in ordinary form.

(a) 3×10^4 (b) 2×10^7 (c) 8×10^{11}

(d) 4.2×10^5 (e) 8.1×10^8 (f) 5.34×10^6

C3 Write these numbers in standard form.

(a) 9000 (b) 5 000 000 (c) 800 000 000

C4 Copy and complete this working to change 6 200 000 000 to standard form.

$6\,200\,000\,000 = \blacklozenge \times 1\,000\,000\,000$
$= \blacklozenge \times 10^{\blacklozenge}$

C5 Write these numbers in standard form.

(a) 63 000 (b) 9 150 000 (c) 76 200 000 000

C6 This table shows the countries with the largest populations in the world in 2006.

Write each population in ordinary form.

	Country	Population (approx.)
1	China	1.3×10^9
2	India	1.1×10^9
3	United States	3.0×10^8
4	Indonesia	2.5×10^8
5	Brazil	1.9×10^8

Calculators display numbers in standard form in different ways.
These are examples of how 2.5×10^{11} is displayed on three different calculators.

$2.5 \quad 11$	$2.5\text{E}+11$	2.5×10^{11}

Use your calculator to work out

- $200\,000\,000^2$

- $30\,000^3$

- $5\,000\,000 \times 900\,000\,000$

How does your calculator display the answers?
Write the answers in standard form and as ordinary numbers.

D1 Use your calculator to evaluate each expression on the left and
so find five matching pairs.

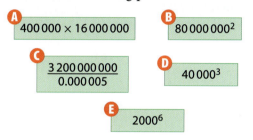

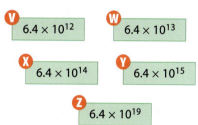

A $400\,000 \times 16\,000\,000$

B $80\,000\,000^2$

C $\dfrac{3\,200\,000\,000}{0.000005}$

D $40\,000^3$

E 2000^6

V 6.4×10^{12}

W 6.4×10^{13}

X 6.4×10^{14}

Y 6.4×10^{15}

Z 6.4×10^{19}

D2 Write the answer to each calculation in standard form.

(a) $2\,000\,000 \times 30\,000\,000$

(b) $3\,000\,000^2$

(c) $\dfrac{600\,000\,000}{0.0002}$

(d) $5\,000\,000^2 + 7\,000\,000^2$

(e) $300\,000^3$

(f) $6\,000\,000^2 - 3\,000\,000^2$

(g) $2 \times 400\,000^2$

(h) $(2 \times 400\,000)^2$

D3 Use your calculator to evaluate each expression on the left and
so find four matching pairs.

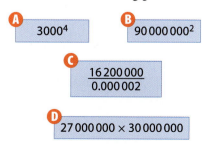

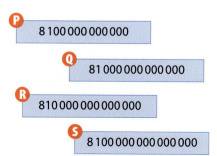

A 3000^4

B $90\,000\,000^2$

C $\dfrac{16\,200\,000}{0.000002}$

D $27\,000\,000 \times 30\,000\,000$

P $8\,100\,000\,000\,000$

Q $81\,000\,000\,000\,000$

R $810\,000\,000\,000\,000$

S $8\,100\,000\,000\,000\,000$

E Keying-in numbers in standard form

To work with numbers in standard form, calculators sometimes have a key with EXP on it.

Using this key to enter, say, the number 4.5×10^9 the sequence of key presses is

| 4 | . | 5 | EXP | 9 |

(When you use the EXP key, do **not** key in '$\times$' or '10'.)

Use your calculator to work these out.

- $(6 \times 10^6) \times (2 \times 10^8)$
- $(1.2 \times 10^{11}) + (3.4 \times 10^{11})$
- $\dfrac{1.5 \times 10^{14}}{5}$

How does your calculator display the answers?
Write each answer in standard form and as an ordinary number.

E1 Use your calculator to evaluate each expression on the left and so find three matching pairs.

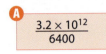

A $\dfrac{3.2 \times 10^{12}}{6400}$

B $\dfrac{6 \times 10^{13}}{1.2 \times 10^{11}}$

X 500

Y 500 000 000

C $\sqrt{2.5 \times 10^{13}}$

Z 5 000 000

E2 Evaluate each of these. Write each answer as an ordinary number.

(a) $\dfrac{4 \times 10^{12}}{1.6 \times 10^9}$

(b) $\dfrac{1.2 \times 10^{13}}{960\,000}$

(c) $\sqrt{8.1 \times 10^{15}}$

Test yourself

T1 Write these numbers in ordinary form.

(a) 4×10^5
(b) 3.9×10^8
(c) 2.16×10^6

T2 Write these numbers in standard form.

(a) 7 000 000
(b) 90 000
(c) 62 000 000

T3 Write the answer to each calculation in standard form.

(a) $20\,000^3$
(b) $500\,000 \times 30\,000$
(c) $600 \times 30\,000^2$

T4 Write the answer to each calculation in ordinary form.

(a) $4 \times 10^5 + 5 \times 10^5$
(b) $\dfrac{8 \times 10^{12}}{2 \times 10^3}$
(c) $\sqrt{6.4 \times 10^{11}}$

33 Volume and surface area of prism and cylinder

You should know how to find

- the volume of a cuboid
- the area of a triangle

This work will help you find the volume and surface area of a prism (including a cylinder).

You need triangular dotty paper.

A Finding the volume of a prism by counting cubes

A **prism** is a solid shape with a cross-section that is the same all the way through.

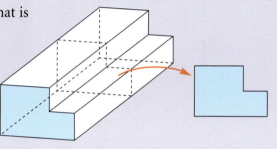

Each of these solids is a prism made from cubes.

- How many cubes are there in each solid?

A    B 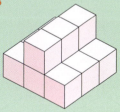   C

A1 Each of these solids is a prism.
How many cubes are there in each one?

(a) 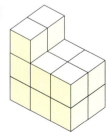   **(b)**    **(c)**

A2 Each of these drawings shows a prism made from centimetre cubes.
Find the volume of each one in cm³.

(a)

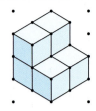

(b)

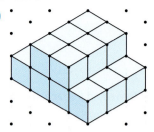

(c)

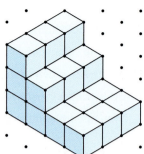

(d)

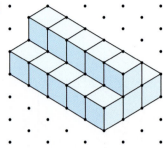

(e)

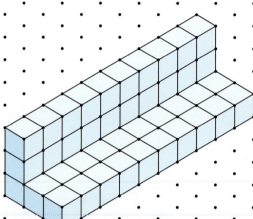

(f)

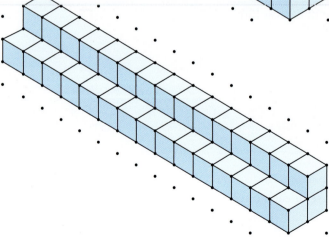

A3 On triangular dotty paper, draw a prism made from 24 cubes.

A4 On triangular dotty paper, draw prisms with these volumes.

    (a) 16 cm³   **(b)** 25 cm³   **(c)** 35 cm³   **(d)** 33 cm³

B Calculating to find the volume of a prism

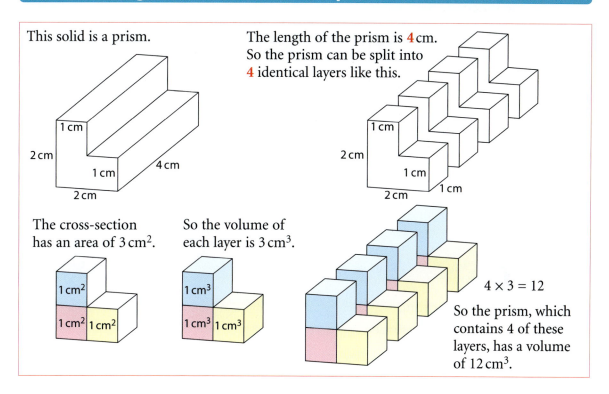

This solid is a prism.

The length of the prism is **4** cm.
So the prism can be split into
4 identical layers like this.

The cross-section
has an area of 3 cm².

So the volume of
each layer is 3 cm³.

$4 \times 3 = 12$

So the prism, which
contains 4 of these
layers, has a volume
of 12 cm³.

B1 Find the volume of each prism.
You may find it helpful to sketch each shaded cross-section on squared paper.
Remember to include the units.

(a)

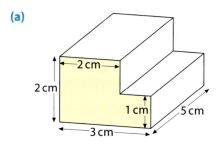

(b)

B2 Find the volume of each prism.

(a)

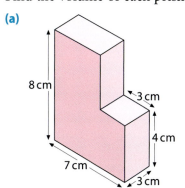

(b)

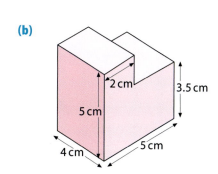

The area of the cross-section of a prism gives the volume of one layer.

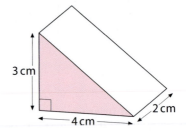

So the volume of a prism is found by

volume = area of cross-section × length

C1 This is a triangular prism.

(a) Find the area of the shaded triangular cross-section.

(b) Find the volume of the prism.

C2 Find the volume of each prism. Remember to use the correct units.

(a)

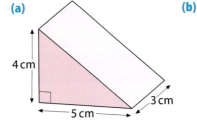

(b)

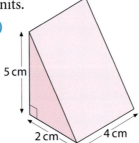

(c)

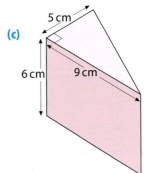

C3 Find the volume of each prism.

(a)

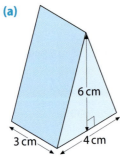

(b)

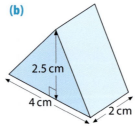

(c)

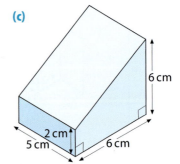

D Surface area of a prism

The surface area of an object is the total area of all its faces.

Example

Find the surface area of this prism.

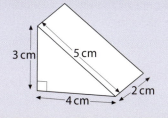

> It can help to sketch the prism and label each face.
> Faces B, D and E are hidden.

Area of face A = $\dfrac{3 \times 4}{2} = \dfrac{12}{2} = 6\,cm^2$

Area of face B = area of face A = $6\,cm^2$

Area of face C = $5 \times 2 = 10\,cm^2$

Area of face D = $4 \times 2 = 8\,cm^2$

Area of face E = $3 \times 2 = 6\,cm^2$

Total surface area = $6 + 6 + 10 + 8 + 6 = 36\,cm^2$

> It can also help to make a sketch of each face. A and B are right-angled triangles. C, D and E are rectangles.

D1 Find the surface area of each prism.
Remember to use the correct units.

(a)   **(b)**   **(c)**

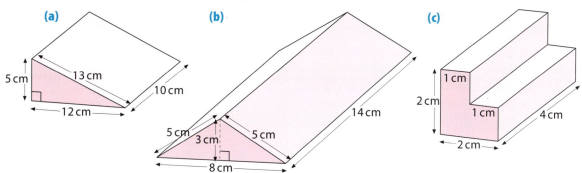

D2 (a) Use Pythagoras to find the length of the edge marked x.

(b) Find the surface area of this prism.

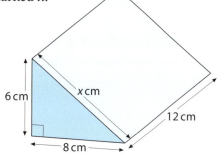

E Volume and surface area of a cylinder

A **cylinder** has a cross-section that is a circle.

For any cylinder, volume = area of the circle × height
$$= \pi r^2 \times h$$

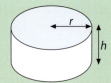

Example

Find the volume of this cylinder.

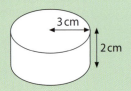

Area of circle = $\pi \times 3^2$

$= \pi \times 9$

$= 28.274\,33\ldots\,cm^2$

Volume of cylinder = $28.274\,33\ldots \times 2$

$= 56.5\,cm^3$ (to the nearest $0.1\,cm^3$)

Remember to include the units.

Give the final answer to an appropriate degree of accuracy.

E1 Find the volume of each cylinder.

(a)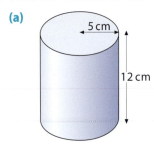

5 cm

12 cm

(b)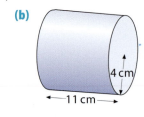

4 cm

11 cm

(c)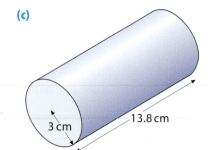

3 cm

13.8 cm

E2 Chocolog is made in cylinders as shown.
The diameter of each cylinder is 4 cm.
The length is 10 cm.

Find the volume of chocolate in this cylinder.

4 cm

10 cm

E3 This tin is a cylinder with radius 7.5 cm.
It is filled with coffee to a depth of 15 cm.

Work out the volume of coffee in the tin.
Give your answer to the nearest whole cm^3.

A cylinder has a curved surface and two flat surfaces.

Each of the flat surfaces is a circle with an area of πr^2.

Unrolling and flattening the curved surface gives a rectangle with width h.

The length of the rectangle is the same as the circumference of the circle, which is $2\pi r$.

So the area of the rectangle is $2\pi r \times h$.

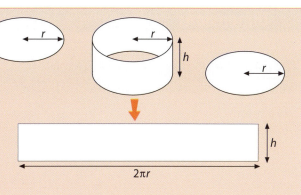

Example

Find the total surface area of this cylinder.

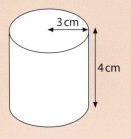

Area of one circle $= \pi \times 3^2$
$= \pi \times 9$
$= 28.27433\ldots \text{cm}^2$
Curved surface area $= 2 \times \pi \times 3 \times 4$
$= 75.39822\ldots \text{cm}^2$
Total surface area $= \mathbf{2} \times$ area of one circle + curved surface area
$= \mathbf{2} \times 28.27433\ldots + 75.39822\ldots$
$= 131.9 \text{cm}^2$ (to the nearest 0.1cm^2)

E4 Find the surface area of each cylinder.

(a)

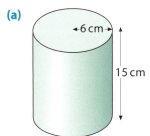

(b)

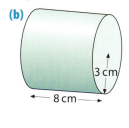

(c)

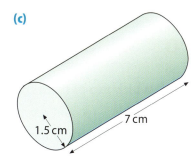

E5 (a) Find the volume of this cylinder.

(b) A label is wrapped round the curved surface. It covers the whole surface and does not overlap at the ends. Find the area of the label.

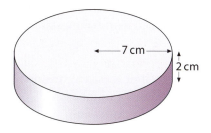

F Dimensions

The perimeter of this rectangle is $2(l + w)$.

We know that $2(l + w)$ can represent a length.

2 is a number.
l and w are both lengths.

So $l + w \rightarrow length + length \rightarrow length$.
So $2 \times (l + w) \rightarrow 2 \times length \rightarrow length$.

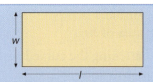

The area of this triangle is $\frac{1}{2}x^2$.

We know that $\frac{1}{2}x^2$ can represent an area.

$\frac{1}{2}$ is a number.
x is a length.

So $x^2 \rightarrow x \times x \rightarrow length \times length \rightarrow area$.
So $\frac{1}{2} \times x^2 \rightarrow \frac{1}{2} \times area \rightarrow area$.

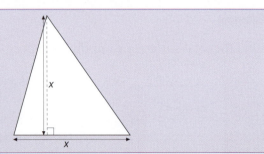

The volume of this cuboid is abc.

We know that abc can represent a volume.

a, b and c are all lengths.

So $abc \rightarrow a \times b \times c \rightarrow length \times length \times length \rightarrow volume$.

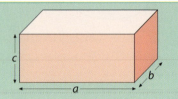

F1 In these expressions p, q and r are lengths.

 A $p + q$ **B** pqr **C** pq **D** r^2 **E** $q + r$ **F** p^3

  (a) Which two of them could represent lengths?

  (b) Which two could represent areas?

  (c) Which two could represent volumes?

F2 In each of these expressions r is a length.
3, 5 and $\frac{1}{2}$ are numbers.
For each expression, state whether it can represent a length, an area or a volume.

  (a) $5r$ **(b)** $3r^2$ **(c)** $\frac{1}{2}r^2$ **(d)** $5r^3$ **(e)** $\frac{1}{2}r^3$

F3 In each of these expressions r, l and h are lengths.
2 and π are numbers.
For each expression, state whether it can represent a length, an area or a volume.

  (a) $r + h$ **(b)** $2h$ **(c)** rh **(d)** rlh **(e)** πr

  (f) $2r + l$ **(g)** $2rl$ **(h)** $r^2 + h^2$ **(i)** $\pi r^2 h$ **(j)** $rh + hl$

F4 This is a sphere with radius r.
One of these is the formula for its surface area.
Which one is it?

A
$A = 2r$

B
$A = \pi r^3$

C
$A = 4\pi r^2$

Test yourself

T1 These prisms are made from centimetre cubes.
Work out the volume of each prism.
Remember to include the units.

(a)

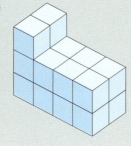

(b)

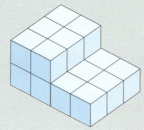

T2 The diagram shows a cylindrical tin of tomatoes.
The tin has a diameter 7.4 cm and height 10 cm.

Calculate the volume of the cylinder.
Give your answer correct to the nearest cm^3.

T3 Work out the volume of this triangular prism.
State the units in your answer.

T4 Work out the surface area of this prism.
State the units in your answer.

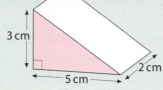

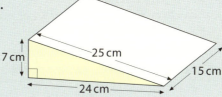

T5 In each of these expressions x, y and z are lengths. 2 and 3 are numbers.
For each expression, state whether it can represent a length, an area or a volume.

    (a) $x + y$ **(b)** $2y$ **(c)** xy **(d)** $3yz$ **(e)** xyz

34 Expanding brackets

This work will help you multiply out brackets such as $(x + 2)(x + 5)$ and $(x - 2)(x + 5)$.

You will need sheet F2–16.

A Review: multiplying out expressions such as $x(x - 5)$

We can find expressions equivalent to those like $2(n + 5)$ and $n(n - 4)$ by multiplying out or **expanding** the brackets.

$2(n + 5) = 2 \times (n + 5)$
$= 2 \times n + 2 \times 5$
$= 2n + 10$

Each term inside the brackets is multiplied by 2.

$n(n - 4) = n \times (n - 4)$
$= n \times n - n \times 4$
$= n^2 - 4n$

Each term inside the brackets is multiplied by n.

A1 Multiply out the brackets in each of these expressions.

(a) $2(x + 4)$ (b) $3(x + 2)$ (c) $5(x - 3)$ (d) $4(n + 2)$ (e) $8(n - 10)$

A2 Expand the brackets in each of these expressions.

(a) $x(x + 5)$ (b) $x(x + 1)$ (c) $x(x - 3)$ (d) $x(x - 2)$ (e) $x(7 + x)$

(f) $n(n + 4)$ (g) $n(n - 5)$ (h) $n(n - 1)$ (i) $n(1 + n)$ (j) $n(3 + n)$

A3 Expand the brackets in each of these expressions.

(a) $x(x^2 + 5)$ (b) $3(2y + 1)$ (c) $5(p^2 + p)$ (d) $n^2(7 + n)$

B Simplifying expressions that have like terms

When simplifying expressions, we can only add or subtract **like** terms.

Examples

$n^2 + 5n + 2n$
$= n^2 + 7n$

We can simplify '$+ 5n + 2n$' to get '$+ 7n$'.

We cannot simplify $n^2 + 7n$ by adding.

$x^2 + 8x - 3x - 6$
$= x^2 + 5x + 6$

We can simplify '$+ 8x - 3x$' to get '$+ 5x$'.

We cannot simplify $x^2 + 5x + 6$ by adding.

B1 Simplify each of these by adding like terms.

(a) $x^2 + 6x + 3x$ (b) $x^2 + 5x + x$ (c) $6x + 3x + 5 + 3$

(d) $x^2 + 2x + 8x + 9$ (e) $x^2 + 2x + 5 + 4x$ (f) $x^2 + x^2 + 6$

B2 Simplify each of these.

(a) $x^2 + 7x - 3x$ (b) $x^2 + 3x - x$ (c) $9x - 2x + 7 - 1$

(d) $x^2 + 6x - 2x + 9$ (e) $x^2 - 2x + 5x - 3$ (f) $x^2 - 7x + 10x + 4$

B3 Find three pairs of equivalent expressions.

A $x^2 + 4x - 5x + 6$ **B** $x^2 - 3x - 8x + 6$ **C** $x^2 - 7x + 2x + 6$

D $x^2 - 5x + 6$ **E** $x^2 - 11x + 6$ **F** $x^2 - x + 6$

C Multiplying out expressions such as $(x + 1)(x + 3)$

We can sometimes break down a multiplication into simpler calculations.

For example,

×	50	8
50	2500	400
2	100	16

52×58
$= (50 + 2)(50 + 8)$

52×58
$= 2500 + 400 + 100 + 16$
$= 3016$

We can sometimes break down an algebraic multiplication in the same way.

For example,

×	n	8
n	n^2	$8n$
2	$2n$	16

$(n + 2)(n + 8)$

$(n + 2)(n + 8)$
$= n^2 + 8n + 2n + 16$
$= n^2 + 10n + 16$

$(n + 2)(n + 8) = n^2 + 10n + 16$ is called an **identity** as it is true for all values of n.

C1 In each of these, expand the brackets and simplify the result.

(a) $(x + 2)(x + 3)$ (b) $(x + 3)(x + 4)$ (c) $(x + 4)(x + 2)$

(d) $(n + 4)(n + 5)$ (e) $(n + 6)(n + 3)$ (f) $(n + 2)(n + 9)$

(g) $(x + 3)(x + 3)$ (h) $(x + 12)(x + 1)$ (i) $(x + 4)(x + 1)$

C2 Show that the area of this rectangle is $x^2 + 8x + 15$.

$x + 5$

$x + 3$

This grid of numbers has ten columns.
A 3 by 3 square outlines some numbers.

1	2	3	4	5	6	7	8	9	10
11	12	13	14	15	16	17	18	19	20
21	22	23	24	25	26	27	28	29	30
31	32	3	34	35	36	37	38	39	40
4		43	44	45	46	47	48		

- Multiply the numbers in opposite corners.

$14 \times 36 = 504$
$16 \times 34 = 544$

- Find the difference between the results.

$544 - 504 = 40$

- Let's call this the 'opposite-corners number'.

The opposite-corners number for this square is **40**.

D1 A copy of the grid above is on sheet F2–16.
Find the opposite-corners number for some 3 by 3 squares in different positions on the grid.

What do you think is true about these opposite-corners numbers?

D2 Imagine the grid above going on for ever.
This square is on the grid.

- **(a)** Copy it and fill in the corner squares without filling in the other squares.

- **(b)** Work out its opposite-corners number.

D3 (a) Copy this square for the grid above.
Fill in the two empty corner squares with expressions in terms of n.

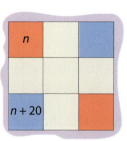

- **(b) (i)** Multiply out the expressions in the red corners.

  (ii) Multiply out the expressions in the blue corners.

  (iii) Hence find and simplify an expression for the opposite-corners number for this square.

- **(c)** What does this show?

D4 **(a)** Investigate for 2 by 2 squares on the same grid.

(b) What do you think is true about the opposite-corners number this time?

(c) Can you show your result is true?

D5 Investigate for squares of different size on this grid.

E Multiplying out expressions such as $(x - 1)(x + 3)$

A table can also be used when the multiplication involves subtraction.

Examples

×	n	8
n	n^2	$8n$
-2	$-2n$	-16

$(n - 2)(n + 8)$ ➡

$(n - 2)(n + 8)$
$= n^2 + 8n - 2n - 16$
$= n^2 + 6n - 16$

×	n	-8
n	n^2	$-8n$
2	$2n$	-16

$(n + 2)(n - 8)$ ➡

$(n + 2)(n - 8)$
$= n^2 - 8n + 2n - 16$
$= n^2 - 6n - 16$

E1 In each of these, expand the brackets and simplify the result.

(a) $(n - 2)(n + 5)$ **(b)** $(n - 3)(n + 6)$ **(c)** $(n - 1)(n + 9)$

(d) $(n + 5)(n - 3)$ **(e)** $(n + 7)(n - 2)$ **(f)** $(n + 10)(n - 1)$

E2 In each of these, multiply out the brackets and simplify the result.

(a) $(x - 6)(x + 2)$ **(b)** $(x - 7)(x + 3)$ **(c)** $(x - 5)(x + 4)$

(d) $(x + 2)(x - 4)$ **(e)** $(x + 1)(x - 5)$ **(f)** $(x + 2)(x - 12)$

E3 In each of these, expand the brackets and simplify the result.

(a) $(x - 3)(x - 2)$ **(b)** $(x - 4)(x - 3)$ **(c)** $(x - 3)(x - 5)$

Test yourself

T1 Multiply out and simplify each of these.

(a) $(x + 3)(x + 2)$ **(b)** $(x + 1)(x + 5)$ **(c)** $(n + 4)(n + 4)$

T2 Expand and simplify each of these.

(a) $(n - 3)(n + 8)$ **(b)** $(x - 2)(x + 7)$ **(c)** $(n - 5)(n + 2)$

Review 5

You need a pair of compasses, and an angle measurer or pie chart scale.

1 This is a full-size drawing of a key.

Which of these keys is similar to the key above?

A

B

C

2 Here are some patterns made from matchsticks.

Pattern 1   Pattern 2   Pattern 3

(a) Draw pattern 4.

(b) Copy and complete the table for this sequence of patterns.

Pattern number	1	2	3	4	5
Number of matches	6	10			

(c) How many matches will there be in pattern 10?

(d) Find an expression that gives the number of matches in pattern n.

3 This fair spinner is a regular octagon.

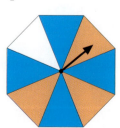

(a) The arrow is spun.
What is the probability that the arrow lands on

  (i) orange   **(ii)** blue   **(iii)** green

(b) The arrow is spun 80 times.
How many times would you expect the arrow
to land on white?

4 Write these fractions in order of size, starting with the smallest.

$\frac{2}{3}, \frac{1}{2}, \frac{2}{7}, \frac{1}{10}$

5 Expand $3(5x - 2)$.

6 The table on the right shows the heights and weights of some runners.

Height (cm)	Weight (kg)
165	45
164	55
159	49
170	62
168	58
161	47
180	69
174	55
197	77
165	55
177	68
167	58
178	58
162	48
155	40
200	82
180	65
168	50
174	60
186	71

(a) Draw a scatter diagram using these scales.

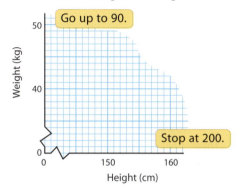

Go up to 90.

Stop at 200.

(b) Describe the correlation between the height and weight of the runners.

(c) Draw the line of best fit on your diagram.

(d) Use your graph to estimate the weight of a runner who is 190 cm tall.

7 Bag A contains n sweets.
Bag B contains 10 more sweets than bag A.
Bag C contains three times as many sweets as bag A.

(a) Write down an expression for the number of sweets in bag B.

(b) Write down an expression for the number of sweets in bag C.

(c) Show that the total number of sweets in bags A, B and C is $5(n + 2)$.

8 Helen and Gina have a total of £30.
Helen has twice as much money as Gina.
How much money does Helen have?

9 The table gives information about the favourite breakfast drinks of 60 students.

Tea	Coffee	Hot chocolate	Orange	Other
16	24	5	12	3

(a) What fraction of the students like orange best?
Give your answer in its simplest form.

(b) Draw a pie chart to show the information in the table.

10 This diagram is a scale drawing of a lawn and two trees A and B.

   (a) The scale is 1 cm to 2 m.
   In metres, how wide is the lawn?

   (b) A bird table T is:

   - equidistant from A and B

   - 8 metres from corner S

   Make an exact copy of the diagram.
   Using ruler and compasses only, construct and label the position of T.
   Leave in all your construction lines.

   (c) How far, in metres, is the bird table from corner P?

11 This two-way table shows information about the hair colour of 120 students.
Some numbers are missing.

	Black	Brown	Red	Fair	Total
Male		39		5	59
Female	10	26		21	
Total			7	26	120

   (a) Copy and complete the two-way table.

   (b) One of the students is picked at random.
   Write down the probability that this student will have red hair.

12 A tin of treacle has these dimensions.

   (a) What is the radius of the base of the tin?

   (b) Calculate the volume of treacle it contains when full.

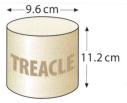

←——9.6 cm——→

11.2 cm

13 Find the value of $2x - 5y$ when $x = 3$ and $y = {}^-2$.

14 Leo bought 1.5 kg of stewing steak for £9.15.
Pete bought 700 grams of the same steak.
How much did it cost?

15 In Berlin in November 1923, a loaf of bread cost 201 000 000 000 marks.
Write this price in standard form.

16 Graham catches the bus to school each day.
The probability that the bus is late is 0.15.
What is the probability that the bus is on time?

17 Factorise each of these.

    (a) $5x - 20$ **(b)** $4x + 14$ **(c)** $x^2 + 3x$

18 Write 3×10^8 in ordinary form.

19 n is a whole number.
    What type of whole number is $5n$?

20 The diagram shows a prism.

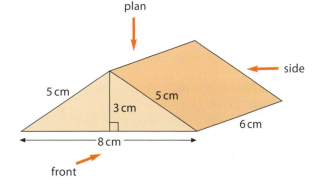

    (a) How many planes of symmetry
           does this prism have?

    (b) How many triangular faces
           does the prism have?

    (c) Find the volume of the prism.

    (d) Draw these full size.

           (i) A plan view of the prism

           (ii) A side view of the prism

           (iii) A front view of the prism

    (e) Calculate the surface area of the prism.

21 Expand and simplify $3(x + 4) + 2(3x - 5)$.

22 A pump operates at a rate of 1.8 litres per second.
    Calculate, to the nearest minute, the time it will take to empty a tank
    that contains 2540 litres of water.

23 Find the nth term of the linear sequence 5, 8, 11, 14, 17, …

24 The membership of a badminton club falls from 58 to 47 members over a year.
    What is the percentage decrease in the number of members over the year?

25 Expand $x^2(x + 4)$.

26 Write these numbers in order of size, starting with the smallest.
         60% $\frac{2}{3}$ 0.8 $\frac{1}{4}$

27 Expand and simplify   **(a)** $(x + 4)(x + 5)$ **(b)** $(x - 2)(x + 4)$

28 p is an odd number and and q is even.
    What type of number is

    (a) $p + q$ **(b)** $p + 1$ **(c)** pq **(d)** p^2

29 In the following expressions the letters r, s and t all represent lengths.
    3, 2 and π are all numbers.
    State whether each expression could represent a length, an area or a volume.

    (a) $3rs$ **(b)** rst **(c)** πr^2 **(d)** $s + t$ **(e)** $2\pi s^3$

Index